Loyal Sons and Daughters

May these pages stir
up your most cherished
Notre Dame
memories —
With best wishes,
Sr. Jean Lenz, OSF

Loyal Sons and Daughters

A Notre Dame Memoir

SISTER JEAN LENZ, OSF

ROWMAN & LITTLEFIELD PUBLISHERS, INC.
Lanham • Boulder • New York • Oxford

ROWMAN & LITTLEFIELD PUBLISHERS, INC.

Published in the United States of America
by Rowman & Littlefield Publishers, Inc.
A Member of the Rowman & Littlefield Publishing Group
4720 Boston Way, Lanham, Maryland 20706
www.rowmanlittlefield.com

PO Box 317
Oxford
OX2 9RU, UK

British Library Cataloguing in Publication Information Available

Library of Congress Cataloging-in-Publication Data

Lenz, Jean, 1930-
Loyal sons and daughters : a Notre Dame memoir / Jean Lenz.
p. cm.
ISBN 0-7425-2274-1 (cloth : alk. paper)
1. Lenz, Jean, 1930- 2. University of Notre Dame—Students—Biography. 3. Franciscans—Biography. I. Title.
LD4112.9 .L46 2002
378.772'89—dc21 2002009697

Printed in the United States of America

∞ ™ The paper used in this publication meets the minimum requirements of American National Standard for Information Sciences—Permanence of Paper for Printed Library Materials, ANSI/NISO Z39.48–1992.

Written in thanksgiving
for these and all the cherished memories
that fill the minds and hearts of
Notre Dame families and friends
around the world.

Contents

Foreword

I believe this book will become a classic in many ways. And for all of those ways, we are grateful to its author, Sister Jean Lenz, OSF, a Franciscan nun from the College of St. Francis (now the University of St. Francis) in Joliet, Illinois. She did her graduate studies in theology at the University of Notre Dame and, with the dawn of coeducation here in 1973, we invited her back to the campus to be the rector of one of our first halls for women undergraduates.

Sister Jean has been with us ever since, serving now as assistant vice president for Student Affairs, after more than a decade of rectoring at Farley Hall. No one is better suited than she to recall our early days of coeducation after a century and a quarter of being an all-male school. In fact, she has been at the heart of all of our coeducational efforts over the past quarter century, and above and beyond anyone else she has guided us to a new life of peaceful coexistence between men and women students here.

It is difficult to think of anyone in a leadership role at Notre Dame who is not a dear friend of hers, who has not been enriched by knowing her and watching her work with our men and women students, particularly the women she guided for over a decade, thousands of whom spent their four Notre Dame undergraduate years under her guidance in Farley Hall.

I believe it is fair to say that we had minimal problems in this wonderful transition from an all-male to a coeducational school. Sister Jean and an increasing number of her fellow rectors in women's residence halls guided us in a way that no one else could have—certainly not as well as Sister Jean and her colleagues who helped with the transition that has now achieved a close fifty-fifty status.

Until now, this story was a warm and rich bit of history that has never been told. Now Sister Jean has told it in such a superb way that I believe her book will become a classic among the books that chronicle the history of this wonderful institution. It would be an understatement to say that Sister Jean's influence affected only the female side of this historical adventure. I would have to admit that all of us men (as professors, administrators, and students) were affected profoundly by Sister Jean's presence, her leadership, and the inspiring ways she lived her life here as an integral part of a bold adventure. We have all been enriched by the presence of women but deeply enriched by the presence of Sister Jean, who could easily be called the First Lady in this time of transition.

This is, above all, a very personal account. Jean speaks bluntly and frankly as she leads us through this revolving wonder of a great university profoundly changing its reality from all-male to coeducational, both on the level of professors and women administrators, particularly in the residence halls. Sister Jean was a godsend in this somewhat daring endeavor that turned out beyond our hopes and dreams. She should get the lion's share of the credit as we entered this unknown world in Notre Dame's development.

As you wind your way through the chapters that follow, you will find yourself laughing and possibly crying. She did a great deal of both by always being there, always being open and friendly and inspiring, even dealing with impossible situations with wisdom and humor. Once when some streakers arrived at the door outside her offices, she simply stepped into the cold night and told them, "You don't think I'm going to let you come into this hall *dressed* like that?" She immediately defused a very difficult situation with all those young men scattering into the bushes, and they did not try it again.

What will appeal to most people is the fact that she has been so open and honest about the problems she faced, the failures and the triumphs which face all of us, with a deep spirit of prayer that simply enriches everything that she does, making tragic moments less tragic and inspiring moments more inspired.

I must admit that this is an unusual history because of her total honesty and obvious dedication to the task at hand. She does not spare herself or any others with whom she had happy and somewhat less happy moments. She is always a dedicated nun, a superb educator, and a woman who leads by her example much more than by her words. All who read this book have a great treat coming—an unusual insight into the life of students (especially women) at this university which was all-male for a century and a quarter before women began to arrive in ever-greater numbers as professors, administrators, and students. Sister Jean represented all of these realities at Notre Dame.

Again, we are vastly enriched as a Catholic university because of her fruitful and endearing presence in our midst. I want to give her heartfelt thanks from all of us for all she is and all she has done and to thank her for her honesty, humility, and love that gave birth to this wonderful book.

Rev. Theodore M. Hesburgh, CSC
President Emeritus
University of Notre Dame

September 4, 2001

Acknowledgments

This book never would have seen the light of day without a group of individuals who shared their many talents in a variety of ways.

Very special thanks go to Walt Collins, former editor of the *Notre Dame Magazine*, for his continual encouragement, from the moment I invited him to lunch to ask him if he honestly thought I could write a book, to the e-mail I received from him after I told him I had a publisher: "I can't wait to hold that book in my hands." At the outset of my sabbatical year, Walt sent me off to start the storytelling, "Go put that streaker story onto paper, and you'll be on your way, Jean." Walt read everything I wrote. He never did any extensive editing, but he continually kept me on track, asking questions, giving me feedback and pointing me in the various directions of my own experiences. I never would have dared this project, or continued it, without his support.

I am also grateful to the staff in the Office of Public Information who opened files for me, allowing me to collect names and dates, and read old news releases. Special thanks go to Michael Garvey ('74), assistant director of the office, who read much of what I wrote and offered valuable critical suggestions as the manuscript developed. He, like Walt Collins, stayed conscious of the historic value of my experience. I seemed always after the truth of the matter simply because I realized our alums, the firsthand eyewitnesses, would be "looking over my shoulder" at the printed version of their colorful escapades.

I am indebted to Chuck Lennon, associate vice president for University Relations and his staff in the Alumni Office, and to John Heisler, associate director of Athletics, for the information they supplied along the way. My thanks to Charles Lamb, assistant director of the Notre Dame Archives, and to Greg Swirz, photo editor of the *South Bend Tribune*, both of whom supplied material that added a visual history to the manuscript.

It was always a pleasure to work with my administrative assistant in the Office of Student Affairs, Joan Hutchin, who prepared the manuscript for the publisher. Her careful work and genuine enthusiasm for the project from beginning to end was deeply appreciated. How providential that my editorial assistant at the publishing house should be a former *Observer* editor, Matt Loughran ('95). His assistance added still more local color.

I am especially grateful to Vice President Father Mark Poorman, CSC, whom I assist in the Office of Student Affairs, for the time he gave me during a sabbatical year, 1999–2000, and the place to write in room 417 on the fourth floor of the newly renovated Main Building.

I am also wonderfully indebted to all who challenged me over the years to take the time to sit and think and write, including some good friends who have gone to God before the rest of us: Father Robert Griffin, CSC, who wrote a column in the *Observer* for some twenty years, and Edward Fischer and Thomas Stritch who left behind some of their memories in *Notre Dame Remembered* and *My Notre Dame*, respectively.

Finally—and forever—I will be indebted to Jim Langford, former director of the Notre Dame Press and presently an agent for Rowman and Littlefield Publishers, Inc., who approached me one spring day in 2001 and said, "I've been going to call you. I hear you have a manuscript. I would like to read it." And that he did—right into a book.

Introduction

How often I shrugged it off with a nervous laugh, "Write a book?" But people kept after me, teasing me, chiding me to tell those Notre Dame tales. Some embarrassed me at times for not having already done it. Others suggested colorful content: "Be sure to include that streaker story." Some folks offered chapter titles. Now and then, a few colleagues found ways of quoting from the imaginary book that existed in their minds, like Father Bob Griffin, CSC, who insisted that I stood tall in Farley Hall's doorway, shouting to those infamous streakers, "You're not coming in here dressed like that!"

The thought of writing kept haunting me, probably because I was standing hip-high in unending life-giving memories. But I was often surrounded by unnerving moments of doubt that some days got the best of me. Did I really have anything worth sharing? Good friend Michael Garvey, of Public Information Office fame and author in his own right, snapped me out of it one lunch hour in the Huddle when he told me how Flannery O'Connor came to realize that she had to write to find out what she thought. He began to urge me to "sit down and start writing something, anything. Just write. All kinds of things will emerge—and you'll come to know what it means and what to do with it." With strong purpose and to my surprise, I picked up a notebook in Hook's Drugstore on a hot summer day and said to myself in earnest, "I will write!"

As the weeks went on, and a sabbatical year for writing became a reality, I began to understand that my friends knew me better than I knew myself. It was true. I had been harboring a deep yearning for a long time to capture in words what happened to me these past thirty years. I grabbed memories from my heart and mind, from midair at times, while others came from pictures and conversations and files that fell open in my hands and on my desk. Nostalgia often overtook me as I walked a favorite path, stood in a doorway, or sat at a special table. Other memories came to life in the middle of the night, woke me up, and sent me scribbling notes before I could go back to sleep. It was as though the names of people and places and streets and performances and conversations hung in my brain like a bunch of rich grapes ripe for the picking.

As I wrote my way through a year, often in a booth in the lower lounge of LaFortune Student Center with morning coffee, but mostly on my PowerBook 520c on the fourth floor of the Main Building, I began hoping more and more that you, the reader, would come to recognize yourself in these pages, or someone you know, or events you witnessed and emotions you felt when and if you were a Domer, or the parent of a Domer, or a regular visitor on campus, or someone who has simply listened to Notre Dame stories most of your life and gradually inherited the place through the miracle of osmosis. Whatever the relationship, you pushed my pen along. You were on my mind as I kept writing and hoping that my memories would stir up yours—and the unending grace that goes with them.

So here's the book you saw in me before I did, all because we shared so many stories at the University of Notre Dame du Lac.

ONE

"Come Share Life"

(How I Got Here)

I never really wanted to come to Notre Dame (ND). I was finishing a master's degree in journalism at Marquette University in 1965 when I was assigned to further theological study in order to understand the many changes in emphases following Vatican Council II which had ended in 1965. My sense was that I would continue in the Jesuit tradition and remain at Marquette. I had already been bred on Council insights through homilies and lecture halls by a variety of Jesuits, often fresh from Rome with the latest Council developments. I first heard the name Karl Rahner, SJ, during a young Jesuit's moving account at an ordination retreat given by the German theologian. There were stories of Henri de Lubac, SJ, and Yves Congar, OP, and others who had pioneered the teachings that emerged in the Council. I stayed on the lookout for anything these men of God wrote. In general, Marquette's theology department was graced with exciting teachers and a waiting list of religious and lay people wanting to do graduate work that focused on Council proceedings and documents promulgated for the Church at large. I was always slipping into a theology lecture after journalism class, convinced that Marquette was the perfect place to take on postconciliar studies. But the waiting list was long, and my application was put on hold. I was forced to apply elsewhere.

While theological studies at that time generally belonged to the world of priests and seminarians, a number of religious women began to get involved. The director of studies in my Franciscan community and I examined programs at Fordham, St. Louis University, and Catholic University. We also requested information from Notre Dame where a new graduate theology program had been specifically created for religious women and lay women and men. I could complete an M.A. in two summers and a full academic year. That's where I headed. There were moments, however, when I seriously wondered if the newness of Vatican II would have a hard time getting through the strong, longstanding Catholic traditions of Notre Dame.

Father Paul Beichner, CSC, director of Graduate Studies, signed and sent my letter of acceptance with a scholarship attached. ND was beckoning women to come. So, in August 1966, I arrived on campus in full Franciscan brown habit, with a modified veil that allowed a few locks of hair to show. I spent the first summer session living in Keenan Hall and the regular academic year and final summer in Lewis Hall, which had originally been built for graduate women from religious communities.

My Jesuit yearnings for Marquette slowly diminished as my confidence in the ND program grew stronger with each class. I was taught by fine professors, including Jesuit biblical scholar John McKenzie, and surrounded by bright, articulate lay and religious colleagues. The ink on Vatican Council II documents was still wet and live reports from the Vatican were daily fare, since there was more open discussion of the Church appearing in world media than ever before. Stable religious realities were questioned and change was in the air. With each passing day I grew more grateful for such a setting in which to tackle church and societal issues and garner insights from scholars and colleagues. It was as though I was making a solemn novitiate for a changing Church.

Along the way, I was asked to give some talks to undergraduate men, which brought me into contacts with priests of the Holy Cross. Fr. Jim Buckley, CSC, invited me to be one of three Lenten speakers for the men of his hall who filled the basement middle room of Farley Hall. The theme of the series was "living out relationships." Fr. Henri Nouwen, fresh from the Menninger Institute, was a visiting professor in the psychology department at the time. He was also one of the speakers. The third was a Benedictine theologian, Luke Johnson. We attended each other's presentations. At the end of the series, Fr. Buckley invited us to his room for light refreshments. We chatted away, recounting some of the local color of our presentations. At the time I didn't have a clue that in six years I would be in that same room hosting similar gatherings as the rector of Farley Hall. Fr. Nouwen walked his bike and me back to Lewis Hall, and we talked about the light spring snow that was falling and how good it was to spend time at ND. At that point in his life, Fr. Nouwen was on the verge of writing his first book, *Intimacy*, which included essays based on his Notre Dame experiences. Thirty-eight other books would follow, the final one published after his sudden death: *Sabbatical Journey: The Final Year, 1997.*

Later in that semester, with springtime in full bloom, I stood listening to the Notre Dame orchestra practice near the front steps of the Administration Building when I was interrupted by Fr. James Burtchaell, CSC, a member of the theology faculty recently returned from studies in Cambridge, England. He asked if I would give a talk at a weekend retreat that he was giving for some twenty students at Old College. My answer was an immediate "I'm sorry I can't at this late stage of the semester." It was early May and I had a major paper to finish and exams around the corner. But that didn't stop him. He pointed out that there had to be some Christian topic I could speak on without a lot of preparation. Before I could respond, he referred to a talk I had given earlier that year. I explained it was on relationships between women and men. He said, "Fine, it would be good to have you address these young men on such a timely topic in their lives. We'll see you Friday." It was a done deal.

I showed up at Old College and introduced the "timely topic" by expressing my deep thanks for the good men in my life starting with my dad and two brothers and good friends, one of whom I almost married. I assured the students that these men influenced me greatly. In fact, I told them that if they didn't like what I had to say, they could blame it on the men in my life! I further explained that, since I didn't know any of the students personally, I just might be able to share some of my deepest thoughts more freely, reminding them—and myself—that it can be harder at times to share some of the most intimate things with those closest to us. And so the evening proceeded.

I decided to speak with them about the men in my life and what they meant to me as both a lay and religious woman. As I sat in their midst in full Franciscan robes, I told them that I entered religious life after graduating from college, right on the fringes of becoming engaged. These students, aged eighteen to twenty-two, asked some stunning questions, filling the room with a series of serious and fun-loving exchanges.

They asked what women looked for in men and what they liked and disliked. They questioned the significance and the differences between women and men when considering each other's appearances, personalities, and characters. Early on and often, I had to explain that I was not in a position to speak for all women, but for myself.

I challenged the students to get to know the larger feminine world by going beyond the confines of their female peers—those they were dating, flirting with, or trying to meet. I told them that they should take time with their little sisters, their teenage and married sisters, and their mothers and grandmothers. I called their attention to the delightful exchanges between the older women making and serving sandwiches in the Huddle and the students who greeted them daily. I wanted them to know that there are great complementary energies in all of us, whatever our ages, and that, as long as we live, we have deep powers to influence each other as men and women.

Quite naturally, a series of their questions centered on dating scenarios at Notre Dame. Challenging them to get to know the women on campus as friends before asking them on a date moved one young man into a sensitive area. He confessed that he was really trying to get to know an individual but found it hard to judge what she really liked to do when it came to activities and sports. "Recently I asked a girl to go horseback riding, but she said she would rather not. I thought she would like horseback riding so I began to wonder if maybe it was the bad time of the month for her. So, then I suggested miniature golf, but she said no to that, too." At this point in his query he looked me straight in the eye and asked, "You can do that at the bad time of the month, can't you?" Laughter let loose among his peers. In utter frustration he declared, "I just want to know if I should just ask her if it's the bad time of the month so I'll get to know what she really likes to do." I attempted to bail him out, commending him on trying to do the best thing. But it was a thoughtful chap in the crowd who offered the most fitting tip on the topic—from his experience: "Just slow down buddy, you'll get to know what she really likes to do without getting that personal too soon."

Later, we gathered for the Eucharist and reflected on Saint Matthew's words regarding the use of talents. A reading from George Eliot's *Middlemarch* was added, depicting a middle-aged man looking back on his life and relationships. I felt the impact of the evening most when I heard prayers of the faithful coming from these young men, thankful and full of requests for women of all ages in their lives.

I sat alone in the chapel in Lewis Hall later, trying to "decompress." So much had gone on in such a short time. I was most amazed at how ready and willing the young men were to listen to the likes of me—in full habit—discuss the topic of woman. Their questions were deep and good, and some so full of fun. We laughed together and grew quiet listening to each other. As it turned out, I was able to say a few intimate things to these male students, mostly because I believed in them and in all the relationships they would enter and shape. But I remember surprising myself by telling them what it means to a woman to come upon a man at prayer, as I had often done at ND. I was not referring to someone celebrating sacraments, but rather a man alone, kneeling or sitting in a chapel or church. I didn't realize I had such deep feelings about this and I could hardly finish what I began. While I hoped our campus paths might cross again, I knew that they had their suitcases packed and that I probably would never have contact with any of them again. But I did.

Five years later I received a letter from Fr. Jim Burtchaell, CSC, who conducted that Old College retreat. He was now the provost of the university. I was the director of Campus Ministry at the College of St. Francis in Joliet, Illinois, also teaching theology. The University of Notre Dame had recently declared itself a coeducational institution and Fr. Burtchaell was writing to invite me to come to campus and talk about the possibility of doing pastoral ministry as rector of a residence hall for some of the first women admitted to Notre Dame. The Old College springtime retreat that I tried so hard to say no to caught up with me again.

This time there was not an immediate "no" in my mind, only a heavy hesitation. I was happy at St. Francis. I liked the students, the staff, and teaching classes. The more I thought of the Notre Dame invitation, the more I realized that I would never respond to an advertisement for the position of rector of a women's residence hall. Sister John Miriam Jones, a Sister of Charity, hired as the assistant to the provost at ND in 1972, also wrote encouraging me to come. We had met in Lewis Hall while she was completing her doctoral studies in biology. Since this invitation involved a possible ministry outside of our Franciscan community commitments, I talked at some length with my general superior, Sister Francine Zeller. She urged me to "write it out"; to list my reasons for staying at St. Francis or going to Notre Dame. We would pray about it and talk some more. She encouraged me to make a trip to South Bend.

I listed thirteen reasons for staying at St. Francis and two for going to Notre Dame. The two reasons were heavyweights. I was strongly committed to Catholic higher education and its mission. I also admired the university for its decision to admit women after 125 years as an all-male institution. I would be willing to support that move and help with the challenges involved. However, the residence hall position remained a big question mark. I did a double take when I discovered that there were infamous rules in place but no job description. It all, no doubt, came naturally to Holy Cross rectors who served for decades and passed such ministry on to the next generation through oral tradition.

Provost Burtchaell challenged me to set fears aside and "come and share life." At the end of the year, he explained, "we'll write up a job description (based on what happens!) and use it for future reference." But I queried further, "What if I can't do what you're asking? What if I get to Christmastime and realize this isn't going to work?" "If that should occur," he assured me, "you can leave and we'll find someone else to carry on." The mere thought of a "bailout hatch" gave me the final bit of courage I needed to accept the invitation. Dr. Frank Kerins, president of the College of St. Francis where I was teaching theology, granted me a one-year leave of absence to offer a hand at Notre Dame as undergraduate women came to campus.

Sister Francine and her council supported me in my final decision. A French scholar in her own right and a college professor, she was willing to lend Franciscan support to the University of Notre Dame as it moved forward as a Catholic coeducational institution. She realized it was a significant step into the future that would cause a ripple effect across the country, attracting many educators from single-sex Catholic colleges and universities.

In time, nine more Joliet Franciscans, all good friends, became hall rectors and worked in related ministries on campus: Sisters Vivian Whitehead (Breen-Phillips Hall), Kathleen Rossman (Walsh Hall), Verene Girmschied (Badin Hall), Patricia Dowd, Mary Lou Marchetti and Nadine Overbeck (Breen-Phillips Hall), Annette Giarrante (Pasquerilla West Hall), Mary Jane Griffin (Farley and Howard Halls) and Susan Bruno (Pasquerilla West Hall).

Then, of all things, we Franciscans began to uncover more and more of our historical roots on the ND-SMC campuses, since the woman who founded our Franciscan congregation had been a Holy Cross sister in the middle of the nineteenth century. Mary Catherine Moes came to America from Remich, Luxembourg, to do missionary work. A record in the Holy Cross sisters' archives describes her as a woman "born to command." Written history indicates that she received her Holy Cross habit from Father Edward Sorin, CSC, president of the University of Notre Dame in 1856, while he in turn received her final vows in 1858. Some six years later, for a variety of pioneer reasons in those days, Mary Catherine left the Sisters of Holy Cross and made another novitiate with the Allegheny Franciscans in Olean, New York. Following this she went to the Archdiocese of Chicago where she founded, in nearby Joliet, the first congregation of Franciscan women in Illinois, working closely with the Franciscan friars of the Sacred Heart Province.

A small band of Franciscan Sisters traveled north to Minnesota in 1887 to establish schools at the request of the local Bishop there. In 1878, due to a series of complications, Mother Alfred, with twenty-five of her Joliet Sisters, branched off and founded another Franciscan congregation in Rochester, Minnesota. It was there that she worked with the famed Mayo Brothers whom she strongly influenced to establish their world-famous clinic. A closer look at history indicates that it was the Sisters' "crochet money" that played a big part in building the first hospital staffed by the Mayo Brothers and Franciscan Sister nurses.

Fr. Ted Hesburgh was always a bit intrigued with these historical facts. He explained once that the Holy Cross priests had always had a close association with the Mayo Clinic in Rochester, Minnesota, in part because the Holy Cross sister who was integral to the foundation of the clinic had come from Notre Dame–St. Mary's territory. He had no idea that she founded our Franciscan congregation first. Once he went out of his way to introduce me as a Holy Cross Sister. When I quickly spoke up for my Franciscan identity, he simply quipped, "Oh, I know Jean, but you're Holy Cross, too," rolling me into such double identity with great ease.

And so it is that the spirit of Mary Catherine Moes, known in religious life as Mother Alfred, steeped in both Holy Cross and Franciscan tradition, came alive again at Notre Dame more than a century later when the first undergraduate women arrived on the scene.

TWO

A Hallowed Hall Called Farley

"Don't get me wrong, we're happy to have the women on campus and living in Farley Hall," Fr. Jerry Wilson, CSC, vice president for Business Affairs, assured me, "but of course everyone has their fingers crossed as to how it will all turn out." I had no comeback. I was too new to know when to cross my fingers about anything. It was all I could do to listen carefully as he took me on my first official tour of Farley Hall.

At the south entrance, where tiny leaves of ivy crawled across the wooden doors, I was anxious to get inside. Fr. Jerry handed me the master key, warning me that if I lost it, I would have to go home. There was humor in his voice, but he made it clear that the university had just finished rekeying the library and that there was absolutely no money for more rekeying. I never imagined then that ten years later we would lunch at the University Club with that same master key in hand, celebrating one of Farley's many miracles and our long-lasting friendship.

A few days before meeting Fr. Jerry, I sat with my family in a fish fry restaurant in Sister Lakes, Michigan, some thirty miles north of Notre Dame. Half of the south side of Chicago vacationed there and ate lots of perch and walleye at Ade's on Friday nights. In the midst of lifting fork to mouth, I watched three strapping male figures come toward me in dark blue t-shirts marked with large white letters spelling FARLEY. Someone shouted to me, "Get ready, they lived in Farley last year." While the sight of them brought me to a standstill, they didn't have a clue of my identity and went on their merry way, proud of their Farley t-shirts. But my imagination ran wild as I gulped down my last mouthful of vacation fish and tried to imagine rectoring some 250 young women who were destined to usurp the Farley t-shirt world. I hadn't quite figured out how to pray about it all. I just kept an Our Father on my lips and in my heart as I begged for the strength I would need to turn Farley Hall into a reality in my life, beginning with Fr. Jerry's grand tour.

Fr. Jerry came across as a very competent and delightful man, but I could tell he was a bit unnerved with the thought of parents arriving on the scene within hours. He had concerns that they might be upset with the rather meager furnishings that had been added to this former male residence hall, including large, awkward, plywood wardrobes designed and constructed in the Notre Dame carpentry shop; white cottage curtains for the bottom half of windows; and new plumbing fixtures to replace the urinals. Hallways were not repainted, nor was new carpeting laid for this historic occasion due to limited university finances. Shower stalls still needed final touches. Rooms seemed crowded with furniture. It was evident that three students and all of their furniture were not going to fit in the two-room configurations. "Best you stay close to the parents and let them know you're here for their daughters," he strongly hinted at every turn in the hallways, as though I could make all the difference for whatever else was missing or proved to be an obstacle. I felt the weight of his expectations down to my toes.

Staff orientation involved a series of meetings for old and new rectors at the summer home of the vice president for Student Affairs, Philip Faccenda, and his wife, Kathy. In addition to getting to know each other, we were meant to discuss a newly minted "mission statement." I received a copy of it earlier in the summer and was impressed. That's why I was stunned to hear that it was only a first draft and needed more discussion. In my heart I knew that the first draft was all I needed to proceed my rectoring way, so I sat back, learned a lot of names, studied a variety of rich personalities, and soaked up as much positive energy and goodness as I could.

It was in a sailboat on Klinger Lake, between the various orientation sessions, that I heard my first Farley stories from outgoing rector, Father Jim Shilts, CSC. He relinquished the hall's reins as smoothly as he sailed the rig we sat in, making it clear that Farley had grown extremely rich in tradition. It produced its share of student body presidents, and, through the years, residents were proud of the generations who lived there. Farley leaders were responsible for initiating the "stay-hall system" which allowed students to remain in Farley throughout their four years instead of changing halls each year according to their class. This stay-hall arrangement became a way of life for all residence halls.

While the majority of Farley men strongly favored coeducation, they were hardly overjoyed with losing their hall to "the cause" as they scattered to other housing. In fact, Fr. Jim warned that there was a good dose of animosity in the air, since Farley was not one of the halls proposed for conversion by the so-called selection committee. Word was out that some former Farley residents expected the women to carry on the popular coffeehouse (that the men had created in the basement) and the famed Farley Striders, a jogging club of sorts. As the wind blew across Klinger Lake, the sails flapped and Fr. Jim sketched more Farley fables, I felt as though I was about to land on another planet when suddenly our sailboat hit the side of the pier where we docked and then headed for Faccenda's grand front porch and more meetings. Feeling disoriented, I found it hard to listen. Farley filled my head.

Once the women arrived on campus, Fr. Jim came by the hall almost every evening during that first week of classes, "just to see how things were progressing." He taught me the layout of the hall: the basement space, tunnel area, closets, route to the roof, fire alarm, chapel area, sacristy, and all I needed to know about supplies. There was no end; there were hiding places everywhere, which to his surprise were still filled with traces of a man's world, including oversized winter auto tires, a few big bikes, heavy grills, and a collection of electrical tools—enough to build a home.

One evening, as Fr. Jim entered by the south entrance, he noticed what looked like a long rip in the carpeting. It ran a zigzag pattern down the length of the first floor, almost to the windows at the north end. I immediately assured him that the carpet was not torn but just pressed down. As I bent over and tried to rub and raise matted fibers, I explained that the trail led to room 133 where I discovered two residents who had become the proud owners of a very large upright piano purchased that day from "Piano Pete." It took eight of their male friends to move the instrument. After a nervous pause, I inquired of Fr.

Jim if students were permitted to have pianos in their rooms. He patted my arm and said, "Just be glad it was a piano; I came home one evening to find Farley men trying to get a horse in the elevator. You can handle a piano, Jean." The piano turned into pure pleasure. Mary Dondanville ('76) and Shayla Keough ('76) were accomplished pianists who kept the piano on the outer wall and learned when the best times were to entertain us all. But there were many moments when I found myself daydreaming about the Farley horse.

From my earliest days at Notre Dame, I began to court a deep hunch in my heart that someone had laid a great inheritance of ministry at my feet. It seemed to be passed on by much storytelling from one generation of graduates to the next: from fathers to sons and grandsons to great-grandsons. Now daughters would begin to add their heritage.

I was intrigued by the fact that over the years graduates had entered the Congregation of Holy Cross and found themselves in a variety of academic, administrative, and staff positions—handing the university down through the years. The same with various lay faculty who, I discovered, had done their undergraduate work at Notre Dame, only to go on to graduate studies elsewhere with an eye to returning to teach at their alma mater. Yet, in the midst of such generational intrigue, some families arrived with sons and daughters who had never laid eyes on Notre Dame before they arrived for freshman orientation. New bloodlines were always welcome.

I learned quickly that I should lean hard on this "inheritance" and let myself feel the strong support, as well as the incredible expectations of those around me who were anxious to bring Farley Hall into a unique moment in Notre Dame's history. It was destined to become a hallowed hall for some 250 bright, articulate young women—pioneers of a sort—who trekked across the nation to the Indiana hinterlands.

During a Morris Inn reception for new women faculty and staff, Provost James T. Burtchaell, CSC, took me aside for special instructions. I settled nervously into an overstuffed wingback chair as he sat on the edge of a large coffee table. He told me that he was sure that I would make it at Notre Dame if I did two things. He asked if I knew how to change fuses. I didn't. He proceeded to distinguish between circuit breakers and screw-type fuses and then commissioned me to track down all the fuse boxes in the basement, on all the floors, and in all wings of Farley, immediately. His second directive was short and to the point. "Never miss a meal; you will need all the energy you can muster." I was a bit puzzled and probably frowned, but as time went on, I learned to translate his directives into their deeper meanings: stay practical and use your good common sense. I passed his words on to every staff member I trained.

When the moment came to welcome that first class of some 130 freshmen to Farley Hall, two former hall presidents were at my side in the chapel, Ders Anderson ('74) and Bob Murphy ('74). Their presence had a special message for all of us; they came in person to entrust us with "their hall." They stood tall, welcomed the women, and challenged them to carry on "Farley College," as they called it. They were gracious and generous, offering us $150 "to get us started," advancing Farley's fame. Before their welcome was over, they were scouting for runners among us to ensure the continued prominence of the Farley Striders (who had already made a name for themselves by sending monogrammed t-shirts to the Pope, the emperor of Japan, and TV show host Johnny Carson, among other notables).

Of all the topics that I dared to touch upon that night, and on many succeeding arrival nights, two have stood the test of time. I remember strongly stressing that I hoped I wasn't going to have to tell them too often to grow up. The time had come for them to give a great dose of effort to growing deep. This got to be known as my "grow up, grow deep" talk, which I have been reminded of affectionately in Christmas cards and countless reunion conversations.

I also invited the new students to do what I had done walking between the maples on Notre Dame Avenue: pray the Our Father with all their hearts for the life they would need to receive all that Notre Dame would offer them and expect from them. It seemed a fitting prayer for freshmen.

Through my first weeks of rectoring, Farley turned into my home as I slowly grew more realistically aware that hall ministry was going to be a twenty-four-hour way of life. It had been a full-time job for generations of rectors before me, including the Reverend John Francis Farley, CSC, native of Patterson, New Jersey, the hall's namesake. From all the stories it was clear that he had strong pastoral influence on a long line of Notre Dame men who affectionately called him "Pops" or "Pop Farley." The best eyewitness accounts were often spun by Father Charles Sheedy, CSC, Edward "Moose" Krause, and Professor Paul Fenlon, all of whom remembered Father Farley as their rector in Sorin Hall, where, as Krause used to tell us, "He was always one jump ahead of the most clever lads he supervised."

Father Farley stood at the heart of student life, living by that crucial rector adage, "Be there." One favorite photo shows him in a horse and buggy, scouting local bars in town and looking for students who were "off-limits." Another depicts him in full Holy Cross habit playing ball, with catcher's mitt and all. He was infamous for conducting mail calls in person, handing every letter to his boys twice a day. Here and there, I'm told, he would catch a perfume scent on an envelope and make a fuss. The more I heard, the more I realized Pop Farley's hallmark was his pastoral presence. I had a lot to live up to.

I remember my first visit to his grave in the community cemetery, near the large crucifix that overlooks all the graves. His tombstone indicated his birth in 1876 and death in 1939. Many of the Farley women found their way there too, some with flowers. In the fall of 1975, one of them returned from a grave visit out of breath with the news that Pop Farley's 100th birthday was a few months away. With great fanfare the hall celebrated that year and every year since, with a January Pop Farley Week. Each year, residents discover ingenious ways to keep his memory and influence alive.

Farley's first women blossomed into strong pioneer women at ND. The media was always asking them the question, "What does it feel like to be a woman at ND?" Sometimes their responses made it sound like we had just landed on the moon. For example, often a woman was one among many men in a class. I have no doubt that these coeds managed some difficult, stressful, and humorous situations, with a host of stories to tell their grandchildren. What seemed to frustrate them most was being asked questions on a variety of topics for the woman's point of view—as though all women were looking in the same direction.

While male students generally approved of the university's move to admit women, a small percentage thought it was a big mistake. From what I heard in friendly campus conversations, the male faculty felt the change the most in their classrooms. They cast a resounding positive vote, since the women came with outstanding academic credentials and "weren't just looking for MRS. degrees."

I quickly learned that I wasn't rectoring Farley alone. Over the years, my assistant rectors and RAs (resident assistants) were a veritable lifeline for me. Together we knew every resident in Farley and, more often than not, their families and friends as well. We were able to touch lives daily. Generally, the assistant and the RAs were strongly motivated and gifted, with an array of talents including innate people skills. They put precious energy into their work, bore the burden of late hours on duty, and served well in difficult situations. Good RAs unconsciously beckoned underclassmen to follow in their footsteps. Year after year, RAs learned unexpected lessons that would serve them a lifetime.

Just as I was getting to know the nooks and crannies of Farley, I was called to the Office of Student Affairs for a meeting with Vice President Philip Faccenda. He had a plan for a few rooms I hardly knew existed in Farley's basement, back in the T-wing section of the building: two large rooms and four smaller ones, plus a bathroom with a single shower. A plan was afoot to house the girlfriends who came to visit their ND boyfriends, sometimes for campus dances and football games. These young women would stay the night in the "Farley Motel" for one dollar.

Five double-decker beds were placed close to each other in the two large rooms, while two such beds were placed in each of the four smaller rooms. In student hostel fashion, we accommodated thirty-six people. This arrangement released a barrage of telephone calls from across the country. I turned into an innkeeper instantaneously, but within days I realized that I needed a motel manager to take reservations, including one from a corporate executive from the Ford Motor Company who had heard about "the new motel facilities." It became quite obvious that our campus motel merchants failed to offer basic accommodation information. One midnight a student's grandmother knocked on my door to tell me that she couldn't make it onto the top bunk.

The Farley Motel thrived for four years until we needed the space for ND women students. Parents of the first seventeen freshmen assigned to the motel facility registered a series of complaints, many quite legitimate. But the problem still remained—there were no more available rooms on campus. My only peace offering was to explain that their daughters would be moving out of the motel area gradually, as beds became available across campus, and that all of them should be relocated by Christmastime. This was a bit of solace for some parents. However, what I never counted on was the amazing influence of RA Carol Lally ('78), who was assigned to oversee this basement enclave. Overnight she stirred the population into community. She called each student by name, created clever social events, and designed attractive green t-shirts marked with white letters formed out of steam pipes that spelled "Cellar Dwellers." She turned the space into prime property. While rooms opened up across campus, the cellar dwellers refused to budge, even as housing officials beckoned them to move above ground. In time, stories of cellar dwellers grew into legends and filled photo albums.

Curiously, RAs always seemed destined to carry their title for life. Long after their Farley days, I would hear them affectionately referred to as "my RA." One football weekend Mary Ellen Burchett Fausone ('79), a former RA and now an obstetrician, stopped by to visit Farley and spun a fanciful tale. She was on intern duty at Northwestern Memorial Hospital in the Chicago area when a call came through that a woman was on her way to the emergency room to deliver her baby. Surgically dressed for intern duties, she rushed to meet the gurney as it rolled along the hallway. In the midst of the urgency and excitement of the moment, the expectant mother looked up at the budding physician and queried, "Aren't you from Farley Hall?" The intern quickly owned up to her heritage, "Well, I am," only to hear a very nervous retort, "You were an RA, and I was a freshman. Please take good care of me." And the drama carried on.

Farley Hall was never in want for drama. From the moment students settled in each fall with all their stuff, including all their gifts and talents, stories unfolded. Before homesickness became a memory, something remarkable happened to the freshmen. In high school most had been known for their brains, but here everyone was smart. All of a sudden they encountered new acquaintances who wanted to know them for who they were, regardless of their grades. New worlds appeared on their horizons, and the freshmen discovered new pieces of themselves and recognized the wonders in others. As one coed put it, "I felt as though I was being turned inside out."

Without a doubt, it is in the area of relationships that Notre Dame students "grow up and deep" at dizzying rates. Eighty-five percent of my rectoring time was spent talking to students about roommate problems, romances, and friendship. I also gave great doses of conversational energy to stressful relationships involving parents, professors, and, on occasion, an administrator or two. While there were times when I felt steeped in such late-adolescent struggles, most of the time I viewed this role as a front-row seat at an award-winning Broadway drama.

I certainly refereed my share of shouting matches between roommates who, having left their private rooms behind at home, had to learn to talk to their roommates about such things as whose turn it was to clean. Everyday life had a way of becoming terribly tangled with, of all people, their peers. After hours or even days of not speaking to each other, they would finally take the time to reflect on some basic approaches to successful roommate relations. Best of all, these struggles were often the beginning of lasting friendships. I've watched a parade of Farley women walk into each other's lives for a lifetime.

Some families took up a long residency in Farley Hall. Kathleen and Bob Burtchaell of Portland, Oregon, hold a record for sending five daughters to live their ND days here: Molly ('89), Megan ('91), Melissa ('93), Margo ('95), and Monica ('02). Most of them had occasion to fly across the country, transporting their college gear with their father at the controls of his Beech Bonanza private plane.

From the moment I opened my rector's door, the topic of man-woman relationships became a front burner issue. I listened to students declare what Notre Dame "absolutely had to do" to make it a place where male-female relationships could flourish. Though some of the suggestions had merit, many were a cover-up for the students' fear of talking to their fellow classmates. On serious reflection, students agreed that it takes a healthy dose of courage to step out of yourself and let another person come to know you—to accept or reject you. I remember lots of delightful evening talks and walks around the lake, when someone discovered that age-old truth and began to understand that it's those who accept you who change you the most.

Of course there were romances and there were romances. A Farley freshman or sophomore would fall so much in love with a young man, and he with her, that she'd soon imagine herself walking down the aisle, "probably a year after graduation." Then after a semester or so, a phone call or note brought devastating news: suddenly this fantasy man needed "space." There were always precious pieces of life to pick up then. We would put our heads together and look closely at the fact that intense relationships do not stand still and wait for "a year after graduation" to come around; they go forward or backward at a pretty healthy pace, and a person has to be ready for life's complications. Though I often counseled students that "people get you ready for other people," some found it hard to learn from the experience of limping relationships, and some found it harder still to turn away from them smarter and stronger.

As time went on I grew uneasy about the couples who met here, became engaged, and got married before the ink on their diplomas was dry. It seemed crucial to me that couples know each other beyond their undergraduate years. Graduates told me that ND romances and engagements need the impact of the workday world to help them prepare for their journey into life.

Sometimes there was hard news delivered of divorces or illnesses or death—the real stuff of life. One day a call from home brought news to Therese D'Angelo ('82) that her father, a man in his forties, had died of a heart attack. The shocked young woman packed quickly and flew home to her family, leaving behind a stunned, numb, and devastated residence hall community.

A second call came late in the evening. It was from the grieving resident to her roommates. That very morning, she told them, she had received two letters from her dad, which he had written, as he always did, while he was on a business trip. She had read them, welcomed his words, and then threw the letters away. She begged her friends to try to retrieve them.

Somehow they did, with the help of RA Mary Murphy ('81), and others wearing boots, carrying flashlights, and digging their way through all the day's trash in the giant garbage bin behind Farley Hall, not giving up until the letters were recovered. I distinctly remember an RA remarking, "I think everyone in this hall called their dads today."

On any day I could find myself in the midst of a healthy family crisis. I recall a freshman who had struggled valiantly for six or eight weeks to stay on campus even though she claimed that she didn't want to be here. Whenever we met, she reinforced her simple message: "I want to go home." One night I knew she meant it; she was ready to tell her father that she had decided to leave his alma mater, even though he had made a special trip to the campus to convince her that she belonged here.

Now, in a bit of hysteria, she phoned her folks and got her message across. Her dad told her he was proud that she had given it a good try, but he agreed that it was time for her to come home. There was an affectionate exchange of words between them and a thank-you to me before we hung up our phones. Her heavy sobs tapered off into normal breathing as we began to make final plans for her to pack and move home.

Five days passed. I met her going to class "to see friends before I leave." But she never stopped going to class. On that night of cathartic tears, she had put aside her father's decision and replaced it with her own.

At times my emotions rode a roller coaster. I remember a young woman rushing into my room in hysterics after hearing shocking news from home. A moment later someone stood in the doorway looking for paper plates.

There were times when sorrow and joy collided in my soul. On a summer Saturday, I found myself walking back from Cedar Grove Cemetery following the burial of a lovely sophomore, Cynthia Cole, who had suffered an aneurysm. My next stop was Sacred Heart Church for the wedding of our most recent hall president, Donna Crowley ('76), who had just graduated and who had lived across the hall from Cynthia. I never got used to such emotional collisions.

Farley women faced death in their ranks five times during my rector years. Cindy Cole was the first one to go to God before the rest of us. Her American parents lived in Saudi Arabia where her father was employed. Her mother flew to Indiana to visit her daughter and other relatives when Cindy died so suddenly in the summer of 1976. Her funeral Mass was celebrated in Keenan-Stanford Chapel and the burial took place in Cedar Grove Cemetery.

Terry (Mary Therese) Gwynn, senior, from Santa Fe, New Mexico, died alone in a one-car accident on an icy January night in 1977, driving back from Chicago near mile marker fifty-two on I-80. Father Louis Putz, CSC, who knew the Gwynn family well, and I flew southwest as university representatives. I had taught Terry that fall semester, and she had been to the class retreat days at Old College, where she was a huge help in the kitchen.

Kathy Guthery was a few days away from returning to campus in August 1979 for band practice. Before heading north, she kept a date to attend a going-back-to-college gathering with friends in Jasper, deep in Indiana farmland. She left the group early, accepting a ride on a motorcycle from a boyfriend. A two-vehicle accident occurred not far from her home. Father George Wisckirchen, CSC, assistant band director, and I drove down for the funeral, taking time to be with her parents, Ruth Ann and Frank Guthery, who annually visit Farley Hall.

In the fall of her junior year, Mary Craig learned she had cancer. Her dad, Dr. George Craig, a world-renowned biologist who taught and did research at ND, and her mother, Betty, along with Mary's siblings, all stood tall in the mystery of it all. Mary's classmates were shocked as their dear friend desperately worked to finish her classes before Christmas. On February 4, 1978, as South Bend dug itself out of a record-breaking snowfall, Fr. Mario Pedi, OSB and rector of St. Ed's Hall, picked up the holy oils for the sacrament of the sick at the east gate early in the morning and together we went to St. Joseph's Hospital for Mary's last anointing.

On another cold night in January 1983, I answered the phone around midnight to find out that Michelle and Rita Murphy of Casper, Wyoming, had been in a tragic car accident on their way back to Notre Dame as the result of poor visibility, a snow squall, and a traffic pile-up of more than twenty vehicles. Rita died instantly; Michelle was in critical condition, not expected to live. Rita was a sophomore from Pasquerilla East Hall and Michelle was a junior from Farley. They were two of Rita and Joe Murphy's twelve children.

I could see Fr. Hesburgh's light on in his office in the main building, but I couldn't bring myself to call him. I had such a hard time living with what I had just heard. I wept and I prayed and I so resisted having to let this news loose on the campus. The Murphys had made their mark at Notre Dame. Dr. Joseph Murphy graduated in 1945, with sons Patrick ('76), Don ('78), and Kevin ('80), and Rita and Michelle following in his footsteps. Later, another son, Robert, and daughter, Ann, would also earn ND degrees. Within hours, Fr. Don McNeill, CSC, director of the Center for Social Concerns and friend of the family, planned to head for Casper as the university's representative. During an unexpected meeting with Fr. Hesburgh the next day, he explained that two of us should go in light of the difficult situation, directing me to pack at once and travel with Fr. Don. By the time our plane landed in Casper, Michelle had died.

I had never realized the impact of so much grief. Vivid images stay stored in my memory of huddling in the cemetery with the Murphy clan and Fr. Don, bundled against bone-chilling January winds whipping across the plains of Wyoming, starkly aware of how good people live and love and face loss. Years later, I stood in that same spot on a warm spring day with flowers blooming everywhere with Rita Murphy, the mother of the girls. They were more alive in us than ever.

The deaths of Farley women have offered all previous residents of the hall a precious wisdom and grace that keeps emerging in our stories about each other, in the memories we cherish, and in our struggles to understand the deepest meanings of loss and grief, hope and resurrection.

There was always someone at my heels asking questions about religion. Although I never took a survey of the students' religious attitudes or practices, I knew from some very lively conversations that they were at various points of development in the life of the spirit. Many had argued endlessly with high-school religion teachers and CCD instructors about what the Church teaches. Some described classic scenes with parents at their kitchen tables. As a result, many were able to couple their intellectual pursuits with a consistent practice of faith. Yet a number of underclassmen openly stated that they had stopped going to church in high school. Many of these students found themselves "back around the altars" at Notre Dame.

I began to think of a portion of the student body as catechumens, in the very best sense of the word. Many had known little cultivation of their faith life, and they unabashedly initiated conversations that drew them into asking the deepest and simplest questions about spiritual things. When I first came to Farley and taught theology, I was often asked to explain the changes resulting from Vatican Council II. By the 1980s, "change talk" gave way to precious ignorance. It was no longer a matter of explaining why altars were turned around to face the congregation or why it was proper to take the Eucharist in hand instead of having it placed on our tongues. Now questions and concerns arose because students weren't always able to name and explain the seven sacraments.

I'm convinced that one of the most profound things that happens to students here is that they watch people, including their peers, simply kneel down and pray. This occurs in the residence hall chapels, at the grotto, and on retreats. They grow startlingly still and reflective during a good homily, touching the spiritual side of their daily dealings. Our students are not strangers to prayer. In addition, they are a real grace in one another's lives, and I suspect many of them realize it—or will in time.

There was so much joy and pain and daily existence to share. Amazingly, the life of the hall produced its own "peer ministry" activity. Farley women found endless ways to care for each other in the face of minor illnesses, upsetting news, difficult relationships, academic stress, and decision making. Of course, there were some selfish moments, but in general I watched peer ministry thrive and prayed that it would continue year after year. In fact, I came to believe that often it was the outcome of our prayer together around our Farley altar that made us more caring and compassionate toward each other.

The altar of our residence hall chapel was a place where many students gathered to celebrate the Eucharist, in large groups on weekends and in smaller groups for daily celebrations. And it wasn't unusual for students to meet in advance with Eucharistic celebrants to plan upcoming celebrations. Many music ministers trained with Campus Ministry, played a variety of instruments, and led the hymns. Others baked the Eucharistic bread. Some practiced with those who volunteered to read the Scriptures. One year, to my surprise, Farley had a team of sacristans who "wanted to learn how to take care of Church things." At another juncture a young woman came carrying the large sacramentary from the sacristy with a simple request: "Would you please teach me the parts of the Mass. I want to become the liturgical commissioner of Farley." And she did. Watching the hall's liturgy commissioners in action put hope in my heart, since I was convinced that much of their experience and energy was destined for the Church at large in the years ahead.

Hardly a Sunday night went by without someone standing up at the end of Mass to inform the congregation about someone or some group that needed help. The request might focus on Logan Center or the Center for the Homeless or someone needing a wheelchair or food. It might be an announcement about a deadline for applying for Holy Cross Associates or Summer Service Projects or an Urban Plunge. There was always some student or student group associated with the Center for Social Concerns, recognizing a need and asking for assistance in the form of time, money, or other material support.

Helping others receives a strong and consistent press on campus. This gospel value was, no doubt, alive and well in those Holy Cross pioneers who arrived here in covered wagons back in 1842, and it has hung in the air and lots of hearts ever since. As rector, I stayed close to that inheritance which had its own way of getting into my bones and changing my heart, too.

All in all, rectoring was an extremely purifying experience. Many residents knew all of my idiosyncrasies, weaknesses, and strengths. Amazingly, there were also some who sensed when I needed to be ministered to. One young woman hit the mark every time. Somewhere along the line she heard me say that "violins soothed my soul," and she would remind me of it whenever she saw me standing knee-high in some stressful situation: "Maybe it's a violin day?" Another resident often returned from the Huddle with an extra double-decker ice cream cone. A sophomore once told me that I looked as though I could use a long walk around the lake, so she stayed and covered the office and phone. One of the most compassionate moments came when an RA, Sheila Murphy ('77), who had lost her mom to cancer, met me returning from a weekend visit to my dad who was dying of the same. I told her I thought I might not see him alive again. We wept together.

As a rector, I was doubly conscious of my emotions, especially those of anger and grief. I never knew such anger could rise inside of me so suddenly when faced with conflict and confrontation; nor did I anticipate experiencing so much grief in the midst of student tragedies that became my own.

Like other human beings, I've been tired in my life but tried to carry on without giving others too much occasion to notice. That was hard in Farley where residents read me well and knew when the need for sleep had penetrated my bones. I became accustomed to their knowing: With a yawn I sometimes introduced myself as "Jean Farley," wore two unrelated shoes, fell asleep during a phone call, and insisted to others that I was "just Farley" instead of "just fine."

Living in the rector's quarters was like living in a fishbowl, but I gradually became adept at finding free time and secret places to serve my solitude and sanity. Some days a long, quiet walk around the lake made all the difference. I corrected theology exams perched on a pile of pillows next to my shower stall or sitting in a shadowy pew in Sacred Heart Basilica. Sometimes I hid in the hall sacristy.

But my days in Farley brought me some of the deepest living experiences I have known in a lifetime. A generation ahead of the first Farley women, I simply moved into their midst and opened my door. They came in, questioned me incessantly on endless topics, picked my brain, and searched my heart, asking me to share my wisdom. They let me confront them with strong words and congratulate them with deep joy.

We laughed and cried and discussed and danced and argued and ate and cheered together. We prayed together and forgave one another. They let me worry about them. Best of all they let me believe in them.

THREE

Parent Watcher

A haunting question circled me constantly as a rector. Sometimes it woke me up in the morning. It had a way of settling right in the front of my brain, especially when there was counseling to do that needed tough-love packaging: What would I do if this were my son or daughter? This query never grew into a complicated paragraph or took on any colorful adjectives, but it did make me stand tall. It always gave me strength and courage to speak up, reach out, call a doctor, make a cup of tea, say some hard things, laugh at the right time, listen to unending "he said/she said" stories, welcome tears, congratulate, cajole, get students to class on time and home for the holidays. It was the question that had an engaging way of pointing me in the right direction and getting me to the heart of issues. It also turned me into a parent watcher.

It was simply impossible to sit where I sat and not see what I saw. Thick family histories unfolded chapter after chapter. While I was not surprised at the kinds and amounts of energy that parents poured into the lives of their offspring, I became enthralled with the opposite flow of energy, the drama of how children shaped their parents. There were signs of it everywhere.

Parents arriving on campus for the first time opened themselves to an emotional stretch that carried a four-year guarantee. They attended every meeting, took the tours, built lofts, purchased and laid carpeting, hung curtains, put up pictures and posters, and bought a pantry of goodies—all the time hoping that they were doing the right things as they rolled their eyes and wondered how their firstborn daughters would adjust to all of this, as well as how they themselves would.

One freshman's dad took me aside quite confidentially to explain that from the moment he and his wife seriously thought of sending their child off to college, he began to fret over where it would all lead. "You think of everything, the best and the worst, but we had to learn to trust," he explained. "The junior college in our backyard was not the best choice for her. We just had to let her go." He deserved my best handshake and congratulations.

I watched an African American couple meet a white couple as their daughters became acquainted in a third-floor Farley room they would share. There was uneasiness, especially since the individuals involved had no experience in meeting members of another race and cultural background. In a similar instance, white parents were civil in the presence of the students, but later requested a room change for their daughter. Most daughters in these scenarios spoke up and said that they were fine with the arrangement and wanted to stay where they were assigned. There were friendships in progress that spread to include parents over time.

During freshman orientation a presentation on international programs available to Notre Dame students stopped many parents in their tracks. "You would like to study where?" "Cross which ocean?" New fears filled parent faces and confusion clogged their voices. They walked smack into another lurking decision with an emotional charge and, with good reason, pushed it into the future, "We'll talk about that later!"

A celebration of Sunday Eucharist always marks the close of formal orientation events. Hundred of freshmen gather as the spanking new class, seated on the Joyce Arena floor, at a good symbolic distance from parents who circle them in padded seats. The scene marks a major moment in the family dynamic—a son or daughter is leaving home—and parents feel it powerfully.

Farewells are the last hurdle on such an orientation weekend. Some parents leave quickly, like plucking a Band-Aid off a raw wound hoping for the least amount of pain. Others drag it out by taking the long way to the car and getting lost in rather insignificant conversations. But the moment has to come. Many parents struggle to take the lead, and stand tall, saying their farewells with lingering affection in the air. Students tend to turn away fast and head into their new life.

Parents know that they are headed back home to stare at empty places. Some deliver a series of staccato phrases at each other as they walk to the car: "I can hardly stand this," "Let's get going, now," "He's too young for all this freedom," "I'm going to miss her so much." Often there are tears and loud silences. If a daughter or son is still within earshot as the family van pulls out of the parking lot, a last minute flow of affectionate commands trail off into a garble: "Call, write, e-mail, get your sleep, take your medicine, write to Grandpa-a-a-!"

As parents drive away, they can't know that the distance between them and their children will afford them a whole new space and level of communication. Right now, they bear only pain with all its rich shaping powers. Some parents record surprise at the impact of the separation. Others felt it coming for weeks.

Occasionally lingering dramas followed separation ceremonies. One mother traveled back and forth to campus for a succession of weekends, driving several hundred miles with her vacuum sweeper in the trunk, prepared to clean her daughter's room. When her husband finally refused to make the trip one more time, the physical separation finally took hold.

If truth be told, in the midst of all the mixed emotions that go along with sending a child off to college, many parents welcome the thought that there will be adults at Notre Dame—faculty, staff, employees—who will come to know, educate, mentor, and care about their children. "We need all the help we can get in this parent business," one dad admitted. Many parents quite consciously invite others to look their offspring in the eye and challenge them with "No, you can't," or "Yes, you can," or "Great job. Do that again!"

While parents pass on most of the responsibility for their son or daughter's education to those at the university, they also continue the challenge of long-distance parenting. There's not a doubt in my mind these days that Farley Hall and every other residence hall is wired to the world, well-connected to kitchens, bedrooms, family rooms, office extensions, car phones, cell phones, and computers, and wherever else ND parents dwell and struggle to be better parents.

Some phone conversations are terribly entangled with intricate plots. Oral "paragraph summaries" on a Monday morning that cover a change of a major area of study, travel plans for spring break, a serious new boyfriend, and applications for working with an inner-city team next summer, leave parents little room for breath. "Mom, how about if I just write you and Dad, and explain what's going on inside me?" These letters are read repeatedly and form a kind of mutual understanding. Some parents actually discover that they also like writing letters. More and more of them join the e-mail route. They get "stuff" off their chests, too. The McGuire family sent their hometown newspaper from Holstein, Iowa, which became a primary source for city dwellers who knew little about country life as it attracted a fairly wide readership in Farley and was often quoted.

Whatever the medium—phone, letters, e-mail, fax—it was communication compressed by the limits of time and space. There was really very little room to beat around the bush or produce a large framework for reference. This often meant that facts and feelings were untimely forced to the surface in inopportune ways. Both parents and children struggled with sudden flares of temper, or expressions of love and affection with words instead of hugs. However, these new forms of communication had some unique advantages over long talks at the kitchen table. Any way you looked at it, everyone involved stood to learn more and more about each other.

Summaries of telephone conversations continually drifted into my office from the hallway. "My dad yelled at me over the phone last night. He was really upset—but at least he didn't drag it out. He told me to quit whining and get to the counselor about my calculus class. He knows me too well. I just hate math."

Some messages were reported to me directly. "I just found out from my mom that I can't go to Cancun for spring break. It was really hard for my mom to tell me. My Gram is terribly sick. I feel so torn, but I know Mom's right, I should be home with the family."

Now and then, even a sophomore got a peek at how she and her parents were shaping each other. She was standing near the chapel door with a hefty package from home at her feet, reading a card filled with greetings for her nineteenth birthday. She looked up long enough to share classic surprise, "You know, I think even if my parents weren't my parents, they would be good friends of mine."

Many parents have yarns to spin about how they sent their son or daughter off to Notre Dame feeling such a loss, only to find Notre

Dame come back to them with a great force of life—three roommates and their families, sectionmates, the hall staff, professors, mentors, and lifetime friends along the way. However, space and time away from home nudges the relationship between parents and young adults to another stage—and more change. Ready or not, what parents hoped for in their sons and daughters begins to happen and can be full of surprises.

Many are amazed at how their daughters and sons, who had rooms to themselves at home, adjust to living in a quad with three others and all their combined paraphernalia. It took some planning, sharing, forgiving, patience, good humor, understanding, and honesty to turn these individuals into lifelong friends.

Selecting a major area of study carries with it early signs of independence. Some households reach happy compromises early on, which satisfies everyone. "I just knew she would be drawn to architecture," one mother whispered to me. "We're thrilled. You know that was her grandfather's trade."

However, life gets more complicated when parents step forward and pressure offspring into specific areas of study for their own reasons. Parents were always on my tail, seriously upset because I supported a son or daughter who was going against their wishes. One lad said rather desperately, "You've got to talk with my dad. This is driving me nuts. I don't want to be a doctor. I want out of the sciences. It's not my world." But this father wouldn't give in and his son conveniently stopped going to class and ultimately dropped out of school. Such influence can be so ugly and long-lasting.

For the few parents who won't give in, there are many who do. It can take some tall talking by phone, during holiday visits, or in long letters. Ideas can become tangled with ego struggles. When all is said and done, there's an unselfishness that many parents learn. It has a lot to do with letting their offspring search for the right path in their lives. Gradually parents come to learn more about their offspring, their talents and gifts, and what they have a passion for. Repeatedly I have heard parents admit that they were wrong as they watch their sons and daughters change their majors, slough off minor depression, and wake up enthused again about life and learning.

Through it all, parental wisdom emerges. Parents patiently learn to give up subtle controls and grow more peaceful and proud in the process. Their conversations are poignant giveaways. "I just can't believe how happy our daughter is since she moved into her ecology studies. We kept telling her that it would be too much for her, but she kept insisting, so we backed off and let her go. She keeps surprising us in such good ways at every turn. The other night at dinner I kiddingly said to my husband, 'Is she really ours?' " Parents watch and hear it all like auditors in a classroom as they shadow their John or Mary along the way. One mom summed it up during a graduation reception, "I feel like I 'did' Notre Dame by phone."

There's a special delight in watching parents recognize unselfishness in so many of their offspring, an amazing grace at work. It starts at home, becomes planted here, and increases and multiplies. One mother confided that the most important things that happened to her daughter at Notre Dame began when she volunteered at Logan Center. As a visitor this mother watched in amazement as her daughter moved with grace and ease among physically and mentally challenged children and young adults. And her daughter had no second thoughts about what this work meant to her, "My Logan days gave focus to my whole education."

While some experiences clarify so much, other developments in a student's life can be perplexing for everyone involved. For example, more than one parent has sat in total denial with me about a daughter's eating disorder. "She's a vegetarian and will be just fine" is where it often begins. There are a lot of phone calls. The daughter's friends worry and circle her. Often good friends alert the rector. Parents arrive, some angry at the intrusion of others into their daughter's life. Some threaten lawsuits—until they see their daughter's physical condition. After agreeing to an exam at the University Health Center and facing facts, many young women have had to withdraw from school and seek immediate outpatient help. Such plots can have happy endings once everyone becomes more educated about the condition.

Parents also find intriguing ways of taking on an inordinate amount of blame and shame for their children's imperfections and mistakes, often desperately trying to hide them. My best words to them may seem cold and direct, but they are the same words I find best for their children at times: "Why are you doing this to yourselves?" There may be anger and tears. Some parents leave my office quickly because their nerves get too frayed, however many stay and admit quite simply, "We need some help with all this." How quickly they accuse themselves of being poor parents and of letting a situation get out of control. Occasionally a son will refuse to talk with either parent, causing a full-blown logjam. The parents are duly embarrassed, yet they grow stronger than ever as they reach out for some professional know-how. Many times I have watched a good counselor take advantage of such a critical moment that might have led to years of not speaking to each other and turn it into a truthful conversation that made all the difference.

While packing up a young scholar to spend a year in Ireland, France, Austria, Japan, or a semester in London or Australia can pose some major hurdles, it often entices parents to follow their kin abroad. What a shock it is for many parents when they find themselves flying across oceans, let alone being whisked around London by tour guides—their sons and daughters. "Without a doubt," a dad recounted, "our daughter made us very daring in our middle age. In fact, before we left Heathrow, we began making plans to tour France next summer."

After traveling through Europe, one father confessed that he would still be sitting on his front porch out west if he hadn't driven across the United States to visit his sophomore son at Notre Dame. "It gave me a great case of wanderlust that I have never recovered from—and for which I am deeply grateful."

Even parents who are unable or choose not to visit their offspring abroad vicariously come to cherish highlights of their offspring's journey. "I feel like I've been there and back" is a common refrain. Phone conversations, e-mail ramblings, a trail of photos, videotapes, souvenirs—they all spin colorful stories that create long memories. Parents surprise themselves as they became map readers right at their kitchen tables. They turn into local authorities on international geography—all because their kids are peripatetically educated in and out of classrooms, jumping buses, catching trains, hanging out at the Hebrew University, backpacking, biking, sailing, camel riding, snorkeling, deep-sea diving, mountain climbing, skiing, and interviewing aborigines. Needless to say, parents quickly learn to check global currency exchange rates and weather reports.

The moment does come when seniors seriously begin to look beyond Notre Dame. Parents often watch them from the shadows. While many make good, honest choices for more education or promising careers, there's a group of some two hundred students who stop in their tracks and embrace a decision that baffles many—volunteer service in God-knows-where in the United States or some far-flung village across the world.

Such decisions shock many parents who expect their offspring to snap up a job in corporate America or continue with their education in law, medicine, or scientific research. It seems the more promising the students are, the more stunning it is to watch them set sights on undeveloped parts of the world, where they might live and work with unknown peoples in challenging living conditions.

Parents easily and convincingly raise a host of questions: "Where did you ever get this idea?" "You're not really serious about this, are you?" "Could it be you're afraid you won't make it in the real world?" "You have loans to pay off!" They arrange and rearrange reasonable obstacles until some of them just give up and give in, then they become silent about it in uncomfortable ways. Other parents simply put the future on hold. "Let's just wait and see if this is really what he's going to do."

Many responses to future career plans hang in the air until graduation day. The truth of the matter becomes clearer during a simple morning ceremony, hosted by the Center for Social Concerns, as the university celebrates the sending of Notre Dame volunteers across the country and the world. A great mix of parents, grandparents, friends, staff, and administrators gather in Washington Hall with colliding emotions, evident in the mixture of smiles and heavy frowns.

The university president attends with special guests, perhaps an internationally known cardinal and/or a U.S. statesman—possible candidates for honorary university degrees—all present on campus for graduation ceremonies a few hours away. Although an honored guest may make some short remarks, the main address is given by a former Notre Dame volunteer, such as Andrea Smith Shappell ('79 and '85), M. J. Murray Vachon ('84), or Lou Nanni ('88), all now married and with children, who never miss the heart of the matter: "My volunteer years changed my life forever. I can't imagine my life without them. I received so much more than I ever gave." Then one by one the new volunteers take the microphone, introducing themselves and the people and part of the world they will serve. It's a charged moment, during which generosity and goodness and prayer are unleashed in the universe.

The audience grows very quiet, lost in thought, studying faces and sizes and strides of young bodies crossing the stage, listening to the declarations of their identities and destinations, one after the other. It's more than a procession. It's more like a walking litany, grace-filled. Parents watch and whisper back and forth to each other. This is all so different from observing their offspring play in a piano recital, collect a science project award, or deliver a valedictory. These are young generous hearts stepping into a commitment that will directly affect the lives of others. It's an energy-filled scene that takes the parents' breath away and moves them thoughtfully into the final moments of the ceremony where they are called upon to do something many have never done before—bless their child, aloud. Invited by Father Don McNeill, CSC, director of the Center for Social Concerns, they stand and place their hands on or arms around their son or daughter's shoulders, begging God's endless, life-giving blessings.

It never fails. As parents leave the ceremony, there's a new spirit in the crowd and a new look in many eyes. Parents cannot help but let their children give their gifts and their grace to those in need. As one father said, walking down the steps with his arm in half a hug around his daughter, "Well, damn it, I can't say I won't worry about you, but this last hour put me in a different place. I'm really proud of you."

One of the grandest surprises will come for parents when they visit a Chilean parish or an African school or home for unwed mothers to watch their offspring in action—perhaps offering a visitor's hand to the cause.

While parents spend graduation weekend at Notre Dame lost in thoughts that often focus on their children's growth and accomplishments, I strongly believe that many of these parents also realize that they have been at the heart of an educational adventure, shaped at every turn, and all the wiser for it.

FOUR

The Legendary Pay Caf

She discovered that I was the new rector at Farley Hall, and I realized that the Pay Caf was nothing without Sophie, who rose each day at 3:00 A.M. to get to campus, make coffee, and get breakfast going. Her smile and small figure were always behind the serving counter, with its breakfast and luncheon specials. She made your eggs just the way you liked them. At first we said short hellos as I made choices and pushed my tray along the silver bars to the cashier. In time we greeted, adding words about each other's well-being. That's when I detected her slight European accent.

I was told from Pay Caf regulars that Notre Dame had opened its doors for employment to a long line of immigrants and refugees over the years, including those who fled from the Hungarian Revolution, Vietnam, and Cambodia. Many were hosted by South Bend families of ND graduates and began new lives again. Notre Dame was well served in the process. Sophie was a Polish woman who immigrated to the United States after World War II. That's all I knew about her for a long time, until a very bitter cold Saturday in January. I stopped in the Pay Caf at midmorning for coffee and a sweet roll. It wasn't busy, and some of the women I knew from the kitchen and the serving line were taking their coffee breaks. So I joined them around one of the large, circular oak tables, choosing to sit next to Sophie.

Somehow we began talking about different nationalities, a variety of which were represented around the table, and arranged-marriage customs. Lots of local-color vignettes emerged quickly, mixed well with laughter. Sophie got that faraway look in her eye as she recalled how her parents had paired her off with a young man in her village. "And I was so young and immature. I didn't even know the facts of life," she said rather shyly. "My mother first taught me what I should know only after I came running home to her all upset and afraid and filled with questions—days after our wedding ceremony. That's how we learned all about life in those days." One of her friends added, "Well, it looks like it worked. Here you are married all these wonderful years to that some young man." She agreed.

Then I asked a question quite directly but so innocently that it led us into a story we could hardly bear hearing, "Did you have any children, Sophie?" She admitted that she did. Then she lowered her head almost to the tabletop and grew speechless. I put my arm around her shoulders. Softly but clearly she explained that they were killed in a concentration camp. No one dared to ask how many. She began to weep. We were all so startled and silent. Then our tears came.

Someone reached for her hand and said, "You never told us this before, Sophie. Help us understand. How long were you in the concentration camp?" She offered a holy day count, "four Christmases." Slowly and deliberately she continued, "I lost my parents and my brothers and sisters in the camp, too." And she wept harder as she added these words to her others.

In so much deep grief, for some reason Sophie felt safe and let it surface in our circle. She was able to let some of her sorrow go, spill out of herself and into our ears and eyes and imaginations. I could feel her shoulders and her small body shudder now and then. We sat quietly with her and each other. From the corner of my eye, I could see the manager of the Pay Caf across the room, reminding everyone as congenially as possible that coffee break was over. When she saw our faces and our tears, she walked away and watched from a distance. It was such a holy moment in such a public place.

Then Sophie moved us away from her sorrow to some of the joy she knew at the time of her liberation from the concentration camp. She explained that she and her husband lived in separate quarters, although they both worked in ammunition factories. "That's why we were still alive. We were young and strong and could work." One particular day the women in her bunker weren't allowed to leave for the ammunition factory because of heavy bombing going on all around them. Gradually it stopped.

They expected the usual signal that would send them back to work, but instead there was a banging on their door and a loud cry, "Come out!" The door was flung open, Sophie explained, and as soon as they saw the tall silhouette they knew it was an American soldier. "I remember, we rushed to embrace him, to kiss his feet, his big boots." For some moments the drama of it all hung in Pay Caf air. She brought us all back to the round table when she said, "After that, my husband and I came to America, to South Bend. Then I came to this place," she concluded, as she took in the Pay Caf with one sweeping glance. Coffee break was over, but not before everyone around the table embraced Sophie.

Call it what you will—the Pay Caf, the Oak Room, the Legendary Oak Room, or the Night Oak—it was a public cafeteria situated between two student cafeterias in the South Dining Hall. This colorful eatery was where the university community intersected, mostly because of hunger for food and good company.

A bit of history stretched across the walls in large murals—to the east, John Zahm's expedition with Theodore Roosevelt to South America and Julius Nieuwland discovering synthetic rubber in a Notre Dame chemistry lab; to the west, a depiction of Notre Dame's growth from its beginning to campus expansion following World War II.

Almost every evening near six o'clock, I locked the rector's room and headed in diagonal fashion for the south quad, eager for a warm dinner and a chance to relax with friends. There were no kitchenettes in rector rooms at that time, which led women rectors from different religious congregations to join each other and the Pay Caf community. At one time, the Holy Cross priests gathered in a community dining room above the Pay Caf. Later they moved to Corby Hall where they now take their meals together.

It was a healthy trek to the south quad, whatever the weather. In spring and summer it was like walking through a grand state park, ducking frisbees here and there, often keeping one eye on a blazing sunset. In early spring, I sometimes took flower tours on the way, sighting clusters of quince blossoms, crocus, tulips, dandelions, bursting magnolia buds, forsythia, crab apple blossoms, and jonquils along the way. Then came the dogwood and lilacs. Here and there were yucca plants. On some fall days, a driving rain produced slippery leaves of all kinds and colors underfoot. In a wink, umbrellas blew inside out. It was hood weather.

But it was the raw, zero-degree weather that carried the drama with crunchy snow and heavy boots. Homemade ice patches enticed their designers to take long, running slides to the dining halls, getting them there more quickly and possibly more hungry. On those bitter, cold nights, crystal-clear skies stretched over the campus filled with constellations of stars that we often tried to sight and name—Orion's belt, Cassiopeia, or the Pleiades—with our warm breath puffing visibly into the air, a syllable at a time. Some evenings it was impossible to see through the driving snow of a full-blown blizzard. A long, woolen, hooded coat (complete with boots, gloves, and a woolen scarf that wound around my neck and covered half my face) returned me unfrozen to Farley. How many times I thought of Jack London and his stories of the Yukon.

In nicer weather I tried to picture the navy midshipmen in full ranks during World War II, filling and marching the quad, right where I was crossing. Dramatic photos of this scene stay locked in my mind, probably because as a child that war seemed all around me. My mom and dad bought my school shoes and meat with rationing coupons. And I learned how to act in a bomb raid (by hiding under my grade-school desk in St. Martin's school on the south side of Chicago), and what to do in my home during a city blackout. Once while crossing "the Navy Quad" back to Farley, I counted the number of wars that had affected the students, faculty, staff, and administrators of Notre Dame over the years, listing too many: the Civil War, the Spanish-American War, World War I, World War II, the Korean War, and the Vietnam War. At close range I watched the Desert Storm War reach out for our graduates.

On any given evening much more than eating was going on in the Pay Caf, as about fifty to one hundred diners gathered around familiar Romweber oak tables with matching chairs, made in Batesville, Indiana, decades ago. Graduate students, most of whom lived off campus, lingered long after dessert, discussing engineering projects underway, linguistic papers they were writing, or comprehensive exams awaiting them. For many international students, the Pay Caf was a place to meet, relax, and speak their native languages. In addition, there were always clusters of law students on the scene, sometimes with Dean David Link or Professor Bob Rodes, continuing a discussion that had started a half a block away in the halls of the Law School.

I first met jurisprudence professor Anton-Hermann Chroust in the Pay Caf at the start of a fall semester. He had just returned from his annual trip to Europe with his sports car that miraculously took him through the European mountains. Coming to the end of his teaching career, he was full of reminiscence that jumped from one continent to another, and from graduate to undergraduate teaching tales. Famous for his definition of history, he called it "the rhythmic repetition of human stupidity down through the contingency of time." One evening in the midst of all his storytelling, he came to a personal juncture. He told me about his young wife who met with a tragic accident while horseback riding. She lingered for some time with severe head injuries. They were hard days for Professor Chroust. Many years later, in the midst of an after-dinner coffee, a flood of dormant grief surged through Chroust, surprising both of us, blessing us. The Pay Caf was made of such moments.

I wanted to tell him of Charlie Phillips that night but I couldn't. Perhaps Chroust had known him; I never found out. They were soul brothers of a sort, at least in my mind. Bachelor Don Charles Phillips was the subject of an "Unforgettable Character" essay by Notre Dame's Richard Sullivan, which included a photo of an outside view of his turret quarters in Sorin Hall. The essay appeared in a high-school American literature textbook and I took a fancy to it. Once on campus, I was hoping to meet Charlie, but I learned from his friend Paul Fenlon, who was also a turret dweller in Sorin, that Charlie had died. Paul also explained that Charlie was not a bachelor don, strictly speaking, though official publications said it was so. As a young man Charlie had married, only to have his wife suffer a mental breakdown, institutionalizing her for the rest of her life. He embraced a so-called bachelorhood and gave his life away as a professor for the young, although very few knew such details, Paul insisted.

For Paul Fenlon, the Pay Caf was as good as an annex to his first-floor turret rooms where he lived for more than sixty years. It was his dining room, where he picked up the morning paper with breakfast and often met with friends. Frequently swamped by alums on a football weekend or during summer reunions, he would sum up his exhaustion by muttering, "I've lived so damn long I've turned into one of those Notre Dame legends. They just want to see if I'm still alive."

Paul remembered Edward "Moose" Krause and Fr. Charlie "Chick" Sheedy, CSC, as "freshmen lads" running up the steps of Sorin Hall for the first time. He was also a great source of information on John Francis Farley, CSC, our hall's namesake, originally from Patterson, New Jersey. Farley women interviewed Paul in preparation for what would have been Pop Farley's 100th birthday celebration in 1976. For the occasion he came for tea and Girl Scout cookies, donning a dashing straw hat, carrying a cane, and wearing spats. Women of Farley had never seen spats before and thought he had a foot problem.

Beloved Moose Krause, who now sits in bronze on a matching bench outside the Joyce Athletic Center, dined frequently in the Pay Caf with his wife, Elise, who had suffered a serious taxicab accident in the 1960s and never completely regained her full physical and mental capacities. The three of us hailed from the south side of Chicago, and on many occasions as I came through the cafeteria line, Moose would invite me to dine at their table. They also had close relatives, Elise's father and her sister Dorothy, who lived, as we say in Chicago "just across the alley" from my parents.

Moose's fine reputation only improved as we sat together in the Pay Caf and I watched him and Elise work their way through many difficult conversations, some of which progressed calmly, while others triggered emotional outbursts from his wife with very little warning. These scenes had embarrassing edges for the Krauses, but Moose counted on everyone around them to understand, and most of the Pay Caf community did. Elise's emotional fragility and Moose's care and fidelity became an inspiration for many who knew them.

Various stages of family life were represented at Pay Caf tables. Many young couples, often on tenure track, met there for dinner with small children, teaching one how to hold a fork and another how to chew food with a closed mouth. Some parents used the high chairs that stood along the wall near the coffeemaker for toddlers too small for regular chairs but very able to make their way through mashed potatoes.

Some of these children grew up right in front of me until they could push their own trays through the cafeteria line, becoming Domers themselves, like Elizabeth and Sarah Moriarty, and their younger brother, Daniel, for whom I became a godmother.

On special nights tables were pushed together and tablecloths appeared. Regular patrons knew that Coach Digger Phelps would soon arrive with his basketball team for steak dinners, which would hopefully convert into big wins on the court. You could hear people all around trying to put names to faces as team members made their way to their tables, towering and smiling over some of their favorite fans.

Lunchtime created another scene in this public cafeteria. It was filled with a bustle and a rush of life for many who were on a lunch-hour schedule, moving quickly through the line, waving to friends, looking for a table where they might catch up with gossip and news of the day. Bill Thistlewaite, his grounds crew, and friends often circled a table where they very informally reviewed plowing procedures after a major late-night snowstorm, or discussed the art of trimming trees, cutting them down, or planting new ones. Secretaries designed shopping tours into Chicago and family parties. Security personnel drew immediate attention if a two-way radio disturbed the noonday chatter. Some diners picked up the *Observer*, hot off the press at the Pay Caf entrance, and read their way through soup and salad.

Friends of Professor Jim Robinson, beloved Shakespeare scholar for some forty years at Notre Dame, and Michael Garvey ('74), assistant director of Public Relations, could converse about subjects from Shakespeare and Samuel Beckett to the Kansas City Chiefs and the Chicago Bears. One day they were discussing the topic of tombstone epitaphs. Jim Robinson made it clear that his should say: "Half of what he said meant something, / And the other half didn't mean anything at all. Forever and anon." Since Robinson also told his wife, Maggie, of his wish, she graciously had those words carved on his tombstone in Cedar Grove Cemetery when he was laid to rest.

A walk between lunch tables uncovered new faces: members of visiting athletic teams and their coaches, interested high-school seniors and their parents, tourists with bookstore bags bulging with sportswear, and a textbook salesman or two scheduled for an appointment with

Brother Conan, the grand manager of the old bookstore, a stone's throw from the Caf.

Sunday morning brunch also had its own ambience. Few people were in a hurry, strolling across campus from Sunday Mass in Sacred Heart Church or driving in from nearby parishes. Some local families (such as the Chuck Wilburs and Steve Moriartys, the Phil Faccendas, the Chris Murphys, the Michael Garveys, and the Frank Cunninghams) regularly gathered there, bought the Sunday paper, and spread the sections among their family members. Football weekend crowds formed in long lines, while lots of friendly visiting went on among the patrons. Families from out of town had reunions around tables that they pushed together as they showed off new babies. Often Notre Dame priests met in the Pay Caf with engaged couples in town for football weekends, anxious to work out preliminary wedding plans between eating Notre Dame waffles.

One Sunday morning following a victorious cliff-hanger football game against a chief rival, the game was replayed on a newly installed large television screen. It turned the Pay Caf into an "eating stadium." Few people left the cafeteria as the game aired. Brunch fans lined the walls eating scrambled eggs. Many had third cups of coffee in the midst of loud cheers, making it seem like a live game that no one had ever seen before. There was standing room only for bacon, eggs, and cherished memories.

One of the large round tables turned into what some referred to as the Algonquin Table, a takeoff on the famed table of the same name in the New York hotel, where you would never sit down unless invited. I never realized that this Pay Caf table had that reputation. Actually, it was a storytelling table. One Sunday morning Jim Murphy, who was in charge of crowd control in the Joyce Center, invited me to bring my tray to that table and in the process coaxed a Farley Hall story from me. It paid my table membership fee.

Among those who also told stories at that table were Bill Corbett ('52) and Pat Farrell ('66), pilots for Notre Dame, and their wives, Diane and Patti respectively. I found out along the way that Bill had served as a Navy pilot during World War II, landing planes on aircraft carriers. This information served me well while flying with Bill in a heavy snowstorm, from Palwaukee Airport to South Bend over Lake

Michigan after representing the Office of Student Affairs at a parent funeral in the Chicago area. Bill calmly reminded me of how fortunate we were not to be traveling the highways in such a storm. His perspective jolted me, but World War II experience gave me confidence as I prayed our way to a complete stop on the Michiana airport landing strip.

There were a number of good readers that gathered at that table who opened up worlds of discussion and storytelling on various topics including Notre Dame and South Bend politics, changes in the Church, new books, movies, and sports. Vito Cinefra, a New Jersey native employed many years by the South Bend school system, could dissect every football game through Ara Parseghian years. He knew the moves from the practice field to their moment of execution in any given game. Vito was always the one to recognize and point out past players eating breakfast near us or coming through the serving line, such as the famed 1966–1967 twosome Terry Hanratty and Jim Seymour, who had offspring attending Notre Dame at the same time.

Pay Caf gatherings and conversations at mealtimes made me more aware of what Fr. Hesburgh meant when I heard him speak once on the quality of campus life. He insisted that a person could be admitted to Notre Dame, never attend class, and still emerge as an educated person four years later if he or she took advantage of the lectures, conferences, and other worthwhile activities outside the classroom and spent some time talking with professors and fellow students about their lives and interests.

I knew what Fr. Ted meant when I saw such professors as philosopher Joe Evans and English scholars Joe Duffy and his colleague Lou Nickolson, from out of the pages of *Beowulf*, hold court regularly at Pay Caf tables. These were men who left long-standing impressions in the lives of those they taught.

Prof. Edward Fischer was a rather soft-spoken man who held his own kind of court. He first walked into my life through the double doors of the Pay Caf, tall and straight, wearing a woolen blazer, carrying a sporty tweed hat, looking for a cup of tea, which he regularly took in the Pay Caf or the Huddle. I surprised myself by approaching his table where he sat alone reading. What I thought would be a few moments of conversation (to tell him how much I enjoyed his writing in the *Notre Dame Magazine*) turned into years of friendship.

Ed lived with his wife, Mary, on St. Vincent Street, just off Notre Dame Avenue, in a home that once belonged to Knute Rockne. He was a great walker, while Mary always rode her bike and never ceased to amaze her neighbors and the Notre Dame community with *The Mary Fischer Show* which she began to host when others her age were considering retirement. After teaching writing for years, Ed took early retirement to do more of his own writing. Along the way, over tea, I learned his history as he traced his life from his Kentucky farm home, to his arrival on the Notre Dame campus with one suitcase, to the professors who taught him and prepared him for a journalism career as a war correspondent during World War II while he served in the army. For years Ed and I had wonderful talks about writing: where to get ideas, how to gather facts, how to organize, and how to tell a story. Writing was in his bones.

Near his seventy-fifth birthday, he showed up for tea in the Huddle with a big surprise. He had a book coming off the press that dealt with the U.S. Army's activities during World War II in the Burma theater in India. "No," I said in disbelief. How could he remember such details after so many years? It turned out that he and Mary discovered in an attic trunk all the letters he had written to her during that period, enough to write a book. His book was reviewed in the *New York Times* as a valuable addition to war literature on a topic about which little was written. It was Ed's last book.

Soon after that, Mary died suddenly one morning, without a struggle, on the second floor of their home. She did not want a wake or funeral. It turned out that she and Ed had made a pact to give their bodies to science. We planned a memorial Mass for Mary at the grotto on a beautiful August morning. Within the year, Ed walked over from his writing office in the basement of the library for morning tea in the Huddle. He removed his coat, sat down like we were going to discuss a new manuscript, and told me that he had a brain tumor with three months to live. I cried. After tea and talk, he walked me to the main building for work. At the bottom of the steps, I was at a loss for words. He left me with a Humphrey Bogart salute, "Here's looking at you, kid."

Daily, he showed us how to die. He continued to come for morning tea, sometimes to the Huddle, other times to the Pay Caf, as he took on the task of putting his life in order—writing letters, cleaning out files. He became a patient in the nursing home that was just around the corner from his house, and where Mary had often visited and brightened the lives of so many patients. He died in early August, almost a year to the day of Mary's death. Friends met again at the grotto for a memorial Mass that ended with some of Ed's own words from his autobiography, *Notre Dame Remembered*:

> Chesterton said of his life that for the most part it was "indefensibly fortunate and happy." Mary and I feel that way; our lives have been more interesting than we had hoped. We understand how the Japanese poet felt:
>
> I have bought bread
> And I have been given roses:
> How happy I am to hold
> Both in my hands!

And now the Pay Caf is no more. In the final years of the twentieth century, it was renovated into a colorful food court in order to handle a larger student population that appeared at the south end of campus due to the construction of four new residence halls built on the "back nine" of the old golf course. Generations of Pay Caf dwellers never cease to miss it, and they look for another such place to appear on the horizon. As Hugh M. Garvey ('39) once remarked, "That was the most important room in the university."

FIVE

Daring to Teach

I ushered a very uncomfortable silence into my first ND classroom in the fall of 1973 as I walked to my desk and set my books down. Suddenly a lamenting "Ohhh, noooo," rose from the back of the room. I was hardly the expected one. Someone near me muttered, "I think I'm in the wrong room." Catching the mood of the group, I introduced myself by verbalizing the obvious, "You were probably expecting a Holy Cross priest but instead you landed a Franciscan sister." I further explained that if my presence was too much of a shock or caused them undue adjustment, they might want to consider choosing another theology class. I had no idea how difficult it could be, since changing a theology class might upset an entire class schedule, but somehow giving them an escape hatch put us all at ease.

No one ever transferred out of my class. I filed away most of those first-day jitters and learned to live, challenged and blessed for many more semesters, teaching courses that focused on Jewish and Christian scriptures and passing on the recognized treasures of biblical scholarship. At the outset, my classes were composed predominantly of underclass males, since everyone was required to take six hours of theology. They were, in one sense, a captive audience, although some were a bit bored by the topic: "Do I really have to take more religion?" But I didn't feel like a captive teacher. I was filled with a fresh challenge, hoping to surprise them just as my professors had surprised me with what thrives between the pages of the Bible. Scripture scholar John McKenzie, SJ, walked me through the world of Hebrew Scriptures, leaving me full of wonder as to how I ever celebrated the feast of Christmas without a deep look at Hebrew historians and prophets. Edward Siegman, CPPS, and Joseph Blenkinsopp taught me Christian Scriptures, while Jesuit scholar Piet Schoonenberg focused my attention on a Christology steeped in the Gospels.

These were early post-Conciliar days. While Vatican Council II circulated strong directives to bring Scripture back into Catholic life, most students sitting before me had not yet felt the impact of such renewal. Many admitted that while they never held a bible in their hands, they knew their Bible stories. However, on the whole, they were in very unfamiliar territory if a conversation got round to major and minor prophets or Paul's letters or Luke's Acts of the Apostles.

It was clear that I should start from scratch and take nothing for granted. My first assignment was to have each student simply list the books of the Hebrew and Christian Scriptures. A frightened lad quickly announced that he wasn't Catholic and he didn't know the names of "all those books." I reassured him that the Catholics who were gathered around him didn't know them either, so everyone was free to copy straight from the Bible: list the names of the books, copy them correctly, say the names out loud, find the right pronunciation if necessary, place the books in simple historical order, and, if possible, identify them by literary genre. As one fellow put it, "You just want us to chew and digest the whole table of contents from many points of view, right?" His comment made it easy to add a second assignment: they should spend at least an hour with the Bible in their hands. At the time I was using the hardback edition of the Jerusalem Bible, which filled two hands nicely. They were to page through it thoughtfully, get a good look and a good feel for it, and list five things they discovered (like hefty footnotes!) that would help them to better understand the content once they started reading. Usually, they just looked at me and rolled their eyes. I looked back and simply said, "Do this. It works."

They went on to read the Pentateuch, some of the prophets, entire Gospels one by one, and the Acts of the Apostles for the first time in many of their lives. They also met Paul and his bundle of letters. They wrote a few short research papers, such as analyzing the meaning of a favorite or confusing passage. Among their resources, they were to use respected scholarly commentaries. One sophomore reported that while he was at home during the fall break, he asked his pastor if he had a copy of the *Jerome Biblical Commentary* that he might borrow to do some research. On his return to campus, he was delighted to tell me, "I think I shook my pastor up. He couldn't imagine that I even knew about that book, let alone want to use it for research. He said he better start shaping up his homilies for the likes of me—and by the way, he wants a copy of my paper when I'm finished. I gotta make it good!"

Research assignments set students loose in a biblical world they never knew existed. They learned on their own and were amazed at the collection of biblical scholarship in print and so easily available. It was the search for resources that often brought them into my Farley residence as they asked for more definite direction on their chosen topics. Some topics had such personal edges. One young man was drawn to examine Jesus' words to his disciples, on how hard it will be for those who have wealth to enter the kingdom of God, as found in Mark 10:23–27. He knew some lines by heart: "It is easier for a camel to go through the eye of a needle than for someone who is rich to enter the kingdom of God." He repeated the words a second time for me, and he registered astonishment, as did the very listeners recorded in the Gospel. During our discussion about how he might approach the topic, I began to realize that this was more than a mere assignment. I commented on his strong interest in the task. He shyly admitted that he always had everything he needed in life and more. In time, I learned that he had felt the full economic impact and moral challenge of a father, Mr. Donald Keough, who had made it to the top of the corporate ladder as president and chief operating officer of the Coca-Cola Company. From 1986–1992, he served as chairman of the Board of Trustees at Notre Dame.

A class on Scripture had a way of opening doors to unending questions that circle anyone around twenty years of age. What do I really believe? Is there a God? Is there a hell? Why does a God allow all the evil in the world? Who is Jesus really? Why is the Church so bossy? How come priests can't marry? Why confession? Who gets to be a cardinal? Why did the Church give up on Latin? How can a Pope be infallible—even a good one?

Time before and after classes was always at a premium. On some occasions it seemed best to invite students to stop by Farley to finish a given discussion. Those follow-up meetings not only settled academic struggles but they often surfaced personal issues. In trying to clarify a misunderstanding over an assignment, I once confronted a sophomore about the anger in his voice and mannerisms. He shouted in reply, "What anger?" and from there he led me closer and closer to a terrible physical ordeal that he had experienced just before coming to Notre Dame. He was a robbery victim who spent weeks in a hospital suffering from life-threatening injuries, the effects of which hung on him inside and out. And there were racial implications that left him with such raw prejudices. After that honest exchange, we looked at each other in the classroom a little differently, and we were never afraid to fall into conversations that focused on putting life back together and moving on.

In many cases, a class was just the beginning of a wide variety of relationships with students. Some exchanges grew out of the needs of the moment—writing a paper, changing a major, settling a test grade, and maybe taking a semester off to care for a terminally ill parent. Other associations stabilized into a mentor-mentee relationship that filled four years and built bridges into graduate school and continued through life in the real world. Now and then some students stopped by Farley simply to say hello and to find out where I lived. No gnawing academic questions. Their eyes often took in the whole room with one sweep, and quick comments, such as "Nice digs," "Great view of the Dome," or "So this is where you turn into a rector?" hinted at a mysterious double identity. As a group of visitors settled into my room for a meeting one evening, a few students from Keenan Hall filled the doorway. One handed me an article that he thought I would appreciate, while the others introduced themselves as "the Scripture scholars" who lived in the neighborhood.

With time, more women appeared in classes, although we were few in number on either side of the desks. When we discovered each other in classroom settings, it felt good. Farley residents began to increase on my class lists, which made it a delight to go back to the hall in the evening and have my students come down to borrow books or untangle academic questions. What a way to teach. Those were the moments when I sensed that I had the best of both worlds at my fingertips—teacher and rector.

There were always more books and articles to read, lesson plans to review and renew, bibliographies to prepare, assignments to create, tests to compose, piles of papers to correct, students to meet, department meetings to attend, committees to serve on, and grades to figure and turn in to the registrar on time. It was a blessed cycle that I never wanted to trade for the world.

While a classroom brought me to life and gave me a great enthusiasm for theology, so did my colleagues in the theology department who taught me, day in and day out, as I met and discussed matters with them, read their books and articles (which often received high praise across the country), and worked with them on departmental business. There were days when, after I finished teaching my class, I walked down the corridor to audit one of theirs. At times I attended afternoon or evening lectures by Notre Dame theologians, such as Elizabeth Fiorenza, New Testament scholar who has accomplished extensive research and writing on women in the Judaic-Christian tradition. James T. Burtchaell, CSC, often spoke on scriptural topics, the sacraments, the abortion issue, and use of fetal tissue. He often prayed about these same topics in the celebration of late-night Eucharists, celebrated in Dillon, Farley, and other residence halls. Prof. Stanley Hauerwas opened up the world of ethics for me in ways I dared not let myself imagine. I read his books, listened to him lecture, and watched him in action during Notre Dame conferences on topics that ranged from war, abortion, and the physically and mentally challenged, to a discussion of the virtues. I was saddened when he left Notre Dame for Duke University, and I wrote and told him so while I was rectoring in London. With ethics and morality in focus, I also audited a seminar taught by visiting Irish theologian Father Enda McDonagh, from Maynooth University, who not only shared his wisdom but also, in very subliminal ways, delighted his "disciples" with his Irish brogue. It seemed I was always a teacher being taught by my colleagues, led into the deepest part of myself and my beliefs to a clearer vision of what it meant to follow Jesus.

One semester I audited Fr. John Dunne's "Theology and Autobiography" class. As I settled into a lecture hall seat, I heard one student behind me say to his guest, "You should know that some students take this class because they think it's so easy. Others take it—because the word is out—it can change your life." I settled in that day with a hundred undergraduates and rarely missed a lecture afterward.

One semester I spent a short break from London duties visiting

Prof. Bob Krieg, CSC, who hosted me on a theological field trip through the university town of Tubingen, where he was doing research in Christology and gathering data for his biography of German theologian Karl Adam. A day's sojourn to the shore of Lake Konstanz, where the Council of Constance convened in 1414, offered sweeping views of snow-covered alps in Austria, Switzerland, and Germany. We both agreed that in the face of such beauty, it was no wonder the Council lasted four years. After lunch, we set out to get a firsthand look at the Council Hall where the bishops sat in session half a millennium earlier. We walked in circles until we realized that we had just lunched on the Council Hall veranda. Returning for a closer look at the property, I kept wondering if a woman would someday cast a Church council vote.

As a part-time, adjunct instructor, I never imagined that I would participate so fully in theology department activities. Early on, department chairman David Burrell, CSC, invited me to attend a joint meeting of Notre Dame's and the University of Chicago's theology departments, to be held on Chicago's campus. I drove with him into the city, asking questions and getting some background information. Once there I grew speechless at the nonchalantly assembled scholars, including Mircea Eliade, Paul Ricour, Martin Marty, and J. B. Pritchard. I had read some of their books, which were on my shelves behind my Farley desk, and here we were chatting our way through coffee breaks together. I also noticed at the outset that Prof. Elizabeth Fiorenza and I were the only women at the large conference table.

Apparently, the University of Chicago had no women on its theology faculty. One had been hired, but she left, explained Prof. Pritchard, who sat to my left confessing that his theology faculty hadn't yet learned how to keep a woman in their ranks. "Believe me, it's true," he emphasized. I then recalled David Burrell's words encouraging me to attend this meeting, "Please come. Your presence will make a statement." During lunch it was Prof. Pritchard, such a recognized scholar in the area of ancient Near East studies, who took me to task for belittling my teaching role when I explained that "I only teach introductory courses to undergraduates." He admonished me for the word "only," explaining that he was not at all proud of the fact that he had lost his touch for teaching undergrads. "My graduate students choose their field and come to my class ready to listen. They want what I have to offer. Not so with undergrads," he added, "they're looking in at it all for the first time. They're a challenge. You have to have special ways to reach them!"

As the day went on, theological exchanges grew intense with this impressive group of scholars. Now and then I secretly slipped into childhood memories of the neighborhood outside the plate-glass windows of our meeting room. Garfield Boulevard, with its broad expanse of the Midway, brought to mind ice-skating afternoons and evenings in this neighborhood so close to where I was born and raised. My mind flitted off to Saul Bellow and his city novels, then to Stagg Stadium and the fact that the atom was first split in a laboratory under the stadium bleachers. In the midst of my meandering stood the stately gothic Rockefeller Chapel, a theological anchor. All this was as fresh as ever in my mind as I struggled to stay in a theological world with so many of its star scholars.

I drove back to campus with Prof. John Yoder, a Mennonite, widely known for his nonviolent theology. Having just recently met him, I asked some basic questions about what he was teaching and writing. It turned out that he had an interest as basic as mine, but not about theology. His mind was on residence life, particularly Farley Hall, since he had a daughter interested in attending Notre Dame. We both relaxed and traded stories all the way home. The next theology book I read was his *The Politics of Jesus*.

How good for me that I got to know Fr. Charles Sheedy, CSC, who was chairman of Notre Dame's theology department twice during his teaching tenure and dean of the College of Arts and Letters for sixteen years. He was still doing some limited teaching when I arrived on campus. I invited him to celebrate Mass in Farley, since he also had been a rector there during his teaching career. Later, he invited me to one of his classes to speak about how the Vatican Council II affected my life as a Franciscan sister.

Charlie or "Chick," as he was affectionately called, was well-read, well-known, and filled with life's experiences. He lived in Corby Hall during his last years on campus. One summer I asked if he might give me a private, spiritual retreat, but he said that he was just too weak, although he was strong enough to graciously hand me all of the necessary ingredients. "Jean, find a good place, take some good time and read *The Cloud of Unknowing* and Julian of Norwich's *Revelation of Love*." Shortly after, Fr. Charles became seriously ill and took up residence in Holy Cross House across St. Joseph's Lake where he stayed close to the oxygen tank that kept him breathing

Charlie had been like a grandfather to his grandnieces and grandnephews who became Domers, including Kerry who lived in Breen-Phillips Hall. The three of us went for supper to Rocco's Restaurant one evening at Charlie's invitation. He loved pasta. After we settled in, gave our order, and chatted some, he left for a minute to say hello to a friend sitting nearby. On his return from a lengthy tour of tables and booths, he agonized over the truth of the moment, full of apologies, "I'm so sorry, but I know everyone in here."

For two decades I heard Sheedy stories, from him and about him, that held tears, but mostly laughter and unending inspiration. He paid me high compliments when he asked me to be the dinner host for his favorite Pittsburgh sister-in-law who came to visit him when he was so ill. Ginny Sheedy held in her memory the mother lode of Uncle Chick family stories.

On Holy Saturday, 1991, he landed in the hospital still one more time, and his friend and brother in community, Fr. George Schidel, was praying near his bedside when I stopped by to visit. I got down on one knee next to Charlie and placed my hand as gently as I could on his terribly thin, discolored wrist. He opened his eyes and said so clearly, "Oh, Jeannie, I just want to go to God." And he did, a few hours later in the midst of the first Easter alleluias, leaving me holding forever an act of faith, full of grace and Charlie's life. Charlie was a teacher all the way—in how and what he taught, but most of all in the way that he lived and died. Many lost a good friend and colleague in Charlie Sheedy's passing. In his inimitable way, he marked the end of an era in the theology department at the University of Notre Dame.

Sometimes I wander into empty classrooms in O'Shaughnessy just to reexperience the feeling and effect of my past teaching days. I can almost hear voices, sometimes my own, and see faces. Not even heavy administrative duties in the Office of Student Affairs can snuff them out.

What really makes teaching come back to life for me is the sudden appearance of a former student. Just when I thought I was going to meet a complete stranger, the newly hired university controller, Drew Paluf, shook my hand and informed me that we met twenty years ago: "Sr. Jean, I had you for theology. Let's have lunch sometime soon!"

Every June a few graduates emerge from north quad reunion tents with colorful theological tales, "I don't know if you remember me, but I did a paper for your class on those 'Qumran Scrolls' discovered near the Dead Sea. I'm still amazed at how I really got into that cave assignment. They were in the news again just last week!" While another student admitted, "I really gave you a hard time arguing against receiving communion in the hand. Remember, I agreed all the way with Mark Chiles. But then there was Joe, the Italian kid who had the Jesuits in high school in New York. He was into all that renewal stuff!"

I'm always amused that so many former students' memories get tied to the papers that they wrote. Patrick Holmes, a member of Notre Dame's Academic Services for Student Athletes, who I thought was a total stranger at a Christmas dinner, introduced himself and his wife to me only to add, "I don't know if you remember me, but I had you for a theology class on the New Testament. I remember I did an analysis of the Our Father, and believe it or not, I still think about what I found out doing that paper."

I realize now that former students can appear anywhere. A young eye doctor, who had joined Dr. Patrick Leahy's office in the Beverly area in Chicago where my parents lived, came forward to help my mother make some decisions about the glasses she needed. I stood within earshot. At an opportune moment, he leaned over and informed me that I had taught him theology at Notre Dame. While I was embarrassed not to recognize him, those nearby were duly impressed, especially my mom.

After teaching Ed McGinn, he came back into my life before he graduated from Notre Dame, running out of the dark of night into the light of the emergency parking lot of St. Joseph's Hospital, holding up his bent arm wrapped in a towel. I was in the waiting room hoping for a report on a Farley woman's mother who had collapsed hours earlier while on campus for Junior Parents Weekend. The next thing I knew, a familiar nurse stood in front of me, declaring that it was a busy night in the ER, acknowledged me as someone from Notre Dame, and asked if I would stay with Ed until a doctor could see him.

Ed, at least six feet two inches, was stretched the length of the gurney and more, arranging himself in and out of S-formations, heavy winter boots and all. He had slashed his hand trying to cut a carrot with a butcher knife "that slipped." He was a bit dumbfounded when I appeared and stood next to him. The first thing he asked me was not to call his mother until the doctor worked on him and had something to report. He frowned a bit, not quite recognizing me because I was out of context for him. Then he relaxed some and turned into a storyteller, moving both of us momentarily back to the classroom where we met.

"I have to tell you what happened the other day. I walked into church while the priest was reading the Gospel—and I recognized right away that it was Matthew's Gospel. I couldn't believe it." How many times he heard me tell his class that if they thoughtfully read, compared, and analyzed the Gospels, they would get to know the authors as individuals, understand their themes and audiences, and, most importantly, "their" Jesus. Ed said, "It really happened to me," and seemed delighted for the chance to share the marvel of it, even in the thick of this medical moment.

It wasn't long before a doctor appeared, examined him, and ordered immediate surgery that was performed through the night. Dr. Brooks Crowfoot did the honors, saving Ed's fingers and giving him full use of his hand. Ed's mother was informed of his injury. His younger sister from St. Mary's and I met the next morning at the foot of his bed, just to check on him. I found thank-you flowers at my door on Valentine's Day. Each year Ed, his wife, Janice, and two daughters touch me with Christmas greetings.

Sometimes parents quite unknowingly commingle into classroom memories. David Vinson, a gifted Baptist student from Texas, signed up for my class on Catholicism. His reason for doing so partially involved his dad who was a Baptist minister. David quoted him one day in class as almost believing that "all Catholics were going to hell." There was a jerk and turn of some heads in the room, but David continued, "I want you to know that I'm a little more broad-minded than my dad at this point, and I want to find out more about Catholicism since I choose to study at this school." He went on to say and assure us that he believed that "Jesus has a lot going for all of us." His questions were among the best in the class and taught us all. He earned an A in his course on Catholicism.

David became an all-American linebacker, #59, and a member of the 1977 national championship team that won the Cotton Bowl in his native Texas. At the game, I got to meet his Baptist minister dad who traveled from Liberty, Texas, to join his son and ND friends for the game and celebration. Graduating with highest honors, David moved back to Texas for medical school at Baylor, a real tribute to his alma mater, his family, and his Baptist heritage.

It didn't take long for me to realize that classroom teaching was only one of many educational ventures at Notre Dame. While walking to my formal classroom, I began to understand that Farley Hall was as much a place of learning as a lecture hall—not quite so structured, but full of life and learning. Any topic imaginable might surface anytime of the day or night and elicit an exchange of ideas that could last five minutes or half the night.

Each time I signed a contract for another year of rectoring, there were master lesson plans to lay out for the year, among them leadership training sessions for an assistant rector and the resident assistants. Hall officers and commissioners had to be mentored into setting goals, planning activities, and learning how to evaluate the activities they sponsored. Freshmen had to be oriented for life as Notre Dame scholars.

While I gave few lectures to large Farley groups, I participated in endless person-to-person talks, discussions, tête-à-têtes, confrontations, encounters, conferences, and delightful storytelling. There was very little note taking but plenty of time to sit and think. There were always questions, and sometimes tears. I was pressured in good ways to share what I had learned in life, the very important and the not so important. Often students went for facts; other times they dug deep inside of me looking for whatever wisdom they could find, from "How do I go about arranging for an alcohol intervention for my dad?" to "How do you know when you've really met the man of your life?" There was always a Farleyite writing a paper that involved interviewing an eyewitness or taking a poll on a current topic. At times I felt "picked real," forced to share my insights as honestly as I could: "What was it like when the first women came to Notre Dame? Do you think women should be ordained? Do you believe in the death penalty? Why did you become a nun? What was Vatican II all about? Do you think Notre Dame should have an ROTC program?"

I was probably no more than a heartbeat away from an educational enterprise any day of the academic year. There were always program directors like Don McNeill and his staff looking for "assistance." Students who volunteered through the Center for Social Concerns to spend six to eight summer weeks serving the poor and those in need depended on educators to help debrief them in the aftermath, or to assist them in gaining perspective on what they had experienced—"to mine the gold" as someone put it. It was always a challenge for me to listen to students in such a way that enabled them to touch the heart of a matter, spot the "pearls," and garner wisdom. It was a teacher's dream to behold what students could see and take into their lives in such reflective moments, often saying, "I can never be the same again."

There were also student retreats. Some were small groups, meeting at Bulla Shed or Old College or the Crowe House on Lake Michigan. Some were large groups and filled Fatima Retreat House. It was always a grace to lead a retreat group, whether alone or with a team. Retreats were very special territory. Faith—strong or teetering—was the common denominator. A wonderful freedom was consciously extended to each participant to talk about God and share what it meant to be Christian or to follow Jesus. We took time to present some of our deepest thoughts and questions—right in front of each other. It was a time for getting in touch with, and coming to a deeper understanding of, the spiritual realities of our lives. It was not surprising that we prayed together and moved toward the celebration of the Eucharist with a certain holy intimacy.

In the early days of coeducation, university committees always looked for a female member. Many chairmen set out to give their meetings a woman's perspective. There were continual opportunities to meet with male rectors and their personnel, all in the name of "adjusting to each other" after 125 years of male occupation. As one of the first women rectors, I tried hard to accept most invitations to speak to other campus groups, since it was a perfect opportunity to quell rumors and circulate as much truth as possible. There was just no end to the questions: "What's it like to be a woman at Notre Dame? How are the women adjusting to the scene? What do you hear about how professors have adjusted to having women in their classes? Do you think the campus on the whole is happy you're here? How do the alumni treat you? Do the women feel the pressure of being so few in number?" Some questions were turned back on the questioners with intriguing results.

Some male professors spoke quite candidly about the pressures they felt teaching women for the first time. One very respected, middle-aged scholar admitted that he caught himself addressing the first young women in his class by their first names, while he had always engaged the men by using their last name, preceded by "Mr." He quickly made his a "Mr." and "Miss" classroom. Another professor admitted that he was disarmed to face a woman's tears in a classroom setting, which happened when a coed reported a death in her family.

Pressure was felt, no doubt, by both the first ND women and the men who welcomed them. While it was true that the men couldn't really fathom just what it was like to be the only girl in a class, the best thing the first women did that brought a great balance to the coed scene was to go to class each day and do well. Their academic prowess settled the issue.

Although I taught regular theology classes throughout my rector years, it was always a pleasure to support the educational endeavors of the ND Alumni Association, especially by participating in summer reunion seminars, Elderhostel classes, or the "Death, Divorce, and Dismantled Dreams Workshop," working closely with Alumni Director Chuck Lennon ('61) and Assistant Director Kathy Sullivan ('82 and '87).

Seminary education began to attract my attention one Saturday morning in early fall while I was having my first cup of coffee. Someone scratched at my Farley Hall window screen. Tom O'Hara was stuck between bushes thick with burnt-orange leaves that looked like fire in the sun. It was final vow day for some Holy Cross seminarians, one of whom was right outside my window with a question, "Can I come in a minute?"

Tom O'Hara had been walking the campus trying to calm a great case of jitters. Through the night he became overwhelmed with wondering if he should really take this step. We drank a little coffee and agreed that God did not ordinarily, at the very last minute, throw a curve ball carrying a totally different message from the one that steadily came through all the growth and challenges of seminary life from one year to the next. I knew Tom quite well as a seminarian and felt that there was always a deep honesty at the heart of his movement toward priesthood. From where I stood and from what I saw, final vows made all the sense in the world for him. We prayed together, finished our coffee, then he went on his Holy Cross way and never looked back. Many years later, in October 1998, Tom was installed as president of his alma mater, Kings College in Scranton, Pennsylvania, which is near his hometown of Hazleton where he grew up the son of a coal miner. I was in line to congratulate him. Together we remembered "the day of the jitters," but this time with great joy.

Tom was one of the first seminarians I knew, but there were others to follow. I met with some of them regularly to help them look more carefully at who they were and what it meant to develop their spiritual lives. Seminarian Tom McDermott posed a new question during the annual gathering of seminarians at Deer Park, Maryland, before the beginning of one of his new academic years. He wanted to know if he could join with Fr. Tom McNally, rector of Grace Hall, and myself in team teaching a theology class to Notre Dame students? He wanted to fulfill his requirement for field education by teaching. It worked out. All three of us were filled with Vatican II developments. One student commented on our various perspectives. "I liked this class because it was taught by a young priest, an old priest, and a lady." As McDermott, McNally, and Lenz, we continue to miraculously reunite for simple lunches in simple places when Fathers McDermott and McNally return to campus from the missions, still talking like a trio ready to step into a classroom.

Some of the most poignant moments I've spent with seminarians came when they were feeling awkward in their field education placement with the elderly, the unwed mother, the mentally handicapped, the dying, or the grieving. Such moments created a readiness to learn like no other. These seminarians reached out for what to do, what to say, and prayers to pray that carry the meaning of such moments. It always seemed a significant time to lead seminarians back to themselves, to search their own feelings, insights, and hunches as to how to respond before leading them to outside sources. I found it a daunting task to help a seminarian search his life to discover and cultivate pastoral gifts and energies within, and a deeper spirituality in the process.

While I was happy to meet regularly with individual seminarians at their suggestion, I was taken aback somewhat at the request of the seminary rector to become a member of the Moreau Seminary formation team. I was reluctant to step into those ranks, knowing that, while it wasn't easy for young men to answer the call to priesthood at this time, it would, no doubt, also be a challenge to serve on a seminary team faced with the multiple responsibilities of establishing and executing a sound seminary program that met seminarians' needs as they prepared for their critical ministry. The issues of women priests, married priests, the role of the laity—all of these questions and many more Church and societal issues surround seminarians. Walking with them as they followed their call in the midst of these developments made me finally decide to lean hard on my religious life experience and help in whatever way possible as a team member.

Seminary work became an undiluted challenge. Our team, most recently led by Rector Fr. Bill Miscamble, CSC, stays close to seminarians—the teachers and the taught—with roles becoming reversed periodically. We all look for honesty and integrity in each other. We pray for each other. While seminarians can often be affirmed for who they are and all the good things that they initiate and accomplish, there are times when hard, direct, personal questions have to be asked; when requests for further study or specific ministry have to be changed or denied; when a seminarian's decision about what he deems good for himself might be the opposite of what the team perceives.

My Franciscan community life stands for many of the same values and faces the same challenges. At times I have reached for some personal experiences that have helped to keep hard times in perspective. It was with a seminarian I knew quite well who was denied his first choice for future studies that I finally landed one of the lessons of my life, "I never wanted to come to the University of Notre Dame to study theology. I had another school in mind. Look what happened." I sat quietly with him, much more amazed than he at my declaration.

SIX

Funny Bones

It was a balmy spring night in April filled with "AnTostal" celebrations. While students glibly used this Gaelic phrase, I doubt many knew its simple translation: "spring is here." More than knowing what it meant, they felt it. It's a noisy time on campus, bursting with spontaneous eruptions of all sorts, such as an early-morning run by a dozen young men carrying a classmate overhead horizontally to dump in the lake's cold spring waters. A mixture of song, heave-hos, and herd movement mark the moment.

It was in the spirit of such revelry that I received a call from the not-yet-ordained assistant rector in Grace Hall, Bob Wiseman, warning me that a group of young men were running toward Farley Hall "full of springtime." It was near midnight. I had other things on my mind as I corrected theology papers. In the midst of a certain calmness on the floors overhead with dimmed night-lights filling the hallways, I suddenly heard that disturbing, heavily throated chant, "Farley, Farley, Farley." I swished around the corner of my doorway, ran down three steps, and stood guard at the south entrance breathing the words, "They're not getting in here tonight." With the grace of office and rector boldness, I pushed the door open as someone inserted an electronic Detex passcard from the outside, saying with such triumph to the troops behind him, "It works!" And that's when the drama peaked.

I swung the door open toward the crowd that was an arm's length away, only to discover some hundred young men ready to charge the hall in their birthday suits. I remember cupping my hands around my mouth and shouting at the top of my lungs, "You're not coming in here like *that*." Then I heard a great holler, a strong voice rise above the rest, declaring the state of affairs, "Oh no, it's Sister Jean," and a great scrambling retreat was underway. Some made a fast getaway and dove into the nearest bushes next to Farley's doorway. Others ran for the bushes that lined the north wall of Breen-Phillips Hall. Some jumped behind bicycles nearby and peered through the spokes of wheels, while others simply stood frozen on the spot, a bit in shock, with twisted backs facing me.

I stood in the doorway until I heard a leading cry of brotherhood from the bushes that injected bravery into the troops as they began to move back toward Farley. This time they came toward me stumbling backward. Again in this fleshy atmosphere of strong male backsides, I said, "I told you, you're not getting in here like that." There was another retreat and a halfhearted third attempt to enter, upon which I shouted, "I am not moving from this spot until you fellows move on." Then came the final rallying cry, "Let's get Lyons Hall." I dashed to the phone and called the Lyons rector who would have time to gather her personnel and bolt all entrances against these brave marauders of springtime. Her answer was one grand sigh.

When I caught my breath and realized that Farley's security guard, Hazel, had been beside me all the time, I turned to her and said, "Am I dreaming or did this really just happen?" Then I heard the clapping of Farley residents from the shadows of the hallway behind me and I knew I was awake.

The last phone call I made that night was to thank Assistant Rector Wiseman for calling to warn me of the "mob of men" headed for Farley. But I fear that my thanks were lost in trying to explain why he should have warned me that all the "emperors had no clothes on" as they made their dash from the towers to north quad.

For a few weeks to follow, I became quite convinced that I was passing authentic streakers in their daytime wear as I crossed the quad. A greeting of "Hi, Ster" went with a quick head lowering and a face filled with a guilty grin. I could spot them every time. It was that same grin that gave them away as we stood holding candles at a grotto Mass for the Feast of the Ascension, an occasion that brought the best out of all of us.

The streaker story never goes away. It creeps into endless conversations wherever Domers gather. It's an AnTostal saga that is referred to time and again in letters and Christmas cards, in reunion tents, and at banquets. However, at this point in history, all the fear is out of the story. It has been replaced by its own brand of pride, "Yeah, I was in that crowd hiding in the bushes."

Two years after the streaking incident took place, a tall young man and his parents stopped by to see me in Farley Hall right after graduation ceremonies. I had taught him and knew him well. He wanted to introduce me to his parents, I thought. And so he did, but most of all he had a question to pose before he went off into the sunset and his promising future. "Did you not know that I was the streaker that stood near the doorstep right next to you on that night of the great streak? You looked me right in the eye and I thought, 'This is it, I'm a goner.' " It seemed his parents had no knowledge of this whole episode and registered enough embarrassment to make everyone a bit uncomfortable. However, he had his diploma in hand and little to lose in the pursuit of truth. I explained that I hadn't recognized him that night, which was why he was saved from a critical encounter with the dean of students.

This lovely May exchange became a perfect moment to explain to this eyewitness that my energy that night was not in my memory lobe. It was all I could do to stand tall, take charge, and sound strong. I told the same thing to the assistant dean who wanted to set out after the culprits the morning after that midnight run. I was simply unable to identify any individual student—they all looked alike. (I was cautioned not to give that statement to the press!) Furthermore, there wasn't a t-shirt in the crowd that bore the name of a specific hall or organization.

In the end, with graduation ceremonies still in our blood, this newly minted graduate and his parents settled on the truth and bade farewell without a hint of embarrassment in the air. As I watched them leave—by "the streakers' door" no less—I realized I forgot to tell them that on the night of the great run, I did spot a Mickey Mouse hat perched high on the head of one Domer and a colorful Viking helmet on another. Curiously enough, it's these pieces of "streaking evidence" that will forever remind me of how great the expanse of history is that hails the streaking rites of springtime.

AnTostal is filled with historical perspective as homemade chariots appear on campus, built by individual residence halls in all shapes and sizes, makes, and durability. Trendy, stylized togas are the chosen wear for the occasion. However, some chariot riders never make it to the starting lineup due to the loss of wheels en route to the race. Other chariot engineers boast total success as they ride to victory and bring their chariot back to their dorm for display purposes and free rides for hall residents.

Tug-of-war was always a crowd-pleaser during AnTostal ceremonies, especially since it occurred over well-watered mud pits. Regulations stipulated that five bodies were allowed on either side. One AnTostal Saturday afternoon, I predicted the winning team. It paraded right past my window on its way to the fray: four well-built young men ready for the tug of their lives and an elephant, complete with a brilliant red cover and gold tassels stretched across its back. Rumors spread that this four-man team had rented their fifth team member from a traveling circus, and they won the top prize by simply standing in front of an enthralled audience, flexing their muscles.

"Ya gotta regatta" was the cry of Fisher Hall men who also enticed the campus to enter a spring race. Each hall had to bring its own handmade boat. A lot of time and assorted types of craftsmanship goes into construction work. One floating vessel made of very large plastic bottles was tied together on the second floor of Farley right outside my door the morning of the race, while St. Edward's Hall constructed a miniature Noah's Ark over a two-week period, using saws and drills and naval know-how in a great space behind the hall.

On an early spring Saturday morning, racing fans and their guests gathered in shivering fashion at the shoreline of St. Mary's Lake. There's a launching pad where chosen folks heave their vessel into the water. An army of student assistants support ND Security and the Red Cross. Life jackets are supplied, since many homemade frigates can sink quickly as the race proceeds amid great cheers and laughter. The most primitive sailing vessel that I ever saw complete the race had a quaint Tom Sawyer look, while the most amazing sailing vessel was built two stories high, complete with furnished rooms and a veranda where roommates enjoyed a cookout while the race was in progress.

Domers feed each other's funny bones daily with their wealth of wit, and they often share it with those who dare to look and listen. For example, they have a penchant for decorating outdoor statues to meet the mood of the campus or to accompany any given season. The holy Moses, standing twenty feet high and cast in bronze, was a constant temptation for decorations. On the west side of the Hesburgh Library, his size alone attracted attention as he stood in full view from various sidewalks leading to the library. A curious artistic interpretation of "horns of light," due to mistranslation, protruded from his head. His creator, an artist from the Mestrovic school, caught him in a classic Mosaic pose with one sandaled foot holding down the head of a strong bull or calf, reminding onlookers of Exodus 34. One of his arms reaches high overhead with a forefinger jutting straight toward the heavens, signaling the one true God. While Moses reflects the strong, holy, Hebrew man that he was, there have been times at Notre Dame when the meaning of his message was temporarily redirected. As the football team moved toward the national championship in 1977, a huge sign hung around his neck, over his bronze chest. In good Hebrew, the message matched the pose: "We're #1!"

One Halloween Moses' lone forefinger was pushed through a large pumpkin, with a brief declaration under his chin: "I am the Great Pumpkin." During an Easter season, creative Domers tried to make Moses look like the Easter bunny, with large ears, a basketful of eggs, and a large puff of a cottontail. There were times when his toenails were manicured red. My attention was especially drawn to this figure of fame the day he pointed, with such rank and recognition, toward our God in heaven with a Band-Aid on his finger.

Both light and heavy snows fill crevices on campus statues that bring smiles to passersby. Sometimes Domers add seasonal dress for greater effect. It so happened that I was teaching Mark's Gospel through one snowfall, which led to a spell of zero-degree weather. In keeping with the Gospel content, I addressed the theme of Jesus' humanity as seen through Mark's eyes. At the beginning of the next class, one young scholar remarked that the class material took on real meaning for him that morning as he passed the Sacred Heart statue in front of the main building. Jesus was wearing a knitted stocking cap pulled down around his ears with a heavy, long, colorful scarf tied around his neck.

In lovelier weather, a passerby is conscious of the Sacred Heart of Jesus statue with arms outstretched, giving meaning to the words on the pedestal beneath him: *Venite ad me omnes.* One student tour guide offered local color to a group of tourists, "I'm not sure what those Latin words mean, but a lot of students call this the 'Jump, Mary, Jesus' since Jesus seems to be beckoning his mother to take the leap." As I walked past the group, I was hoping they realized that they were hearing a dose of ad-lib not on the official tour script.

While the famous Father Sorin statue on the main quad has modeled his share of clothing, it's the smaller statue of Sorin (now full of cement, I have been told, and bolted down in Sorin Hall) that has the curious traveling reputation. Before becoming sedentary, this Father Sorin statue apparently took trips around the world, sending back cards "signed" and postmarked from exotic and distant places, such as Tibet and the French Riviera. This story is told afresh to "the daughters of Notre Dame": toward the end of one such trip, he wrote ahead to announce the day and time when he would arrive back at the main circle. He was right on time. A taxicab pulled up with the Sorin statue in the back seat.

It is due to the living, breathing Father Edward Sorin that a statue of St. Edward the King graces the courtyard between St. Ed's Hall and Cavanaugh Hall. An ornate crown on his brow and a king's scepter in his right hand depicts his status, while he holds in his left hand a miniature gothic-looking church building, symbolic of his title as patron saint of the Church. Now and then his identity is almost completely hidden when he appears in a high chef's hat and long, white butcher's apron.

A "stylized" piece of property can appear on campus overnight, thanks to the clever students in our midst. When ranch-like fences were created to prevent unwanted paths close to sidewalk intersections, residents of Zahm Hall built a horse with a head made from a large shoe box. They proceeded to hitch the animal to the fence with a sign announcing the development of the "Zahm Corral."

Snow calls forth all kinds of sculpturing instincts and creativity. Some of the best art pieces appeared during the great snowfall of 1978, when forty inches fell from January 25–27. In all, 136 inches of snow were recorded that winter, eighty-six of which fell in January, breaking all South Bend records. The university was officially closed for five days. In addition to the creation of some pretty impressive snowball forts, there appeared a gigantic sculpture of the gorilla King Kong, sitting on his haunches on the north quad near Keenan Hall. He had a stunning head and face. It took weeks for him to melt down to his toe nails. Of another size and stature was a well-packed Charlie Brown, along with huge snow Domers dressed in colorful clothing that froze to their icy skin. For winter daredevils, a "snow chute" was created by packing mounds of snow onto the front steps of the main building. The aim of the game was to see who could get closest to the Sacred Heart statue, riding on a dining-room tray. It was a feat even for the faint-hearted.

Everyday life became a challenge in high snowdrift areas. For example, students had to lean down to open the regular U.S. mailboxes. Some had to be helped up from a residence hall entranceway in order to find the regular walking path in the "snow ledge." The snow was so deep near the swimming area of St. Joseph's Lake that the tall fence that once stood over our heads now dwindled in size, reaching our waists.

Women employees from the north dining hall bunked in with Farley women, sleeping in extra basement rooms. Part of Notre Dame's Channel 16 staff kept the WNDU-TV station operating through it all, also occupying rooms in the basement. When the weatherman Dick Addis knocked on my door looking for some towels, he tried to quell my fears by telling me that it would only flurry through the night. And it did—another foot.

Domers boast a spirit of frolic that often surfaced during football games. They could whip up a "wave" in no time, which sometimes undulated through eighty thousand fans from both directions, putting a delightful dizziness into the crowd during a lull in a game. Since students weren't allowed to throw objects onto the field (such as oranges to indicate Orange Bowl yearnings), they took to tossing marshmallows at each other.

Students had a way of responding to disciplinarian directives with creative antics. They were warned again and again not to "pass up" or "crowd surf" (i.e., passing classmates horizontally over the heads of the student body) during home football games. One Saturday, among thousands of fans on the northeast side of the stadium across from the student section, I watched a student get tossed dangerously high and pass over the heads of student fans. Some acrobatic Domer apparently gave his body for this sideshow. He went up, row by row, very quickly. I could feel the anger starting in my toes. They knew better than this. Someone was going to get hurt. The body reached the last row and was suddenly thrown over the stadium wall. There was an audible gasp all around, mixed with declarations of fright and religious pronouncements, before the crowd realized that it had been a dummy.

During one football season a student found a way to dangle his body from a pole that jutted out over the heads of fans. The student press referred to him as "the stripper." He found a way to hang on to a pole and remove his clothing piece by piece, down to a pair of shorts with a red heart print design. After two of these demonstrations, the dean of students publicly forbade him to continue stripping or face disciplinary sanctions. He quit his display until the last game. The pole appeared again on a very cold day and the stripper suspended himself wearing his heart-studded shorts. He would obey. He would not strip and throw his clothes to the fans. This time, he got dressed in midair with the help of an accomplice who threw him his winter attire piece by piece.

President Reagan's visit to Notre Dame in 1981 as commencement speaker gave special clout to long-standing policy that indicated proper student conduct for graduation. It was the president's first public appearance after the assassination attempt. Faculty, staff, students, and their guests had to pass through metal detectors in order to be admitted to the ceremonies. Students donned their best behavior—no champagne bottles, no corks popping and flying through the air. Amazingly, something of the spirit and discipline of that graduation flowed into 1982's commencement. A sense of good order was in the air. However, as the graduates waited on the official graduation party (which includes the president, other university officials, and honorary degree recipients), they put festivity and laughter in the air as they blew up a dozen beach balls and a large rubber rendition of Jaws that they had tucked away in their pockets, tossing them across the sea of two thousand peers. As one distinguished professor behind me remarked, "they will never be outwitted."

There was always someone in the student ranks ready for fun. During a film showing in the engineering auditorium of one of their all-time favorites, *Singin' in the Rain*, a row of students stood tall and opened their umbrellas as Gene Kelly danced his way through those unforgettable puddles. Watching the film *Knute Rockne—All-American* in that same auditorium was like sitting in the midst of a Greek chorus that voiced the emotions of a developing plot. The students' sound effects and silence carried the meaning of the moment.

Their humor infected each other in the nicknames they gave to friends and those who caused them fear and agitation. Such monikers seemed to pop out of comments, events, or relationships. They either told the truth about a person or just the opposite. For example, Flash was someone either very quick or very deliberate and slow in demeanor. Hoot was a hoot to be with. Bounce was a fellow with a lot of energy. Pee-wee was short of stature or six feet four inches tall. The same could be said of those named Moose in our midst. I especially remember a fellow named Spoon from Zahm Hall whose brother followed him to ND and was called Teaspoon.

Some student humor also felt a bit too close for comfort at times. One midnight hour I was taking a shower when I suddenly became aware that someone was "knocking" on my shower curtain, throwing punches in the plastic. This was a first. My heart leapt at the thought of some serious emergency! I stuck my dripping head out to find a Farley RA in complete panic because someone had stolen her piano. The women in her section hid the instrument as an April Fools' prank.

Farley's laundry room was a perfect setting for a sitcom. Until undergraduate women were admitted to the university, there was only St. Michael's general campus laundry, designed primarily to handle clothing for the male population. Women's residence halls added brand-new laundry facilities to campus, which quickly caught the attention of the men who lived in the vicinity.

Grace and Flanner Halls were each one thousand residents strong, and many of these students found endless ways to sneak into Farley to use one of seven washers and dryers to do their "good slacks and shirts for special occasions." If they had a real emergency, they would often appear in my doorway with a personal request to use the facility. At times I granted it, but I warned them that they had to travel at their own risk and get in line. Some men enlisted their sisters, cousins, girlfriends, and classmates to come to their rescue—and they did. On one of my laundry rounds, I discovered one lad, who was not only new to the facility but also new to the machinery. I stopped him from adding another dose of Tide detergent onto a load of clothes he had stuffed into a dryer.

A Grace Hall senior confessed one day that he actually sneaked into Farley and got away with washing his "good shirts" on more than one occasion. Initially the joke was on him, he insisted, since it took him weeks to realize that he was supposed to add soap to each load. He thought once you inserted the necessary coins, soap was automatically added.

Rectors do put their lives on the line sometimes—all in the name of fun. Dillon Hall Rector Daniel Jenky, CSC, who now clasps a shepherd's staff in his hand as bishop of Peoria, once had an encounter with a group of his Dillon men who boasted that they could raise three thousand dollars for Sr. Maura's Day Care Center. Father Jenky doubted it out loud, but the residents insisted that they could raise the money. Jenky was so sure of his bet that he didn't fear offering them an invaluable personal asset: "You raise $3,000 for Sr. Maura and I'll shave off my beard." He claimed that he had inherited a chin that went best with a beard, which with time became a facial treasure. His Dillon men knew this, as did many others on campus. And so the Sr. Maura coffers filled fast, exceeding all expectation, going over the top. The beard had to go. Dillon men imported Joe the barber to set up his shop outdoors on the south quad, complete with a special platform, barber's chair, and necessary instruments. Striptease stereo music filled the air. The shearing and trimming was all in the name of childcare and a rector's dare. It was a south quad moment filled with great fun and the promise of a good sport who walked away from it with a brown bag over his head.

While professor of chemistry Dr. Emil T. Hofman had demanding ways of challenging his freshmen with Friday quizzes, he would offer pure entertainment when it came to making his way across campus to the north dining hall where he gave his semester exams to hundreds of freshmen at the same time. Dr. Hofman appeared dressed as Indiana Jones and Bruce Springsteen, among other notables of decades past. Each exam period, surrounded by his teaching assistants on hand to proctor the exam, he led his test parade through a surge of students as apropos music blared from windows of residence halls. Once he tried to arrive on the exam scene by helicopter, but the insurance company wouldn't hear of it. A hot-air balloon attempt was also canceled along the way. It took an NBC team to create a national sensation the day it covered the spring exam parade, which was led by Notre Dame's director of athletics, Gene Corrigan, and assistant coach, George Kelly. Emil was dressed in full football gear and introduced as next year's star quarterback.

In the spring of 2001, Notre Dame women created one of the grandest parties in ND's history, putting smiles on everyone's faces. At one o'clock in the morning of April 2, the campus was alerted through e-mail that the champions were on their way home. ND's women's basketball coach and team were flying from the Savvis Center in St. Louis, Missouri, drenched in victory. I had watched other coaches and teams make their way to "the circle" near the Morris Inn after their big wins: Ara Parseghian, Digger Phelps, and Dan Devine. They all had their moments of celebration in the dark of night after driving into throngs of students lining Notre Dame Avenue and filling the circle, cheering teams on to a hunt for a national championship (which some teams did earn during winter holidays when no one was on campus). But this night was different from all the others. Coach Muffet McGraw and her 2001 women's basketball team were about to roll down Notre Dame Avenue in their minibuses with a fully certified national championship, nailed down by cocaptain Ruth Riley when she hit the last two winning baskets in the game against Purdue University from the free throw line with 5.8 seconds left on the clock. I had to get to this parade on time.

First estimates of arrival time (announced in Farley Hall, home of senior starter Kelley Siemon) was 1:00 A.M., but it wasn't until after 2:00 when the minibuses finally hit Notre Dame Avenue and Angela Boulevard, causing an outburst of recognition that marked the start of the parade. As the moon moved across the sky, thousands of fans of all ages milled about in the magic of the moment in twenty-degree weather. Many wide-eyed students shivered audibly, wrapped in their bed blankets as the band filled the air with ND favorites, giving playtime to bagpipes along the way. With flashing lights, campus security cars led the entourage to the first platform I had ever seen for such an occasion.

I fell into conversation with an employee from the *South Bend Tribune* who disappeared briefly, then suddenly thrust a copy of the *Trib* in front of me. It was hot off the press with a front-page photo of Kelley Siemon, Ruth Riley, Alicia Ratay, and Niele Ivey, taken seconds after Ruth Riley hit her free throws that sent the team skyrocketing into history.

Suddenly I saw those same team faces peering out of the minibus windows in total wonderment at the celebration that engulfed them. Steeped in the thrill of the win, the players made their way to the platform with arms waving and faces filled with captivating smiles. Somewhat stunned, Coach McGraw stood at the center of the uproar with megaphone in hand, declaring breathlessly, "Nothing like this ever happened to me before." I was thinking the same thing as my eyes swept across the clear night sky filled with a bright spring moon and a Golden Dome all ablaze. It was a quintessential ND athletic moment, with a woman's touch.

Such Domer celebrities were always in the making. While there were tears at times and mistakes of all sorts and sizes, there were a great number of successes and much joy to be had. And humor thrived. It was always thick and shared in great doses. Not many students left Notre Dame without a sense of achievement and well-cultivated funny bones.

SEVEN

Land of Pound and Pence

One year I was asked to slip away from Farley and go off to London. The ministry of rector/chaplain took on stunning British trimmings when I moved into the district of Maida Vale with a new group of sixty undergraduates each semester from the College of Arts and Letters. There was always drama from the get-go.

The U.S. plane was only minutes on the Heathrow tarmac when junior Michael Flannery was apprehended at Heathrow Airport and detained in immigration by security personnel. "Madam, he is under surveillance," I was informed with very formal British protocol. It turned out that he had the same name as the head of the IRA (the Irish Republic Army), the sound of which put Heathrow security on full alert. As Michael produced passport and papers to prove his identity, I was given phone numbers to call in order to confirm his Notre Dame membership in the London program. His predicament stopped his fellow students in their tracks as they sat on their suitcases waiting for his release from immigration territory. Once he was released, everyone celebrated their London arrival. Farley Hall semesters never began quite like this.

After ten years of walking on the north quad at Notre Dame, I began strolling the streets of London, spending English pounds and pence, and adjusting to new terms: a purchase in the marketplace would cost me a "quid or two." I took the tube and buses everywhere, discovering the best approaches from Sutherland Avenue in Maida Vale (where we ate and slept) to 7 Albemarle, a stone's throw from the Ritz Hotel in the Mayfair district (where classes were scheduled at the Notre

Dame Center). I listened carefully to the English accent and even developed an ear for cockney. One of the first Londoners I befriended was the flower man who stood hip-high in blossoms that filled his cart at the top of the steps at the Green Park tube stop. He and his bouquets turned sacramental in my London life.

Since the Notre Dame London program was in its infancy, there were few files and no official job description for my position. Yet many things fell into place since "a rector is a rector is a rector," home and abroad: students knew I had expectations of them, and vice versa. And so together we held the gift of a London semester in our hands, unwrapping it with great curiosity and much creativity.

In preparing for the opening Mass on a makeshift altar set up beneath the grand winding staircase in the Notre Dame Center foyer, I stood without an altar cloth. And so it was that I met Michael, the concierge at Brown's Hotel off Piccadilly, where Teddy Roosevelt spent his honeymoon. (Almost everything we touched hung on historical hinges!) In tux and tails he met me in the hotel lobby and graciously agreed to lend a linen tablecloth for our special liturgy. He was quite aware of Notre Dame, "a few doors away," and of Father Hesburgh and Chief Justice Burger of the U.S. Supreme Court, both of whom had recently resided at Brown's during the dedication of Notre Dame's Law School program in London. As he sent me on my way, the lady behind the theater desk in the hotel lobby shook her head and called me "a plucky one." While I was charmed by her British "touch," I was desperate for an altar cloth.

Within minutes the cloth was spread across a table, creating an altar under the winding staircase, just in time for Father Ned Joyce, CSC, executive vice president, who arrived with Prof. David Link, dean of Notre Dame's Law School. They gathered with us to celebrate the Eucharist at the beginning of a new academic year in London.

Life had a simple touch as we made our daily way though it. Our Sutherland Avenue three-storied residences, which must have been a century old, were right out of late-night classic movies such as *Gaslight*, complete with high, wrought-iron fences and basement dwellings. There was no central heating, only gas jets set into old fireplaces. A few portable showers were added to the ground apartment, often called the garden flat. Refrigeration was at a minimum and there were no laundry facilities.

All along the way we leaned on each other through minor illnesses and for material needs and emotional support. Students stopped by my room in the evenings "just to talk," only to discover that they were turning to the deeper things going on inside themselves. During the day, there were also quaint pubs serving lunch, with a quiet spot for discussing everything from faith and relationships to poor self-image and concerns that students had buried in themselves back at Notre Dame. Both men and women admitted that their defenses were down on this side of the Atlantic.

Quite naturally there were always some discipline issues brewing. The London bobbies forbade students to play frisbee on Sutherland Avenue. This was not the north quad. Kitchens and sleeping rooms had to be kept clean. Marisol Gonzalez, a native Spaniard who was chief housekeeper, came into our lives with great gusto for keeping things in order. Since students were of legal age to consume alcohol in England, they were expected to behave as adults, use common sense, and drink responsibly—or catch a plane back to the United States. After a few minor fusses, Notre Dame expectations filtered into London life.

Students were steeped in international independence. Most of them used it well. Some stumbled into a bit of chaos, such as the lad who drank too much beer at the Munich October Fest and woke up without his belongings, including his passport. Among other things, he learned quickly about the significance and some of the responsibilities of the American Embassy, which came to his rescue.

While Notre Dame now sends hundreds of students annually to sixteen international academic sites, for Domers there was and is no end to the intellectual stimuli present in one of the largest cities of the world. The late Shakespeare scholar Prof. James Robinson delighted in the rich benefits afforded him as he lectured and led us all to Stratford-upon-Avon to see it all ourselves, including the Royal Shakespeare Company's production of *Julius Caesar*. Someone in our group was always attending Royal Shakespeare productions in London at the Barbican, including *The Tempest*, *Henry V*, or *Much Ado About Nothing*.

There were music classes before and after performances of Mozart's *Don Giovanni* and *The Magic Flute* by the English National Opera at the London Coliseum, as well as Puccini's *La Boheme* at the Royal Opera House. Duly impressed, I watched as students took notes, listening to Beethoven's Fifth Symphony performed at the Royal Festival Concert Hall. For many it was their first opera and first symphony.

Leicester Square's theater specials were within walking distance, including long-standing productions such as Agatha Christie's *Mousetrap*, which played in London for thirty-two years. We added *Singin' in the Rain* to our repertoire, sitting in historic seats in the London Palladium. Andrew Lloyd Webber's genius came alive for all of us in *Cats*.

We were constantly debriefing each other after popular London walks, advertised and led by guides to such places as the Old Bailey, where judges most properly bewigged and robed were hearing cases. While I studied the faces of jurors and heard closing arguments, my mind kept skipping through *A Tale of Two Cities*, catching scenes filled with Sydney Carton and Madame Defarge.

Visible on the shore of the Thames for a thousand years, the Tower of London had its own allure, thanks to William the Conqueror, the king of England in the eleventh century. Many of us were drawn to the tower often, always with more questions and history on our minds. The tower property was filled with Reformation history: for example, Henry VIII's break with the Church, his wives and their executions, the reign of his daughter Elizabeth, and the confinement and martyrdom of Thomas More and John Fisher.

A long visit to Westminster Abbey offered a grand survey of English history, literature, and the lives of kings and queens, novelists and poets. I watched as students stood quietly among the tombs and memorials of writers and rulers. Some of us carried copies of the English monarchy's family trees, which we unfolded into a visual history that stretched back for centuries.

The drama of Fleet Street and the daily presses enticed the journalists in our midst, while budding architects toured Wren buildings. Students always seemed to feel that they were missing wonderful opportunities. And they were; there was just too much to see and do. Each student was forced to make selections.

Almost everyone went to Harrods, the store that boasted the Queen's business, capable of selling customers everything from an earring to an elephant. We learned that Harrods even offered a "funeral package" to assist those responsible for making purchases and plans for burying their loved ones. The Harrods' fish hall, though smelly, was an artistic sight to behold. High tea, served with an elegant touch, was a walk into the world of pastry. On my first visit to Harrods, I was treated to a storewide announcement. It was Christmastime. Introduced by three chimes in ascending tones, a very proper and official sounding British male voice caught the shoppers' attention: "Ladies and gentlemen, please mind your pockets and mind your purses. There's a pickpocket in our midst." It took three more chimes, in descending tonal order, to put hustle and bustle back into the crowds. I felt as though I had posed for a movie clip.

A trip down the Thames River took us to Greenwich, where time is marked for the whole world, on land and at sea. We also posed for pictures on a copper strip that indicated the "Prime Meridian of the World," from which point longitude is counted east and west. As one coed put it, "It seemed I had a controlling hand on all the continents and waterways of the world."

There were day trips to Cambridge or Canterbury, Salisbury or Dover; weekends in Windemere (the land of the Lake District poets in northwest England); and excursions to Edinburgh, Scotland, and Cardiff, Wales. Trains easily connected us to all of England and beyond; in fact, England without Wales and Scotland is about as big as the state of Vermont (although England's culture, power, and influence has been felt around the world for centuries). Now it makes sense to me why some Brits make plans to visit New York, Miami, Chicago, and San Francisco during a five-day stay.

It was a hands-on education for Notre Dame students traveling in Europe. They learned quickly how to keep track of their funds and how to exchange American dollars or English pounds for foreign currency, as they made plans to travel to Ireland, Russia, Greece, Spain, Italy, France, or Morocco. (A few students even put a foot into Bogart and Bacall's Casablanca.) They walked in and out of world-renowned banks like Lloyd's of London and Barclays, passing long-robed oil sheiks in the process. They arranged their travel by trains, planes, ships, and hovercrafts—no hot-air balloons that I heard about. They made reservations in student hostels, bed and breakfasts, hotels, motels, or with family, friends, or fellow Domers studying or working in other countries. The world was more than at their fingertips, it landed in their laps day in and day out.

For each country we visited, I watched our exchange students purchase paperbacks containing basic European travel information. They would then sit in circles in our small and intimate Albemarle pub and carefully tear a travel book apart, chapter by chapter, relating relevant material to travelers' plans and destinations. Periodically I cleaned library shelves of the remains of paperbacks that hung together by front and back covers, a table of contents, and advertisements. The innards had gone round the world.

Often I came across small groups of Domers enthralled as they listened to each other's travel experiences whether to the Greek Islands or West Berlin. They questioned the presenters and challenged some of their insights. They collected names, addresses, and phone numbers and they reached out for hand-me-down maps and train schedules from each other. It was peer education in full bloom.

We were spellbound by those who returned from Moscow full of stories during the fall of 1983, but they were also somewhat depressed by what they had seen and heard. Professors Peri Arnold and Jim Bellis held a formal debriefing session during which they coaxed the deeper impact of the Moscow experience out into the open. Students knew that they were followed as they toured Moscow. There was evidence that their rooms were bugged and that some of their belongings had been searched. They went through three Russian guides before one seemed strong enough to rein them in and answer their unending questions. In daily ways they felt some of the constraints of people under Communist rule. They saw people waiting in bread lines. Young Russians followed them, wanting to practice the English language, inviting them to their apartments. Domers exchanged their clothing, especially their jeans, for Russian memorabilia. One student attended Mass two days in a Russian Orthodox church. On the second day a funeral liturgy was celebrated and he was asked to help carry the casket. The government at that time did not look kindly on those who worshiped God, and this caused those in attendance to be suspect and small in number.

While trips away from London were always fun, there was daily London life to live. We learned to shop for food in our neighborhoods, carrying our own bags and filling them at the counter. We learned to "queue up" at the bakery, even if it meant standing in a line that stretched out the door and into misty weather. Many of us shopped at the Portobello and Church Street markets for second-hand woolen coats to ward off raw cold winds that swept in from the sea. England is an island!

The underground became almost too familiar, and the longer we lived there, the more red double-decker buses we took. Some days, in busy shopping areas, you could count ten buses in a glance. They became a symbol for me of London, which seemed like a double-decker city with its underground filled with tunnels of tracks that connected everyone's life, from Piccadilly Circus to the edges of Zone Six and out to Gatwick Airport. At certain times of the day, great numbers of people moved around in the bowels of the earth, reading and eating, dozing and talking their ways to and from work.

One late hour, after walking down a great flight of stairs to the train tracks, I met an underground employee who tried to warn me of an accident that had just occurred on the tracks in the direction I was headed. Not yet accustomed to thick cockney accents, I asked him to repeat himself—three times. Finally, I realized that he was trying to soften a tragedy with some flowery language, until he clearly blurted out, "Suicide, my good lady, it's a suicide!" He explained that someone had thrown himself in front of a train speeding through the tunnel. As I flinched, he shrugged his shoulders and warned, "You must get used to it. You will see that some among us have other uses for the tube."

While each semester had festive days, it was our Yankee holiday in late November that earned an English Oscar. We planned Thanksgiving dinner for eighty, putting our money, time, and cooking wits into the venture. We divided ourselves into food committees, created a kitty, and chose a keeper of the purse. Each group shopped at their favorite markets, keeping eighty guests in mind, agreeing to create their dish from scratch. Mr. Peter Lowy gave us the use of a large dining room and adjoining kitchen in the Hyde Park West Hotel.

Mark Boennighausen, Paula Beaujailly, Sharon Jones, Jim Carpetta, and Todd Young took care of the string beans. The mashed potato crew involved Phil Allen, Crane Kenny, Brian de Toy, and Pete

White. Supervising the salad, soup, and apples were John Breen, Todd Young, Matt Revord, Tracy Klockner, and Jim Plamondon.

The pie committee, including Patti Riley, Aline Gregoire, and Lisa Kopidlansky, swung into action the night before the feast by following instructions for pumpkin pie on a wrapper from a Pet Milk can that someone's mom had sent. The next best thing to a real rolling pin was a quart milk bottle, which was used to roll out enough dough for twelve pies, which baked miraculously in two small ovens that might have been left over from Queen Victoria's day.

All the food traveled to the hotel by black cab or the underground. Four turkeys were purchased by committee members, were filled with homemade stuffing prepared by professors' wives Marilyn Bellis and Beverly Arnold, and delivered in a black cab to a local French bakery for roasting. At the "well-done" hour, the turkeys returned by cab to the front entrance of the Hyde Park West Hotel, a main dinner attraction with all the trimmings.

We were all cooks for a day. We washed, peeled, chopped, quartered, beat, melted, stirred, ladled, sprayed, dipped, cut, mashed, sliced, and divided. Some students were given charge while others took charge and made the feast come together. Tables were covered with white bed sheets and set with dishes and silverware of all makes and models. Candles burned brightly. We prayed Jewish and Christian prayers filled with Thanksgiving for so many gifts, one of them being the moments we shared—Domer Yanks huddled together, living and learning in London.

It was good to return to London for another semester after the Christmas holidays. I knew in the fall that the semester abroad was such a gift; but it got more precious with time, with every turn. I was in need of a fresh perspective and getting away from Notre Dame for a while was the solution. Those months made it possible for me to rest my mind and body. A quiet settled deep inside of me again. I was desperate for holy solitude, for the kind of solitude that lets thoughts run deep. It was pleasant to wake in the morning without twelve things to do as soon as possible. I loved my ministry back at Notre Dame, so it was hard to pull away. Yet it was useful to clean out my entire room: empty drawers and closets, bookcases and files; clear the walls, pack everything, and leave it behind. There was a voice inside of me that said, "I dare you to go be a pilgrim for a while." Separating myself from people, places, and things so close to me was just what I needed. It turned out to be one of the best insights I ever had into my life.

During this time, it was refreshing to read for long periods. I read biographies with an English eye: Thomas à Becket, Thomas More, Edmund Campion, Charles Dickens, G. K. Chesterton, Hilaire Belloc, Winston Churchill. I also read the Sunday paper. Some weeks I surveyed the whole issue, an unlikely undertaking at Notre Dame. Often I combined it with tasty tea and scones with jelly and clotted cream.

I returned again and again to Farm Street Church for Eucharist for the quiet amidst London life. Some Domers found their way there as well, especially during Lent. It was only a stroll away from our Albemarle headquarters, around Berkeley Square, past scenic London buildings, including an auto showroom that only held one large Rolls-Royce. I gradually learned some of this miniature gothic cathedral's rich, thick Jesuit history, beginning with Fr. John Laurance, SJ, who circled Farm Street Church on my London map one night after he celebrated Mass in Farley Hall. The Jesuits came to London looking for a site for their first London church in the 1840s, and they found it in a back street that got its name from the Hay Hill Farm, which has turned into London's Mayfair district.

During the coldest days of winter, there was a rush among us for hot water bottles as our Sutherland Avenue rooms became raw with cold. We lit portable gas jets in fireplaces of another century. We were strongly advised not to leave them lit through the night. More than once we made public pacts that we would never take central heating for granted again. Some nights turned coeds into frigid models who dressed themselves in fashion-show ambience, wandering into each other's rooms with the multilayered look of winter sleepwear, including socks, hats, and mittens. While we found ways to stay warm with a roof overhead, we became aware of people who spent cold nights living on the streets.

Fortunately, we were able to do some volunteer work in London during this time, joining with the Irish clergy and sisters as they visited and served food to the homeless through the night. Various charitable groups took responsibility on a weekly basis. Ours was a "soup run" from the homeless shelter at Bondsway to five or six stops around the city, including the Royal Festival Hall viaduct area, Fleet Street, Lincoln Inn Park, the Embankment area, and Waterloo Station.

Mostly men waited for hot soup and tea. Some waited at designated spots or benches in the area, while others came forth out of nearby boxes or from under rugs, old furniture, or car cushions. One man made a habit of sleeping in a phone booth on the Embankment. A former disabled military man sang us a lullaby one evening about a mother and her child. A young fellow, standing nearby with his steaming hot soup, began to curse him, adding, "I can't stand it when you sing that song." It led to a skirmish and heavy blows.

One night a rather frail-looking woman walked toward us out of the shadows of a viaduct near the Thames River wearing a flimsy summer dress. "Oh, I have a coat," she announced, "but no shoes." Rose was dirty and bruised, and a bit drunk. All she wanted for the moment was a cigarette, which someone offered. With a bit of an Irish brogue, Sr. Moira also offered Rose new tennis shoes and socks before Rose ambled back into a bed of cushions propped against the walls of a bridge. It had all the ingredients of a Gospel parable.

The soup and tea and human companionship loosened some tongues. A few men spoke out angrily about Thatcher and Reagan. Some railed against churches and their hypocrisy. Others posed questions to us about the United States: "Are there troubles like ours in the colonies?" One man exploded in my face: "You're a Yank! What are you doing here with us? You must be crazy." Some men stayed quietly in the background. Others spoke if spoken to. Many expressed gratitude for the soup. We finished our volunteer work at 4 A.M.

The memories of World War II were a real residue in the memories of older Brits, and these memories showed up many times during our days abroad, most often when we least expected them. One Sunday, as our Notre Dame contingent sat scattered among older neighbors in pews of Our Lady of the Woods Church, the celebrant of the Eucharist reminded us all of Jesus' exhortation to love each other and to lend a hand to neighbors in need. In making his point, the priest reached to the past: "We must get back to that spirit that many of us in this Church knew when we huddled together in the underground stations during bombing raids." His words brought the old and young, the Brits and the Yanks together in conversation after Mass.

While making my way with students to the Barbican Center in London for a concert, I became conscious of high-rise buildings around me, a sight in such contrast to many other parts of the city. When I asked a British professor who was in our party about them, I was told that these buildings replaced those reduced to rubble during World War II bombing raids. In the middle of the concert, I heard a plane overhead and sat straight up with thoughts of bombs. Older people sitting in front of me actually looked up. I sensed that their thoughts were much more realistic than mine.

These thoughts occurred again as I walked through the Cathedral of Chartres in the footsteps of pilgrims whose lives stretched across centuries. I listened intently to the guide as he explained how the Christians who came here to pray to the Virgin Mary also ate and slept in the cathedral space. He added that medieval engineers designed the stone floor with a slight tilt toward the doors, allowing the drainage of water used to wash the church out after pilgrims moved on. The guide further helped us to understand how this medieval church stood as a "book of stone and glass," instructing the many Christians, who could not read, about their faith as they moved among the statues and carvings that depicted the life of Jesus. They also learned from the more than three thousand figures appearing in the stained-glass windows filled with vivid colors. Suddenly, with the turn of a phrase, the guide jumped from the Middle Ages to the World War II bombings, from Chartres' blue stained-glass windows to red military flares that were strategically placed around this historic place of worship to insure continual protection against bombs. It was intriguing to hear that all of the windows were removed during both World War I and World War II and stored in safe places. I was amazed by how country leaders made such plans and agreements in the name of religion and art and historic buildings. I couldn't imagine such rational care and concern in the midst of so much wartime irrationality and inhumanity.

It was always a challenge to catch up with Domers studying in other European programs. I took the long way around Ireland to Maynooth, with its one stoplight, to visit with Notre Dame and St. Mary's students whom I found in the swimming pool at St. Patrick's College. We gathered for a tour, afternoon tea, and an evening Eucharist, where, to my surprise, I gave the sign of peace to Prof. Emeritus Ernan McMullin's brother Eunan and niece Patria Malone. Before the evening was over, and with an Irish twinkle in their eyes, they shipped me off to stay a few days with their cousin in Galway.

In order to catch up with other Domers abroad, I traveled from Salzburg to Innsbruck on the longest train route I could find, a scenic four-hour journey. I wanted to see all of the alps I could. Skiers entertained me all along the route, racing down grand snow slopes looking like black dots on an electronic board game. I became all eyes with a dancing pulse, while the woman sitting across from me slept soundly. With lunch, I watched and listened to four young women in front of me chatting the trip away, oblivious of the scenery. They probably knew it all by heart and yearned to see New York skyscrapers. Young lovers across the aisle stared at each other with each mouthful. We could have been in the Sahara for all they knew or cared. Aware or not, we were all steeped in the beauty of Tirol, and so I took it upon myself to bear the full burden of such beauty and ecstasy.

Then came the day when it was time to climb an alp with Janice Engelhart and Sylvia Reveles, Farley women studying in Innsbruck. First, a cable car (the "Nordkettenbahn") took us to the highest point on its map. From there we trudged through snow, clinging to strong cables that led us to the top of Mt. Hafelekar at seven thousand feet. We stood in bright sunlight on a small piece of mountaintop property completely surrounded by light, fluffy clouds which seemed to pass through us. A large wooden cross stood tall on Hafelekar, and it was the only object in sight as we beheld a sea of unending snow-covered mountains undulating off into the distance. It seemed that the whole world was full of mountains and that I was standing right in the middle of them. It was pure beauty. The three of us caught each other's sighs. When I try to put that scene to words, I feel like I am trying on a gorgeous dress that I am much too small for. It is better if I remember Fr. Terry Lally, CSC, telling me that when he finally reached the peak of Mt. Hood in Oregon and feasted his eyes on the scene that lay before him, he erupted into an act of faith: "I know there is a God."

Later that night, down below in the streets of Innsbruck, it seemed that mountains, with all of their mystery and massive majesty, followed me. There was one at every turn. I felt the coldness of the peak's ice and snow in my face and on my neck. The longer I stayed in the city, the more accustomed I became to such company, but I wondered if Innsbruck citizens ever suffer from claustrophobia.

Thanks to Father Charlie Sheedy, CSC, who had a strong hand in the development of the Innsbruck program years before our visit, we created a Notre Dame scene in the Martplatz as we gathered around café tables for morning "kaffee" and "kuchen." Our group included Dan Klee ('86), Dave O'Neill ('86), and Mark Herkert ('86), along with Sylvia Reveles and Janice Engelhart ('86) of Mt. Hafelekar fame, among others. On one occasion Tom Kronk ('70) explained to me that he was in the first group to study in Innsbruck, sailing on an ocean liner for at least eight days, first spending some time in Paris. Prof. Klaus Lansinger, director of the Innsbruck program at the time, claims that the first group almost never made it out of Paris, since there was so much to see and do there.

A short stay in Luxembourg was filled with thrills. In an outdoor marketplace full of flowers, fruits, and vegetables, and a small outdoor café, I ordered kaffee and kuchen under a sun umbrella. With the first sip of kaffee, a lady in a wide-rimmed hat walked over and hailed me by name. It was Betty Stockover, our former Sister Brian, who had picked up a ray of sun from my gold ring and was drawn to look in my direction! We had lots in common and many of the same friends, but we hadn't seen each other since she left the convent, following those turmoil years after Vatican II. She was now at the U.S. Army base in Ramstein, Germany, not too far away, serving as an official of the USO (United Service Organizations), having just established a women's center on the base for the wives of servicemen, the first of its kind. Her USO history is filled with the accomplishments of thousands of GIs who are indebted to her for programs established around the world on their behalf. Our amazing Sister Brian went on to do all this. She reminded me that she was near forty when she left our community. She made her decision not to marry. Then she went on to minister unceasingly to young American servicemen. She was very bright, articulate, filled with life, and known for her great sense of humor.

In her apartment, I examined a stack of scrapbooks filled with pictures of aircraft carriers and their crews and endless thank-you letters for her work. She often flew by helicopter to waiting subs and ships to help orient servicemen and women about to land in foreign ports. Planned activities kept them from falling prey to unwanted and sometimes dangerous and dicey encounters.

We went to Sunday Mass together, witnessed a First Communion, and sang "Holy God" in German at the top of our lungs. She toured me through Ramstein, then Heidelberg. She had just returned from a U.S. visit and a reunion of all our former sisters held at our motherhouse. "It was an experience packed with emotions. It was so good to see everyone in that setting. I'm so grateful for all the life the community has been for me. And here you are to debrief me on it all." When it was time to say goodbye, I commented on the ray of sun that had touched my ring and drawn her attention. What was more amazing was that Betty was still wearing her gold ring, the one placed on her finger when she made her final vows as a Franciscan.

Another Luxembourg surprise came in Remich where I walked into a store owned and operated for a hundred years by relatives of Mary Catherine Moes, the woman who founded our Franciscan community after having spent some years with the Holy Cross sisters. An outdoor sign drew me to toward the shop "Moes Freres." Milly, the Moes cousin-in-charge, knew of the "the girls" who went as missionaries to America. An interpreter helped me to answer some of her questions and review a brief history. Mary Catherine Moes and her sister Barbara had received Holy Cross habits from Fr. Edward Sorin, CSC, founder and president of the University of Notre Dame, who also received their final vows. In time Mary Catherine went on to found the Franciscan Sisters in Joliet, Illinois, and then the Franciscan Sisters in Rochester, Minnesota, where she became a major influence in the foundation of the Mayo Brothers' world-renowned medical clinic in Rochester. My final words to Milly ballooned into an invitation to come to America and travel in the footsteps of "the girls" who made significant contributions to the American Church and society in general.

Before leaving Luxembourg City, I was pressed once more into World War II memories at the sound of a small military band and the sight of a company of men and a small corps of veterans, some with canes, one on crutches with a missing limb, and another in a wheelchair. With a very silent but obvious pride, citizens circled the group. An American child's piercing questions forced the reality of the scene out into the open, into words and emotions: "Who?" and "Why?" and "How come?" A roll call of those from the area who had died some forty years before was read aloud by a statesman, "the Minister." As the band played and a large wreath of flowers was placed at the foot of an imposing war memorial, veterans pulled themselves up to full attention. Other onlookers wept openly. I picked up a small part of a spring bouquet that fell at my feet and carried it with me for the rest of the day.

My last days in London were similar to the first, only in reverse—so many friends to bid farewell, too many things to see and do, too much to pack. Sutherland Avenue had become home. Domers hardly slept, especially those trying to squeeze the last bit of life out of London before returning to the states. Others made plans for one more trip to such places as Rome, the Greek Islands, or Vienna, often traveling with parents who had never been to Europe before.

The night before I headed for Heathrow Airport, I found myself sitting quietly, taking in the music and the meaning of Mozart's *The Magic Flute*, performed by the English National Opera at the London Coliseum. Oh, the gift of wisdom that gets pressed from human joys and sorrows; it's like fine wine from ripened grapes. As I clapped my way through the last curtain call, I knew that *The Magic Flute* had touched the heart of my London experience.

EIGHT

Office of Student Affairs

I was fresh from London with English pounds in my pocket when I got the call to meet Fr. David Tyson at the Martinique Restaurant near my home in Chicago where I was visiting my family. I had heard that he was about to become the new vice president for Student Affairs, and I sensed that he wanted an update on a few situations needing attention across the Atlantic. London was the furthest thing from his mind.

Fr. Dave was forming a new senior staff and he had circled my name as a possible member. At first I held my hands up in front of me, not wanting the request to get near me as he proceeded to lay out his plans, explaining what my position would involve. Although the intensity of life in the Office of Student Affairs on the third floor of the administration building never attracted me, I agreed to give his plans a thorough look.

Thoughtful questions and encouragement from others who knew me quite well began to cast more light on the situation. During a chance meeting with Fr. Hesburgh on the north quad, I expressed my reluctance when he proposed the arrangement. As president, he strongly encouraged me to gather up my experience and to "come and sit down with colleagues who care about this place as you do and help them make good decisions. It's the hardest thing we do." I prayed hard, let myself grow accustomed to the idea of feeling challenged and unanchored as an assistant vice president for Student Affairs, and finally agreed to start a new job.

But I didn't say yes until I knew John Goldrick would come aboard as associate vice president, a new position that held the same responsibilities as the former dean of students. This meant that he would leave his position as director of Admissions, which he had held for some thirteen years since he finished his Peace Corps duties in Thailand and a teaching assignment in Beirut. Father Frank Cafarelli, CSC, who served as assistant director of Student Accounts and the assistant rector of Zahm Hall, became the fourth member of our team for a few years and then passed the reins to Father Peter Rocca, CSC.

With coeducation at Notre Dame only a dozen years old, I suspect my strongest credential for the position was that I was a woman. It was time for Notre Dame to place a woman at this level of administration in the division of Student Affairs. Add that fact to ten years of rectoring in Farley Hall, teaching as an adjunct instructor in the theology department, and serving as rector and chaplain for the London program. While these experiences would serve me well in this appointment, I sensed that this new ministry would tap into the deepest experiences of my life.

Fr. David's flowchart made it quite evident that we would be immersed in students' lives. Among us we would supervise the major departments that offer support services for students as they go their academic ways: career planning, counseling, discipline, health, housing, international and multicultural student needs, safety and security, and student activities. In time, the Alcohol and Drug Education office was established. Standing central to the faith life of Domers is the Office of Campus Ministry, which continually expanded its staff and programming over the years.

At the outset, the senior staff worked directly with twenty-four residence hall rectors, thirty-nine assistant rectors, and 140 resident assistants who staffed the undergraduate residence halls. A manager and a chaplain served the University Village for married students, while a rector and staff administered the O'Hara-Grace graduate housing complex designed for single students.

All of my hunches about my new position proved true. The Office of Student Affairs was as intense a place as I had imagined. Not knowing what would happen next in a world of almost ten thousand students went a long way in shaping our team for living on the edge, where we spent most of our waking hours. We met weekly, and sometimes more often, as we attempted to keep abreast of developments within the student body and among those directing the various support services. We always covered for each other in case of minor and major emergencies. We learned quickly to use each other's strengths.

Curiously, most students gasped or posed a fearful question at the mere mention of the Office of Student Affairs: "They caught me!" or "What did I do wrong?" As far as they were concerned, discipline was the only thing that happened in our division. Although we tried to shape another image, we had to learn to live with theirs. At least they were on the right track. Good discipline, the best we could muster, was always our concern and ten thousand students kept it in focus. They were, without a doubt, the inspiration behind *duLac*, the student handbook published and updated by our office, for which we held the student body accountable.

For a few years John Goldrick carried the responsibility of the dean of students of earlier decades, but he wisely developed the Office of Residence Life and hired Ann Firth ('81 and '84) as its chief hearing officer. I listened to some of the most serious student discipline cases that came to us, and my participation in the hearings involved hard decisions for me that had far-reaching effects on student lives. Such hearings made it clear to me that an insistence on good discipline was one of Notre Dame's most valuable educational pursuits. I often recall the words of one student who, after his major "alcohol mistake," was suspended for a semester. On his return, he was man enough to come back and say, "The best thing you ever did was to kick me in the butt and get me out of here for awhile. I started to see ugly stuff in my life that I never saw before."

This "ministry of hollering," as I sometimes described it (saying very emphatically, "No, you can't get away with that"), was tough going at times. Serious case hearings could involve long hours with numerous witnesses. Such cases initiated countless phone calls and letters from parents, family, friends, former educators, and clergy. Cases of a public nature often brought local and sometimes national media to the scene. Penalties could range from fines and/or community service to suspension or outright dismissal. An appeals process was in place and used. Now and then we had to go to court. However, it was worth the effort when truth telling was the outcome, forgiveness expressed, recompense made, and offenders learned lessons about themselves that would serve them a lifetime, whether they remained a Domer or had to leave the community.

I heard John Goldrick explain to disciplined students many times that we wanted them to graduate from Notre Dame, but that first they had to take a semester (or two) away from school to get help with their problem, be it alcohol, drugs, excessive anger, or a family issue. Suspension was much more than a penalty; it often held the answer to a problem and a lifelong lesson.

During my first four years in the Office of Student Affairs, we suspended forty-one students and dismissed a handful of others for what we deemed very serious reasons. Those suspended left us for a semester or two and got the help they needed. Forty of the forty-one suspended students returned to graduate. It became obvious that what Notre Dame said it stood for, what it said in its literature, especially in *duLac*, was tested repeatedly. One Holy Cross priest, with years of experience at watching people suffer some of the agonies of growing up, put it on the line with me: "Don't be afraid to be tough on our students. They're the first ones to send their kids back to us." He saw it happen hundreds of times.

I will salute the energies that go into parenting and the wisdom it takes to do it well forever. But curiously, some parents found it difficult when we were tough on the children and expected the best behavior from their sons and daughters. At times they were angry with us when it seemed that they were really angry at their offspring for their mistakes and poor judgment. Some parents were upset with themselves for not seeing the signs in their offspring that led to more serious personal failure. However, other parents joined us in trying to put the best things in place for their children. I suspect there is an intriguing correlation between the growth patterns of parents and their Domer offspring, which so often strengthen family bonds and turn into family legends.

Although there was a time when I was very suspect of the phrase *in loco parentis,* I gradually grew willing to put my life on the line for it. I have come to believe that nothing can take the place of one generation respecting and paving the way for the next generation—not treating them as ten-year-olds, but rather as who they are at nineteen, twenty, and twenty-one, young women and men full of promise, precious energy, keen intelligence, and deep feelings. It has been a distinct grace to share daily life with colleagues who continually struggle to expect the best of our students in and out of the classroom. I know these educators by that expectant look in their eyes and the energy in their attitudes and actions. They simply care, and they find the most engaging ways (often mixed with wit, wisdom, and, at times, a healthy, precious anger) to correct Domers or congratulate them, sometimes in the same breath.

While many students saw our office mainly as the source of rules and regulations, we also earned a reputation, and rightly so, for receiving and responding to emergency calls. Our security department, under the direction of Rex Rakow, kept us informed on events happening locally or nationally that affected or involved the Notre Dame community. Rectors, faculty, deans, and other staff reported their concerns to us about needy, injured, or missing students. Parents, family, and friends contacted us with difficult situations. Phone calls, e-mail, and faxes funneled in from staff members of our international programs regarding various nonacademic student issues that needed attention such as illness, accidents, or discipline matters.

Our world was wired for emergencies. The most difficult call by far was the urgent request to get to the hospital immediately because of a critically injured student. It took all of my energy to turn on the ignition key and drive those few blocks to the emergency center at St. Joseph's Hospital or Memorial Hospital, sometimes finding it almost empty and sometimes filled with students "who saw it all happen."

One late night in 1987 I walked into such a situation, with students ranting and raving over what they had just witnessed. Some observers walked the hallways. Some prayed in the hospital chapel. One young man kept beating his fist against the wall. Some sat in shock while others insisted with loud voices, "He can't die." However, as the night wore on, it seemed that the injured student was going to die. Michael Cogswell, a resident of Zahm Hall, had been struck by a car while walking back to campus from St. Mary's College. He was on a respirator until his parents, Michael and Dorothy, and sisters, Catherine and Amy ('93), could get to his side.

It was one thing to stand in St. Joseph's emergency room supporting a sick or injured Domer. It was another whole reality to be there holding vigil for a dying student. I remember Fr. Dave drawing me aside and saying so thoughtfully, "Jean, this is by far the hardest thing I do." It was as though I heard a piece of a prayer that went straight to God asking for the grace and strength to minister to those depending on him. He had anointed Michael, called his parents in Marcellus, New York, to explain what happened, and then stood in the midst of so many in shock or full of grief.

That night it became evident to Fr. Dave that we couldn't leave the hospital without giving Michael's friends a chance to see him and say their good-byes. "Jean, we should take them to Michael." And so we did. With medical personnel nearby, we gathered Michael's friends around his gurney. We prayed and we cried. I watched with deep admiration as Zahm men took their turns to say some final words to a buddy. Some good-byes were direct, audible, and clear; others were soft-spoken. Some sentences fell apart as knees buckled. Later, one of his good friends, Justin, stopped by Farley Hall and asked if I thought it would be okay for him to write Michael a letter and put it in his casket when he went to Marcellus for the funeral. In my heart I knew that all of Michael's friends lost more of their innocence that somber night.

Sometimes a serious emergency call came in the middle of the day. Out of the corner of my eye, I saw Fr. Edward "Monk" Malloy, then assistant provost living in Sorin Hall, come into the Office of Student Affairs asking for Fr. Dave. I never saw such a look on his face. Fr. Malloy knew the Niland family from Michigan. The Nilands' son Paul lived in Sorin and was ill in St. Joseph's Hospital. Their older son, Patrick, a Notre Dame graduate in medical school at the University of Michigan, was on his way to see his brother, along with his sister, Katherine, who was also a Notre Dame graduate. On a country road they suffered a tragic accident in which Patrick instantly lost his life.

I heard Fr. Malloy say, " Dave, I need help with this." As Fr. Dave motioned for me to come into his office, they stood strategizing. Fr. Dave left immediately for the hospital to be with the father and brother. Fr. Malloy and I went to the Morris Inn where Patrick's mother, Martha, was unpacking before heading to the hospital. His appearance on the scene somewhat startled her as he reached for very simple and direct words to deliver the dreadful message—words no one ever wants to hear or speak. Fr. Malloy and I were helpless, offering only our presence,

"A Modern Nun"

The author in 1967 in full religious habit with a modernized veil that allowed a bit of hair to show, asking a question of Notre Dame biblical scholar John L. McKenzie, SJ, during an informal discussion held in Lewis Hall. Lewis was a residence for members of women's religious communities until 1975, when it became a residence for undergraduate women.

"A HALLOWED HALL CALLED FARLEY"
(Sketch courtesy of Posie Strenz, class of 1986)

"LOYAL DAUGHTERS"
Members of the class of 1978 pose in front of Farley Hall with the author (front row, fourth from left).

"FOOTBALL SATURDAYS"
Thirty years of football Saturdays initiated annual Lenz family reunions in Farley Hall. (Left to right: cousin Jim Crinnion and his son, Patrick, brothers Ray Lenz and his wife, Ethel, and Jack Lenz and his wife, Pat.)

"JUNIOR PARENTS WEEKEND"
Father Ted Hesburgh, CSC, inaugurated the annual Junior Parents Weekend in the early 1950s and continued to join in the celebration years later with members of the author's family. (Left to right: Michael Ford, Fr. Ted, Jenny Ford ('94), Trudy (Lenz) Ford, and the author.)

"TIME TO FLY"

Father David Tyson, CSC (center), vice president for Student Affairs from 1984–1990 and his senior staff before boarding the ND plane bound for an annual Student Affairs meeting on Notre Dame's properties in Land O'Lakes, Wisconsin. (Left to right: O. J. Stewart, former property manager, Peter Rocca, CSC, Fr. Tyson, CSC, John Goldrick, and the author.)

"CELEBRATING MSGR. JACK EGAN"

The author and Jack Egan in 1983 at the fortieth anniversary celebration of his priesthood ordination. Never at a loss for inspiring young people to do the work of the Church, Msgr. Egan died in May 2001.

"Every Campus Needs a Griff"
Fr. Robert Griffin, CSC, strolled the campus daily with Darby O'Gill I, II, and III as he went about his ministry from 1965 to 1995. Fr. Ted best eulogized this Holy Cross priest at Griff's memorial Mass when he simply said, "Every campus needs a Griff." *(Photo courtesy of Holy Cross Community)*

"The Legends"
Rev. John Francis Farley, CSC (left), and a young assistant football coach named Knute Rockne ('14). *(Photo courtesy of Notre Dame Archives)*

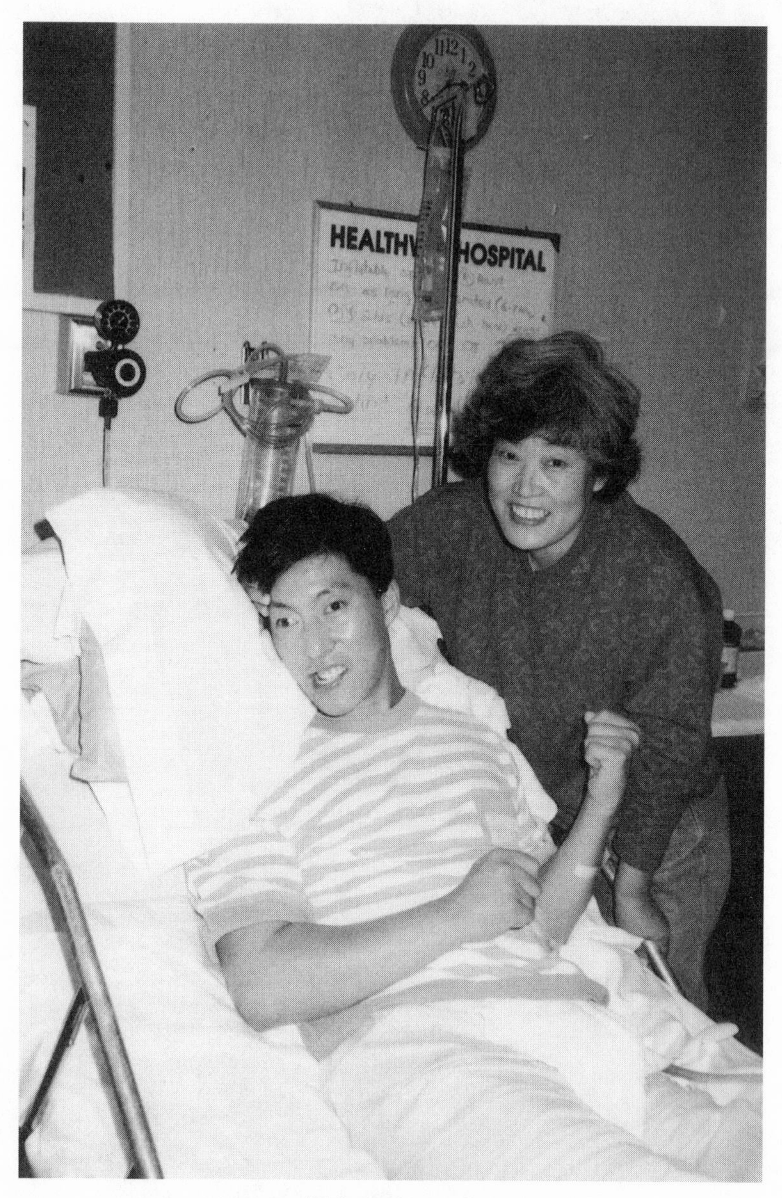

"T-Shirt Therapy"

Former graduate student Zhengde Wang ('89) and his mother, Zueying Wu, in Healthwin Hospital in 1990. Wang received extensive therapy after a serious accident in 1989 on Notre Dame Avenue left him severely handicapped. The ND–South Bend community sold thousands of t-shirts to help defray his medical expenses.

(Photo courtesy of David Durochik)

"RULING THE COURTS . . ."
Former ND law student and assistant rector of Farley Hall, the Honorable Judge Ann Claire Williams ('75) now serves the Seventh U.S. Circuit Court of Appeals in Chicago. Judge Williams has been a member of ND's Board of Trustees since 1988.

(Photo courtesy of NASA)

" . . . AND THE COSMOS"
U.S. Navy Captain James Wetherbee ('74) has logged over 1,200 hours in space. He has served as mission commander for the crews of the space shuttles *Columbia, Discovery,* and *Atlantis*.

"AT HOME 'NEATH THE DOME"

The author, pausing outside of Farley Hall on her way to the Office of Student Affairs, where she has served on the senior staff of three university vice presidents.

our compassion, and some kind words to help Patrick's mother absorb the shock and sense of great loss.

When Fr. David Tyson left the vice presidency after six years to become president of the University of Portland in 1990, he passed his formidable responsibilities to Prof. Patricia O'Hara, a tenured member of the law faculty, who, in accepting the position, became the first woman officer of the university. It was while she was vice president that forty members of the Notre Dame women's swim team and their coaches met with a tragic nighttime bus accident in blizzard conditions on the way back from a January meet at Loyola University in Chicago. Their bus slid off interstate highway I-80, near the seventy-two-mile marker a few miles from campus, and turned on its side in a ditch. The worst had happened. There were two fatalities: freshmen Megan Beeler and Colleen Hipp. Haley Scott ('96), who ultimately had a miraculous recovery, was in critical condition. As members of the senior staff and other university personnel began to help slightly injured swimmers huddled in shock and fear in various hospital emergency centers in the South Bend area, scenes of the accident were being broadcast on television news reports.

Following treatment at hospitals, the swimmers were transported to the University Health Center where a full staff of doctors and nurses, under Anne Thompson's direction, offered further care. Parents, family members, friends, and university staff arrived by car and plane. That night I lost all sense of time. I remember the late-night call to my Farley residence from Bill Kirk (who had succeeded John Goldrick after he left to become the U.S. director for the Peace Corps in Ghana, Africa) to get to St. Joseph's Hospital immediately. The next thing I knew was that it was 8:20 A.M. and I was having morning coffee in the Corby Hall dining room surrounded by people who had stayed at various posts through the night.

There was shock and anger and a multitude of prayers being offered as news of the tragedy swept across campus. The great losses of Megan and Colleen, along with Haley's critical condition, were great burdens within the campus community and for their parents and siblings. There were circles of people going over the details of what had occurred on the tollway. You could hear students wondering out loud, asking each other why things like this happen. Some were overwhelmed. Others joined in prayer vigils. As one swimmer confessed, "I can't handle this. I don't know what to think. I put it all in the hands of God."

The years bear witness to the fact that sudden deaths among students weren't always due to accidents. One Sunday afternoon, Knott Hall senior Justin Brumbaugh ('98) jerked back in his chair, then slumped forward and died while sitting in a computer cluster in the College of Business Administration where he and classmates were working on a class project. On another day, third-year law student Joseph Ciraolo, confined to a wheelchair, was having a late lunch in the Huddle when he suddenly collapsed and died. A group of us kept a brief vigil as paramedics worked on him, then finally transported him to an ambulance.

While I became conscious over the years of the life and vitality in the young women and men who crossed my daily paths, I must confess that I also came to realize how close I was to the mystery of death. As I watched those who had their whole lives ahead of them go to God before the rest of us, I was struck more and more with how short and fragile life can be. My mom's words would remind me: "We treat ourselves like we're made of steel, when we're really only flesh and bone."

Bobby Satterfield died on one of the happiest days of his life—hours after meeting the president of the United States. Father Malloy, Coach Holtz, and the national champion football team of 1988 had met with President Ronald Reagan in Washington, D.C., the day before the president's last day in the White House. The team was being honored for its victory and team members stood tall as Father Malloy presented "the Gipper," President Reagan, with the monogrammed sweater that once belonged to the real Gipper, George Gipp, former Notre Dame star halfback. Bobby Satterfield was standing near the president in the rose garden of the White House in all of the television news reports and newspaper photos that swept the country. At Bobby's funeral, Coach Holtz and his team, hit hard with shock and grief, processed out of the church and huddled for one last time behind the hearse as the church bells tolled.

I never learned the best way to give the news of the death of a parent to a student or receive a parent's report on the death of a spouse. It always took me completely off guard, knocked the wind out of me, went deep and left pain. It was such an ordinary morning the day that Mr. Caswell called the Office of Student Affairs from his place of work, asking if I could find out what his daughter's class schedule was for that day. He wanted "to fly from Michigan immediately to tell her—"; there was an audible silence on the other end of the phone. Hesitating, he was gradually able to tell me that he had just received word that his wife had been hit by a small truck and killed as she jogged around their neighborhood early that morning. We spoke through the shock and shaped some plans for Doug Caswell to come to campus and be with his daughter, Jenny. She was Doug's only child, but the Caswells knew many of the young women of Lewis Hall, as well as the rector, Sister Annette George, OSF. I knew a family would be waiting to share the grief and celebrate the life of Mary Caswell with him and Jenny.

The Office of Student Affairs stayed close to the South Bend hospital scene, as did rectors of the residence halls. In fact, I simply can't imagine my life this last quarter century without a hospital emergency room, attending physicians like Dr. Mark Walsh ('69), a caring staff, and all the latest medical technology available. As rector, my main responsibility involved Farley women; as a member of Notre Dame's senior staff, a call to "get there immediately" was for the sake of all of our students, on or off campus, any time of the day or night.

One noon hour I ran next to a gurney carrying a broad-shouldered junior on his way to surgery. I was just in time to catch a message from him for his mom, grab his watch and Notre Dame ring, and bless him (and his surgeon!). He rolled his eyes, amazed that his appendix could give him such a dramatic twirl. "I'll be here when you wake up," were my fleeting words as he passed through private doors.

Once I went through those doors with a young woman from Farley who had broken both of her wrists when she lost control of her bike and ran into the wall of the old field house. She requested that I not leave her side as her gurney rolled into the casting room, the sight of which made my physical energies wane and my words welcome the medical staff. She was a star tennis player, who was not only off the courts for months to come, but needed help for weeks with her day-to-day tasks.

Another fellow skidded and fell from his motorcycle. It was hard to take in all of his wounds, but his greatest need was for emotional support, for someone to be there as he phoned his parents and admitted that he went against their wishes, bought a bike, and landed in the hospital. For a few days I played phone referee between them. The bike had to go. When it did, there was more than enough reconciliation to go around. He gave recuperation full attention, producing his best academic record to date.

Telephone calls to the Office of Student Affairs were emotional roller-coaster rides saturated with local color. Some students called, mad at their rectors; some rectors called, upset with their residents. Students who were harried by roommates demanded room changes. Parents called, frantic to report a daughter who was ready to leave Notre Dame for no good reason or to report a rector who swore at her son for some misdeed. "And he's a priest!" the woman insisted. I simply tried to explain that when you live with 550 young men, "there are days that come along when you simply lose it."

There were campus neighbors who called because students urinated in their bushes the night before and/or kept them up with loud music, and there were some neighbors who called looking for good, strong young men to shovel their walks after a heavy snowfall. Now and then faculty phoned asking for help in locating a student who hadn't reported to class for days or weeks. Alums called, upset over male cheerleaders who dressed as nuns for the football game and then did back flips and tackled each other on the sidelines. Fans complained about nasty or lackadaisical ushers in the stadium. Shopkeepers called because students hadn't yet paid for a dozen roses or twelve dozen hot dogs or a hundred t-shirts.

Some calls pinned students down by name and residence hall for their boorish manners, selfish ways, or name-calling. Other calls were filled with kudos for good things done: work at Logan Center, help at the Center for the Homeless, or cleaning done at the Catholic Worker House.

Most calls demanded a good listen and a response. In time, and without names, some calls grew into legends, like the story of the mother who called seeking help for her son but wouldn't give me her name, his name, the roommate's name, or the rector's name. She offered nary a clue because she didn't want to get her son in trouble.

However, she got me into some when she reported me to my boss for being unprofessional because I told her there wasn't much I could do for her if she insisted on holding back such basic information. The heart of such information will often put senior staff members in touch with one or more of the eleven directors responsible for Notre Dame's major support services, such as the Counseling Center, the Health Center, or the Security Office.

Over the years I've commented in jest that Vice President Patricia O'Hara was administratively responsible for everyone from the cops to the doctors. In truth, she was. However, on a daily basis she delegated her assistants to work with various directors. I worked closely with Joseph Cassidy, who directed the Office of Student Activities; Iris Outlaw, who steered the Office of Multicultural Student Affairs (earlier called the Office of Minority Student Affairs); and Maureen Fitzgibbon, who oversaw the Office of International Student Affairs. As a rector, I often heard myself say, "Without our directors and their staffs, we are nothing." Within the Office of Student Affairs, I carried the boast even further: "With them we can be all things to all people on this campus—almost."

Many times I thought and sometimes said to Joe Cassidy and his assistants, Adele Lanan, Mary Edgington, and Peggy Hnatusko, "You should all go to heaven in a blaze of glory!" They worked closely with student government officers and staffs, the Hall Presidents Council, the Student Senate, and over two hundred clubs and organizations, radio stations, and print media. Joe's office also supervised the Alumni-Senior Club, Stepan Center, and LaFortune Student Center. The annual JPW (Junior Parents Weekend) is coordinated through his office. His staff was always planning, full of ideas and new developments. He made a dream of mine come true when he established a student leadership training program. Then he began to dream of a new student center.

Joe mentored student body presidents for thirteen years, encouraging the best of them to keep one foot in the world of students and the other at least on the edge of the world of administrators. While learning that balancing act, Student Body President Patrick Cook ('89) and his vice president, Laurie Bink ('88), faced the unique challenge of leading the student body through farewell ceremonies for Fr. Theodore M. Hesburgh, CSC, when he retired from the Notre Dame presidency after thirty-five years in the spring of 1987, only to turn around and organize students for fall festivities that marked the presidential inauguration of Father Edward "Monk" Malloy, CSC.

A grand spring picnic on the south quad attracted thousands of Domers to celebrate with Father Ted and his executive vice president, Father Ned Joyce, with whom he had worked all 35 years. They arrived on the scene as total strangers appearing to crash the party, riding red motor scooters and wearing black jackets and dark glasses. Their scooters whizzed past Dillon, Fischer, and Pangborn Halls and headed for the stage set up for student bands. At this point "the strangers" dismounted, propped their bikes on kickstands, and removed their helmets as they joined the celebration. It was pure drama, with fireworks breaking overhead as the sky darkened and dessert was served.

With the Malloy inauguration a few months later, new territory needed to be covered. In Notre Dame's long history, there had never been an official presidential inauguration. For decades the appointment was made in the framework of "holy obedience" within the congregation of the Holy Cross community. Fr. Ted often described his approach to the president's office. After the annual announcement of obediences (more commonly referred to as assignments) by the Holy Cross Provincial in the summer of 1952, it became official that Fr. Ted would be the next president. It was a six-year appointment. Father John Cavanaugh, outgoing president, approached Fr. Ted and handed him the keys to the office in the administration building. With no fuss, Fr. Ted walked over and began to work. Thirty-five years later, holy obedience would still have its place, but the going and the coming had a very different look.

An official university-wide inaugural committee, consisting of eighteen members, was set into motion with provost Timothy O'Meara as chair. The word was out—the inaugural celebration would be the most complex program the university had undertaken to date, surpassing athletic events and commencements. There were twenty-one different categories of guests. Student body officers Pat Cook and Laurie Bink worked under the supervision of Jim Gibbons, who exuded expertise as director of special events and protocol, organizing hundreds of students to lend a hand by ushering, hosting, driving, serving, waiting tables, cleaning up, and even singing in chorale and glee club and playing in the band.

And so it was that Father Malloy was duly inaugurated with great formality on a picture-perfect Indian summer day, including a colorful academic procession of Notre Dame's faculty and students, and 175 presidents or chief academic officers of colleges and universities and heads of learned societies from across the country. Later in the day he was feted quite informally as the guest of honor at another south quad picnic decorated with an array of handmade flags flying on tall poles. Each residence hall designed and crafted its own coat of arms for the occasion, thanks to the planning and supply services of the student government and the members of the Hall Presidents Council. In the course of the day's events, Fr. Malloy was escorted to a viewing stand with his mother and other members of his family where they listened to both graduate and undergraduate student leaders greet and welcome him as their new president. A visit to the grotto capped the student celebration.

Like his predecessor, Fr. Hesburgh, it didn't take long for the new president to show a special interest in underrepresented students at Notre Dame. With more extensive programming in mind, Fr. Malloy and Vice President Fr. Mark Poorman welcomed Iris Outlaw into the ranks of administrators in 1991 as the director of Minority Student Affairs, later renamed Multicultural Student Affairs.

Having earned her undergraduate degree from Indiana University and an M.S.A. from Notre Dame, Iris brought boundless energy and a deep conviction about the reality of cultural diversity in the world today. While assisting students of color in every possible way, she had an eye for involving the majority of ND students in minority affairs as well. She established relationships with campus administrators, South Bend community groups and leaders, and national officials in higher education who are active in cultural-diversity programs and future planning.

Also strongly believing in a more culturally diverse society, Vice President Patricia O'Hara took it upon herself to make sure Iris was not alone in her work. Throughout her nine years in office, Prof. O'Hara continually examined the ways and means for creating and supporting a culturally diverse campus. She worked to educate the entire Division of Student Affairs. Time, money, and energy were given to retreats, workshops, guest speakers (for the student body in large and small groups), rectors, directors of support services, and staff personnel with deep convictions that a more culturally diverse society was everyone's new world.

Despite efforts on all sides, there were some difficult struggles along the way. Since important things were being said and heard at every level of the university, town-hall meetings, involving administrators and students of culturally diverse backgrounds, made it possible for some of the most honest questions to be asked in public—and often answered. At times there was great uneasiness within an assembled group. There were tears, and sometimes laughter, and often pain. Periodically there were apologies offered from both sides of issues.

One evening I watched Prof. O'Hara, so like St. Sebastian, take students' frustration and anger and never lose her cool. I also saw students struggle to carefully explain their needs and frustrations. While some meetings ended on a downcast note and many left frustrated, a number of good things ultimately came from them. I had a deep sense that there were many students who never gave up on the belief that a culturally diverse world was in the making, though they realized it was going to take hard work.

Senior students of color who were able to stand back and speak of their lives at Notre Dame gave perspective to the situation. One young woman said to a mixed audience, "If I had it to do over again, I would not come to Notre Dame. I knew I was in a good academic place, but I never felt at home as one of so few black students among so many white students. Many of my friends adjusted. I never did." Another young woman admitted, "I didn't know how hard it would get at times, but I learned a lot about myself and others. I think this got me ready for the real world out there." "I felt so lost at first," another testified. "For weeks I only came out of my room to go to class and eat. Even finding familiar food to eat was difficult. I cried a lot. It was the two girls who lived next door to me and my RA who kept reaching out to me, making me feel that being Hispanic from Texas had definite possibilities at Notre Dame. I had so much to learn. Gradually I saw that others were learning things from me. I can't believe I got through all that hurt and stayed." An African American junior explained that he had lived and gone to school in an all-black neighborhood: "Coming to ND was a real twist! I think it's the hardest thing I've done. I quickly learned that I was living with a lot of white men and women who never spoke to a black person. I can see now that we all had homework to do." A group of white students claimed that they learned one of life's lessons after they staged a minstrel show in which they blackened their faces, then sat with African American students to learn why their show was so offensive to them.

Whenever I heard of our students engaging in a "Let's Talk Race Retreat" or a "Prejudice Reduction Workshop," or whenever I listened to a multicultural student panel discuss "What it's like to be at Notre Dame," I reveled in the thought and prayed that these students' experiences would someday get loose in society. April Davis ('99) is an early answer to that prayer. While she claims she has never been sorry that she came to Notre Dame from Los Angeles, she would never deny how difficult it was for her at times. In the midst of her college career, she never hesitated to share her ideas and energy for making the campus a more culturally diverse place. Her decision to stay in the Midwest after graduation made her the top candidate for the assistant director position in the Office of Multicultural Affairs at St. Mary's College, where she began to follow in the footsteps of her ND mentor, Iris Outlaw.

More and more I find reasons to believe that many of our graduates, whatever their ethnic heritage, will have the conviction and courage to address prejudice by initiating programs within their own social, professional, and business surroundings. Some of their convictions about culture have already been felt. During an annual committee meeting with some members of Notre Dame's Board of Trustees, students reported on their diversity programs. During the meeting, a CEO of a major corporation leaned over to another trustee, commenting, "I must start doing something about cultural diversity in my own company."

Maureen Fitzgibbon meets students from around the world as she welcomes and works with approximately nine hundred international students (many pursuing graduate degrees) as director of the Office of International Student Affairs. With the dawn of this millennium, the Internet, e-mail, and fax machines give her easy access to students arriving at Notre Dame from over one hundred countries, the largest number since the late Daniel O'Neill, CSC, first opened the office. The countries with the most students at Notre Dame are China with 150 students and Canada and India each with some 60 students enrolled. Russian representation has increased each year during the past decade with 32 students presently enrolled.

Maureen's office is a safety net for those students struggling to adjust to their new surroundings. However, she also engages the help of student officers from the Chinese, Indian, Japanese, and Pakistani organizations, and she asks other international student leaders to sponsor major events that bring students of the world together.

Maureen continually fulfills requests from campus personnel and the South Bend community for international students to serve as interpreters. Some have stood in courtrooms clarifying the meaning of questions and answers for judges and lawyers and their clients. Others have interpreted for doctors, nurses, patients, and families. One student offered language and cultural interpretation as she assisted during childbirth. Notre Dame housekeeper Magdolna Hunnyad asked if a student could translate her husband's Romanian school record into English since her husband needed it to prove to a potential employer that he had the required educational qualifications. Her request was granted—and so was the job.

International students have always been a source of information for local and national media covering international events. While students, on occasion, may be unable to cooperate for safety and security reasons, they often serve as "ambassadors," offering background information on significant world events. Many have agreed to interviews by newspapers and local TV stations. Through the International Resource Bureau run by Maureen and her staff, students reach out to schools, libraries, and various civic groups in the local community, as did Wie Yusef (who spoke in classrooms about her life in Malaysia) and Achieng Opondo (who told stories of her life in Kenya).

The International Women's Club, which Maureen established for the spouses of graduate students, has created a greater interchange among many of the women who reside with their families in the University Village community. It allows wives and mothers to meet and share experiences, to take advantage of English language classes, and to make trips together to Chicago and other places of interest in the area.

South Bend families, through the Notre Dame Host Family program, have contributed richly to the lives of international students and vice versa, attested to by lifelong friendship and trips to all parts of the world. Connie Peterson Miller, like Sylvia Schuster before her, serves as the Host Family coordinator, continually matching international students with one of the 150 families who have volunteered for this service. While students do not reside with host families, they are often invited to share meals, holidays, and family events in order to learn more about Americans and their way of life.

Students from various countries also take time to get to know one another by watching each other's movies, playing on international sports teams, and rallying around television sets watching world soccer and cricket playoffs. During International Week, which involves the setting up of an International Village, students invite the Notre Dame community "to take a walk around the world" for a look at who they are and where they are from. Maureen is the first to remind us that it's the entire Notre Dame community that stands to gain the most from the influence of nine hundred worldwide student representatives from more than one hundred countries as they mingle daily with the entire university community.

As the new millennium begins, there are other directors in the Student Affairs division who are veritable lynchpins in departments directly affecting the lives of over ten thousand students, including Rex Rakow in Security; Dr. Patrick Utz of the Counseling Center; Anne Thompson of the Health Center; Jeff Shoup in Residence Life; Lee Svete in the Career Center; Gina Firth in Alcohol and Drug Education, and Scott Kachmarik of Student Residences. Rev. Richard Warner, CSC, oversees the Campus Ministry program.

In the spring of 1999, while many were planning for graduation or trying to discover how to systematize their computers for Y2K compliance, the Office of Student Affairs suddenly changed leadership. After nine years as vice president, Prof. Patricia O'Hara was elected dean of the Law School.

This surprise announcement had hardly hit the headlines when rumors swirled that Father Mark Poorman, CSC, was the most likely candidate for the vice president position. There was a chorus of voices that wondered aloud, "Who would ever want that job?" Some folks contend that the position of vice president for Student Affairs is probably, on a day-by-day basis, the most challenging position on campus, since the person in that position deals with emergencies of every kind that can and do arise in the lives of over ten thousand students on campus and in sixteen study-abroad programs. But Fr. Mark said yes to that challenge.

He left his position as executive assistant to the president and moved to 316 Main Building along with other members of the senior staff, including Bill Kirk, Mary Louise Gude, CSC, David Moss, and myself. All of the administration had been temporarily housed in the Hayes-Healy building from 1997 to 1999, while the entire Main Building underwent a major overhaul from the tip of Mary's head on the dome to the depths of the building's foundation. We watched a historic landmark arise anew for the next century.

Mark became the sixth vice president of Student Affairs I have known at Notre Dame, and the third one I have served with on the senior staff. It was clear that he hit the road running. He needed no introduction to his surroundings since he had served as executive assistant to both the president, Father Malloy, and to the executive vice president, Father Bill Beauchamp. After Mark's ordination in 1982, he served three years as rector in Dillon Hall and associate director of Campus Ministry before he went off to complete his doctoral studies in Christian ethics. On his return, Fr. Mark lived in Grace Hall as a faculty member of the theology department where he served as director of the Master of Divinity program for seven years. While serving in his various administrative and academic positions, he has continued to live in a student residence hall and to teach courses in ethics on both the graduate and undergraduate levels. He presently resides in Keough Hall.

One group that welcomed Fr. Mark wholeheartedly when President Malloy introduced him officially at a gathering in the Center for Continuing Education (CCE) were the twenty-seven rectors of the various residence halls. They knew that he had been one of them. Convinced that residence halls were a hallmark of the university, Fr. Mark recognized that the rectors reported directly to the vice president for Student Affairs who hires them, evaluates them, and meets with them regularly at his or their requests. He was ready for their encounters, adventures, and ordeals, which make for twenty-first-century salvation history. As one of our twenty-seven rectors once quipped, "If we ever put our heads together, we'd have the makings in our midst of an award-winning television program, 'As the Dome Turns.'"

On a daily basis, these rectors, a well-educated band of dedicated women and men steeped in a variety of talents and valuable living experience, live and labor on behalf of their hall residents. Rectors of male halls are generally members of the Congregation of Holy Cross, although a small number over the years have been diocesan priests or members of other religious communities. A few male rectors have been laymen. For the most part, women rectors have been members of any one of a number of religious communities, including Holy Cross, Dominicans, Franciscans, Sisters of Charity, Immaculate Heart of Mary, Josephites, and Poor Handmaids. Among the laywomen who have filled the rector position are three Notre Dame graduates Kate Sullivan ('85 and '90), Cathy Lohmuller ('86 and '91), and Heather Rakoczy ('93, M.Div. from Vanderbilt). Dolores Ward of Beaverton, Pennsylvania, mother of Barbara ('79) and James (who died suddenly as a student in 1975), became the first rector of the newly constructed Pasquerilla West residence hall.

During the first quarter of a century of Notre Dame's coeducation, undergraduate residence halls changed demographically from all male to fourteen male halls and thirteen female halls. (In the process, Grace and Flanner were converted to administrative offices and faculty quarters.) Amazingly, the reality of single-sex residence halls survived endless discussions during those years. When I first arrived in 1973, there was serious talk among some of the Holy Cross rectors of creating coed residence halls, which was a result of housing experimentations going on at other major universities. I believed then that the whole residential system was headed for dramatic change in five to ten years. But for whatever reasons (from Fr. Hesburgh's strong commitment to retain the traditional hall system to all the discussions and votes since then), a coed hall arrangement was never established. The traditional system has always survived. It's a strong arrangement, with many advantages and some disadvantages that have been aired and argued along the way. And we've all heard ND graduates say to each other, almost immediately upon meeting, "What hall did you live in?" Some will add, "My mom or dad lived there, too." Some men even boast of living in "my grandfather's hall." Women don't fit in that category—yet.

As hall tradition lives on, there's no doubt that some individuals will always insist on change. However, many graduates look back on their ND days with what they call "a wiser eye," communicating their desires in person, in letters, and by phone: they want the hall system to stay as it is for their sons and daughters. To them, "It works."

I dare not overlook the effect of a muskie in my Student Affairs life. From the moment I hung that mounted creature on my wall, my ministry felt the influence of the fish.

"Did *you* catch that?" people often queried as they caught sight of Bruno, so named by the sons of Chip Stam, former director of the ND Glee Club, whose daughter Clare insisted on being lifted up in order to feed Bruno her jelly beans. "In one sense, I did catch it," I often replied, but, in another sense, I like to think that Bruno went out of his way to catch my hook when I cast my line into Plum Lake on the Notre Dame properties in Land O'Lakes, Wisconsin.

During a visit to the Office of Student Affairs, the father of a freshman stared fascinated at Bruno's size and swimming pose stretched across beige plaster. He was not only interested in whether I caught it, but where I caught it, to which I offered a very general location. He returned that afternoon with a large Wisconsin map asking me to indicate the exact body of water.

I caught the fish with fishing guide and friend O. J. Stewart, or Stu, as he is familiarly called, who is the former manager of the Notre Dame properties (which have been declared ecological territory) where Notre Dame students conduct marine biology research. Stu is a fisherman's fisherman but kind enough to pass on the know-how to a novice. After we caught some walleyes, he announced that he thought I was ready to try to catch a "big one." Whatever Stu decided on my fishing behalf was fine with me, although I wondered just how ready I was, wearing a man's rain jacket made of noisy nylon that was three times too big for me. Every cast I attempted made the nylon sound like swishing waves hitting the boat.

With fishing faith, I declared, "I'll try those reeds over there," only to have Bruno leap out of the water off into the distance. Stu insisted that the fish was on my line, swimming toward me as I reeled away in complete denial, aghast at the size of what I had seen fly through the air. I felt absolutely no tugs on my line, but Stu insisted that Bruno was headed my way, and he suddenly surfaced close to the boat, struggling to unhook himself. His hard tugs at the line and swift swimming, along with my kind of reeling, went on for half an hour before Bruno finally faced his attachment to us.

Stu had no net for scooping the thirty-eight inch fish out of the water, so he used heavy canvas gloves. Down on both knees, he lifted the fish into the boat where Bruno came to a slippery landing at my feet. It seemed so unreal, like so many fish stories I'd heard before. I winced when Stu picked up a small wooden mallet and struck the fish's head to knock it out. It was my first lesson on fish in the muskellunge family, famous for mouths filled with razor-sharp teeth. For effect, Stu added a few colorful tales about fishermen who almost lost limbs to angry muskies. These were hardly blue gill tales to add to my repertoire.

With a hooked muskie stretched out in our boat, Stu declared that fishing was over for the day. We had only been on the water a short time; however, there was a tradition in these parts that we needed to honor: "When you catch a muskie, Jean, you go home and celebrate." And so we did, after we encased my catch in a freezer. That was the first clue I had that this fish was going to have an ND future.

Students invariably do double takes when they step into my office and come face-to-face with Bruno. One morning I walked in on a Chinese graduate student who, in the course of waiting for me in my office, kept running his hand along the muskie's lacquered underbelly, declaring, "What a beautiful piece of porcelain." When I informed him that it was the skin of a real fish, his eyes brightened as he pointed out of my third-floor window, asking if Bruno was caught "in *that* Notre Dame lake out there."

Bruno's influence has made its way through some deep waters at times. Late one afternoon, a very depressed lad entered my office with his head hanging low. As he moved slowly toward a chair, his eye caught sight of Bruno on the wall. We were scheduled to discuss whether this young man was going to drop out of school for a period of time, but instead I found myself deliberately listening to this lad's fish story. He had caught some big ones in his young life, and he sat straighter and held his head higher as he gave me a few of the details. I was pretty impressed by what he knew about fish in general and muskies in particular. I asked a few honest questions. It was evident that something quite fascinating had just happened to him. Bruno had more shock value than either of us might have imagined. He helped to snap this young lad back to a level of reality that led him into some honest storytelling about his fishing adventures, which led to some simple, honest discussion about himself. Before we parted, we were able to confer about some counseling, to which he agreed, and which in turn allowed him to successfully finish the semester.

Few women gave Bruno a second glance. I understood completely. Muskie, or fish talk in general, was not always a large part of my world either. In fact, I remember almost making a fisherman's faux pas when I considered giving my mounted muskie to my brother, Ray, for his birthday. A veteran fisherman interceded, informing me with great gusto and lots of hand language that you never give another fisherman your fish! A fisherman's skill and honor lies only in his catching the prize. A year later, Ray caught a Canadian muskie measuring fifty-two inches that made mine look like a minnow.

Although many women aren't interested in muskie matters, the fish on my wall continually gives many men pause. It's quite clear that some of them think the catch was rather wasted on me and that I should be more appreciative of the prize. Some go to great lengths to make me understand what it means to catch such a game fish. As one fellow adamantly explained, "You should know that some men spend a lifetime trying to land a muskie." Other men ask investigative questions, "Did I actually handle the rod through the whole process of the catch?" I now realize what a favor Stu did for me by never taking the rod from my tired hands, although he did save the day with his canvas-gloved landing.

The truth is that Bruno has gathered more meaning with the years. He captured a curious place in my thinking one springtime as I prepared a talk for a retreat group on the subject of sacraments. I decided to move into the topic by way of discussing "sacramentals." Suddenly I found myself staring at Bruno—his sleek and shiny body, large mouth, sharp teeth, glassy eyes—and the thought struck me as I stretched my theological boundaries: this muskie had become something of a sacramental in my life. I found myself telling the retreat participants that Bruno had become a sign to me of all the gifts in my life that I came to truly appreciate only with the passing of time, often after others called my attention to them. As they so often do, students caught the meaning of my analogy. They continued to make Bruno quips long after the retreat. Some deliberately found their way to my Student Affairs office on the third floor of the Main Building to see if Bruno really was a "mounted sacramental" or just another fish story.

I'm surprised at how often people have said to me, "Nothing must surprise you anymore after all these years in Student Affairs." But that's not true. Every year there's newness to think and pray about. Although I've never spent much time trying to outguess God on the future, I have reflected often on the first time things happened in the past:

I remember the first time I rode in an ambulance with a girl who overdosed and vomited all the way to the hospital emergency room, only to come through it ready for the professional help she needed to get on with her life.

I remember the first time a top student leader yelled at me and then came back and left a note: "I'm sorry I yelled. I know you were trying to help. Sometimes I just blow off steam inappropriately. I will stop by soon."

I remember the first time a weeping young woman said to me, "I'm going to have a baby. No one knows. I'm scared, please help me."

I remember two anxious and concerned students explaining that "we don't want to get our rector in trouble with Student Affairs, but we think our rector has a drinking problem. Where do we go? What should we do?"

I remember the first time a student said, "I think I'm gay," and we talked about it into the night. And I remember the first time a young alum told me he was gay and asked if I had any idea how hard it had been for him when he was a student at Notre Dame. He had lots of questions and lots of pain. "I beg you, please do something about the situation."

I remember an alum's visit as he was driving the interstate to New York after traveling the world on a bike. He had just heard that his godmother had died. Convinced that he needed one, he asked me if I would take her place. He wondered how he should activate such a relationship in the church. We decided that it would probably be best to let it rest as a covenant between us.

I remember the first African American student who came to me and told me how hard it was for her to be one of so few in number at Notre Dame. She had never been in an all-white environment. She cried herself to sleep at night wondering if she was going to be strong enough to stay at Notre Dame and take advantage of the education that was at her fingertips.

I remember a student contacting me after hearing a lecture that convinced her that her mother was an alcoholic and needed treatment. Where should she go? I wasn't sure. Together we researched the best clinics available.

I remember the first time a senior trusted me with his tears because the love of his life—a senior in Farley—would not accept his engagement ring.

I remember the day a member of Notre Dame Security sat like a sentinel at a table near me in a local restaurant because I had agreed to meet with a student who had been dismissed from the university. I met this student in order to discuss some of his personal issues that often caused him to erupt into bizarre behavior.

I remember the day I explained to a sophomore that she could not "kill" her mother for a better chance at financial aid. In the course of our conversation, I discovered that her mother had told her that she could not return to Notre Dame because it was financially impossible: "If you leave home and return to Notre Dame against my wishes, I'm as good as dead in your life." Her daughter affirmed that declaration orally to administrators, stating that her mother was dead. That's when we had a realistic conversation about what it means to be dead. Then we phoned her very alive and dear mother.

I remember the first time I was caught in a food fight in the north dining room. The midnight "breakfast" was a pre-Christmas treat for students during the final exam period. I never volunteered to host that event again, and I cast written and oral votes to cancel the gift because of bad timing, bad manners, and heaps of immaturity.

I remember the first time I heard a senior from Grace Hall stand up in the midst of a large gathering of students and say that one of the best things that happened to him at Notre Dame was that he developed good friendships with women—and everyone applauded loudly.

I remember plugging my first computer into a wall socket in my Farley room in January 1995.

I remember when Notre Dame students elected the first woman as student body president—Brook Norton of Walsh Hall, whose home was Glendora, California. It took a quarter of a century, but it finally happened in the spring of 2001.

And I will never forget the day a student came to me for confession. We prayed together and then she asked, "Do I still have to go to a priest?"

NINE

Zhengde and His 32,000 T-Shirts

Lost in autumn thoughts and a charity benefit, I stood hip-high in the midst of navy blue t-shirts, counting them for distribution in the name of Zhengde Wang, a graduate student from Tianjin, China, who met with a serious accident on Notre Dame Avenue. Football fans and friends from across the United States bought and wore thousands of these shirts bearing Lou Holtz' image as a gesture of support for Zhengde during his recuperation from extensive injuries that left him bound to a wheelchair.

Memories of that cold, stormy October night forever cross my mind like a movie on fast-forward: the startling phone call about a hit-and-run accident, the hospital scene, the doctors and nurses, the unending questions, the search for translators, the call to China. Weeks later, Zhengde's mother and father, Xueying and Goutong, walked toward me down a long hallway in St. Joseph's Medical Center, fresh off a plane. They had never flown before. They knew no English and I knew no Chinese, but we met, embraced, and somehow understood the hundreds of words we wanted to speak to each other.

Zhengde struggled for weeks to regain consciousness and face the extent of his injuries. He had received a severed blow to the stem of his brain. The doctor explained the situation to me the night of the accident: "It's like going into a house and turning off the main switch." Then, after weeks in a coma, when Zhengde seemed to be gaining consciousness, the doctor coached me to say, "Zhengde, it's Sister Jean. If you know me, blink three times." And he did. But Zhengde couldn't move. He would be months recuperating and years in therapy. He had lost all of his automatic reflexes. He would have to relearn how to swallow, eat, speak, and, maybe, walk. That's why t-shirts became a focus for the 1990 Notre Dame versus Miami game. Zhengde needed help.

Word spread to the student body, and the residence halls offered their support, not only to buy but also to sell t-shirts. The athletic department backed the project and spread t-shirt news to the national media. They offered their 800 number through which orders were placed even before the t-shirts existed or had a design. There was little more than a month to produce the shirts. The first shirts were delivered two weeks before the October 20, 1990 game—all seventeen thousand of them—and sold by kickoff time.

Zhengde shirts filled the stadium. The back of the extra large, long-sleeved t-shirt pictured Lou Holtz on a long, slender football ticket, surrounded by green shamrocks and other Notre Dame scenes. Not only was the t-shirt benefit a grand success for Zhengde's sake, but it also served to memorialize a great Irish victory. It was hailed as the game of the decade. It was the last game we would play against Miami until further notice (and for many good reasons). Because of this, stock in Zhengde's shirt began to soar before the field was cleared. In the weeks to follow, student entrepreneurs placed four orders for a total of fifteen thousand more shirts, adding the final game score in large numbers, 29-20, on the front left side, under gold and orange helmets. For both Chinese and American reasons, it became a shirt with a story—a souvenir.

The t-shirt money almost immediately began to affect the lives of Xueying and Guotong. They were financially able to settle into nearby housing and stay close to Zhengde while he was in the hospital for almost a year and again while he was in therapy at Healthwin for at least six months. Xueying, an acupuncturist who had supervised her division of medicine in a Tianjin hospital, naturally was more accustomed to the hospital atmosphere. She made her way quite graciously, learning many English nouns but very few verbs. As much as she and her husband appreciated all that St. Joseph's Medical Center and Notre Dame were trying to doing for them, they struggled continually to adjust to American life in the midst of their doctors and lawyers and their circumstances. They knew stress from many quarters, and before returning to China, each of them needed surgery. Xueying suffered a herniated disc; Guotong had his appendix removed. T-shirt funds helped to eradicate some of those medical bills.

Zhengde gradually grew stronger. He finally became fully conscious and knew everything going on around him. His smiles and tears made perfect sense, always reflecting the meaning of the moment even though he couldn't utter a simple sound. At times he used his thumb or turned his head slightly to say yes, but you could see the frustration in his eyes. He had much more to say.

There were linguistic challenges at every turn. We literally moved language right into his room along with the medical equipment. Walls were covered with lists of Chinese and English words and phrases, making it possible for doctors, nurses, and visitors to communicate with Xueying and Goutong. What started as a small display of medical terms grew into a handy Chinese-English "wall dictionary." There were times when I felt that I was creating award-winning dance routines as I tried to make myself understood, seeking and pointing out various "wall words" to his parents. Some were rather sad dance routines, while others reflected a great sense of joy. When it came to official medical conversations, we were grateful for a neatly typed list of names and numbers near Zhendge's phone that belonged to Chinese faculty and students who volunteered as official interpreters.

In quiet moments during those twenty months, I began to realize that my heart and mind were filling up with Zhengde memories. I could hardly stand to walk by the sidewalk square near Farley where Zhengde and I first met just hours after he arrived in South Bend to begin work on a Ph.D. in sociology. That day he needed directions to Stepan Center. He also needed new shoes, so the next day I drove him to University Mall where, after walking through the main entrance, he declared, "This is a very big store!"

Once classes got underway, there were days our paths never crossed. But now and then Zhengde would appear, always with a bulging book bag, suddenly with a side part in his hair, and with markedly clearer English pronunciation and a colorful sprinkle of American idioms. Often he was holding a letter that unfolded into artistic Chinese characters that spelled news from home. I declared them original art pieces and was always tempted to ask if I might frame one. In the midst of a spectacular snowfall one night, he took a break from his library research and came to Farley Hall for hot chocolate. I knew then that he had settled in at Notre Dame.

Zhengde moved ahead in his graduate work right on time, making friends among a host of both American and international students along the way. As he worked to complete his Ph.D. in sociology, he made plans to combine it with a law degree from Notre Dame. He saw international law in his future. His application and interviews had been completed. After his accident, there was so much at his fingertips that he was never able to touch.

The day dawned when Zhengde's parents knew that it was time for them to return to China with their son. Near their departure date, the university presented them with a check for one hundred thousand dollars to help with Zhengde's care and therapy—all from the sale of a navy blue t-shirt that took Notre Dame fans by storm. While radio, television, and the press highlighted the story across the United States, United Press International ran headlines in the Beijing press.

The trip home involved a medical Lear jet with an onboard nurse. The family flew from South Bend to San Francisco, and then caught an Air China flight on to Beijing. On this flight a number of seats were removed in order to make room for Zhengde, his nurse, and the medical equipment necessary for the long trip home with his parents seated nearby. Once in Beijing, local transportation would transport him to the hospital in Tianjin. In South Bend the Lear jet soared heavenward with a certain drama very early on July 4, 1990, sounding like a great firecracker in the sky. Thirty-five thousand dollars, from the biggest t-shirt sale in Notre Dame's history, made this trip possible. I watched as the sun came over the horizon, beckoning the Wangs to the Far East.

While the navy blue t-shirt moved into history and the funds it garnered ran dry long ago, the story of Zhengde Wang stays fresh. Christmas gifts and greetings, shipments of medical supplies, and a large collection of fax and e-mail messages keep us in touch. Chinese missives needed English translations, while my messages needed a Chinese hand. Xioafeng Liu, a doctoral student in aerospace engineering, would, at a moment's notice, translate a message either way. What now transpires in a matter of minutes by fax or by e-mail, formerly took airmail letters three weeks going and three weeks coming to and from China.

One day a fax of a lifetime landed on my desk—an invitation to come to Tianjin for a reunion with Zhendge and his family. It was suggested that I come, soon, and invite Dr. Sam Valenzuela, chair of the Department of Sociology, and his wife, Erika. After five years, the Chinese connection remained real and strong, only this time I would be the one walking into a whole new world, and the Wangs would be waiting—Zhengde, his parents, his grandparents, his brother, his uncle, and his friends—people I knew only through letters and photos. The trip was arranged quickly once the Wangs checked with the Ministry of Foreign Affairs in Beijing. I applied for a tourist visa from the Chinese Consulate in Chicago, which arrived two days before I buckled my seatbelt on my way to Vancouver, British Columbia, the first leg of the trip.

The night before we left, I searched the travel shelves at Little Professor Bookshop and found a hefty paperback that looked as though it might put me into a Chinese mood and fill my senses with the Orient. (I didn't realize at the time that the very next day I would already be immersed in the culture, sipping Chinese tea poured by a Chinese flight attendant from a Chinese teapot as the captain announced that we were flying over the edge of Siberia!) Quickly perusing the book, I realized that the first eighty pages dealt with "How to Prepare for a Trip to China." I refused to scan the section, worried that there was something I might have overlooked. I began to verbalize this to the clerk who rang up my sale, but she had a head start on me, commenting with a friendly, teasing lilt in her voice, "Oh, it looks like you're thinking of a trip to China." Not quite, I explained. "I'm packed. I'm leaving early in the morning." She simply stared at me with large eyes as she handed me my receipt.

Not until I stood at the O'Hare check-in counter did I really think about my trip in terms of distance. When a perky clerk for American Airlines asked about my frequent-flyer membership, I had to admit that I wasn't registered in the program and that she was right, this was probably the moment to do so. Fourteen thousand initiation miles would make me a well-traveled member. Secretly, the thought of traveling that distance stunned me. But there was no time to stay stunned. I had to quickly focus on being at home with the Wangs.

Home for the Wangs was about a two-hour car ride from the Beijing airport. Our plane was on time and so was Zhengde. He was waiting in the parking lot, standing in the shadow of his wheelchair, supported on either side by his younger brother, Zheng Chun, and his uncle, Guang He Wu, and leaning hard against his white Toyota van, which had been purchased with Notre Dame t-shirt money. The van transported him everywhere. His welcoming embrace was a strong one. He had gained weight and his eyes and skin looked healthy. Most exciting of all, he was making sounds. I heard some throaty words and one whole phrase.

In the midst of this international spectacle, I became very conscious that other Chinese people were watching us closely. At first I thought it was because Sam and Erika and I were South and North Americans. But gradually it became evident that many of the stares were directed at Zhengde—and his wheelchair. He appeared very physically challenged, yet he was in the public eye, visiting in very normal ways. From that moment I grew more conscious as we traveled around Tianjin, a city of seven million people, that I never saw another physically challenged Chinese person in public areas.

Regularly Zhengde took to the sidewalks near his home, all because Notre Dame t-shirt money helped his parents acquire a first-floor apartment that allowed him easy access to the outside. He tried to walk around his block with the strong assistance of two adults. The struggle to put one foot in front of the other was written all over his face and in the sweat of his body. Traffic on the street often stopped. Cabs drove up to the curb to watch him. Some folks gawked, frowned, and whispered. Intrigued bike riders peddled nearby while Zhengde's assistants tried to wave them away. A few neighbors came out of their state-owned apartments not only to watch but also to clap for him.

One of Zhengde's favorite places was Water Park, a summer spot that attracts hundreds of people of all ages every day. He needed a van, a wheelchair, and assistants to get there, but the park belonged to him as much as to anyone else. He cherished the surroundings and all of the highlights—the great expanse of water, the summer breezes, the water lilies and land flowers, the ice cream, and the camaraderie that surrounded him. I watched him close his eyes and let the soft breezes play on his face. There were always people trying to hide their stares and children pointing fingers at him and asking questions. When it was time to leave, he always refused to go home.

It was while stopping on a picturesque bridge in Water Park that I found myself able to share with Zhengde his special mission—I saw him as a paragon for the physically challenged persons in China. It seemed so obvious. There was a real power in his public appearance. I wondered out loud if he had ever given that a thought. His only response was a faraway look and a deliberate bowed head.

Twice I tried to tell Zhengde's mother, Xueying, that her family was an incredible exemplar for all of China as they thoughtfully and lovingly kept Zhengde in the mainstream of life. He was always where the action was—the airport, the welcome dinner in one of Tianjin's finest restaurants, the hotel lobby for a visit, Water Park, and his very own neighborhood. No venue was off-limits with the assistance of his family members and assistants.

As Sam, Erika, and I spent hours visiting with Zhengde, we became very aware that he was unable to care for his person. His mother and a nurse's aide were with him at every turn. Since he had been able to speak and write English fluently before the accident, he had no trouble listening to our news and stories about Notre Dame. We had carried letters, cards, and photos from campus. They produced a lot of laughter, some tears, and a deep sense of friendship.

In the course of our Tianjin days together, I met Zhengde's elderly grandfather, a retired physician who had delivered thousands of babies and worked among the poor. Zhengde had often spoken of him with real pride. I first saw him walking toward me across the dining room of the Wang apartment. As we came close to each other, he broke down into tears, sobbing and speaking Chinese. As we embraced, I could feel his tears on the side of my face and I heard the translator telling me in my other ear, "He is trying to thank you and everyone involved for not letting his grandson die in the street." That tragic moment and all the individuals who came to his rescue are forever with Notre Dame and its people.

While there wasn't much time for sight-seeing, Zhengde's family wanted us to get some sense of their hometown just as Zhengde had come to know Notre Dame and its environs. As we crisscrossed Tianjin streets, I felt out of place among some 3.5 million residents who went to work on their bicycles every day. I starred wide-eyed in the midst of sights and sounds that became hypnotic. I fantasized about Chicago, my hometown, going to work on bicycles. A translator in the back seat of the van declared that we were at the center of the manufacturing world of one of the best bicycles in China, "the Flying Pigeon."

Local bicycle parking lots continually turned my head. On a relatively small plot of land near the large Tianjin hospital, hundreds of bikes waited for their owners. Had they been cars, acres of land would have been needed. I wondered what size lot we might need for a stadium full of fans on two wheels instead of four.

I became much more aware of the appearance of bike riders. No one seemed to have an extra pound on his or her body. Mao clothing had vanished. Many men wore white shirts and dark slacks. Women chose a variety of skirts and blouses, some dresses. Even though it was hot weather, many women wore nylon hose that rolled to just above the knee. Chiffon skirts picked up summer breezes and made bike riding look graceful. Some women had a sophisticated look with neckline pearls and short summer gloves with fingertips cut away. Many women and men wore straw hats that tied under their chins for protection against the sun.

Children rode to school straddling the back wheel of their parents' bikes. They chatted with school chums perched on the back seats of nearby bicycles, as though no one else were around. Some were engrossed in books propped against their parents' backs. A few were in the "grab and go" mode, eating breakfast.

Bicycles, as well as love, made the world go 'round in China. A Flying Pigeon, as well as any other good two-wheeler, was often seen carrying a rider who in turn carried carts and wagons filled with fruits, vegetables, coal, bricks, fish, pipes, bundles of cloth, cases of Coca-Cola, sets of furniture, and stacks of unmarked boxes. The bikers made me want to shout and point at the miracle of management, packaging, and transportation.

Heavy morning and evening traffic on main streets, with all their sights and sounds, was a Cecil B. DeMille dream come true. It was a four-generation "Kodak moment" when I discovered a man pedaling a bike attached to a cart that I learned was carrying his son, his father, and his grandfather. Amazingly, cyclists never wore helmets or used bike lights at night. Left-hand turns were daily miraculous events.

Even I could detect something of the new China on the horizon. The rather recently built broadcasting tower (one of the world's tallest with a revolving visitors center near the top), appeared as a great needle in the Tianjin sky, sewing the world together with news bulletins. New roads were in the making with western versions of overpasses and underpasses taking shape. There were multiple signs of entrepreneurship—new cafés, a leather store, a dress shop—small, but in existence.

Zhengde's mother was determined to give us a glance at Beijing. How cautiously I approached Tiananmen Square. As I slowly walked among people peacefully flying colorful kites, it was hard to imagine the bloodshed and violence of those 1989 student demonstration days that had reverberations as far away as Notre Dame. I stood quietly, looking across the largest square in the world, which measures an unthinkable one hundred acres of concrete. The sheer size was mind-boggling and still more so to imagine the gathering of people upon the concrete.

Standing on the edge of the square, I caught my breath before entering into the imperial past of China. The immense portrait of Mao Zedong loomed much larger than life and dominated the gateway into the Forbidden City. Nearby stood the Great Hall of the People. It was impossible to take it all in. I satisfied myself by agreeing to simply let it "run" over me. I walked through the Forbidden City, gate after gate, palace after palace. I was overwhelmed by a history and a culture of which I knew so very little. To experience Beijing grabs at your heart. Forever I will look and listen and ask questions about her people.

On a cloudless day, I strolled and climbed the Great Wall in a dreamlike fashion as it stretched out across the ridges of the northern mountains beyond Beijing. I remembered the astronauts in space reporting that it was the only man-made object they could see from their satellite. Four thousand miles of brick and stone was enough to circle the earth with an eight-foot-high dike. It seemed like a great piece of scenery on the stage of the world as it undulated into the distance and out of sight. I tried to imagine the ways it served as protection from the barbarian invaders charging out of the north centuries ago. History indicates that while the Wall saved lives, it also took the lives of an estimated three hundred thousand Chinese who died during its construction and were buried within its confines. Perhaps it will be an Orient marker for interplanetary pilots of the new millennium.

I should have known that I would feel most at home in China in a place that I thought I would never experience—the Chinese Church, including her people and their place of worship. Zhengde's mother, Xueying, gave rise to the occasion in her inimitable way by asking, "You—church—Sunday?"

Zhengde's brother drove me across the city to a brick gateway that arched over the entrance marked with the words "Chinese Catholic Church." Behind the brick wall, encircling the church grounds, I stood in awe before a gothic-looking building the size and shape of Notre Dame's Basilica of the Sacred Heart. Drawn to follow the Chinese parishioners behind the church, I veered left, walking slowly in amazement, to a grotto of Our Lady of Lourdes. Mary stood some fifteen feet above the ground in a rock formation with potted plants at various levels. A kneeling statue of Bernadette looked up at her. There were small candles and vigil lights on the ground, with people kneeling nearby saying the rosary. For some moments I lost my geographical bearings and I felt like I was standing at two grottos at once. The mind and heart are wonderful that way, but I had to shake it off and get to Mass on time.

Halfway around the world from my moorings, in a totally different culture, I slipped into this scene like a hand in a glove. There were hundreds of people of all ages who crowded into the church with standing room only. A high altar, with side altars dedicated to the Sacred Heart and Mary, dominated the nave. A great swell of adult voices sang a familiar Gregorian chant from a high loft behind me. Eight altar boys in red cassocks and white surplices carried out their duties, sometimes standing in place on red pillows. As the Mass went on, I realized I was gently slipping into a pre-Vatican II celebration. The priest prayed with his back to the people while some parishioners tried to follow the Mass in their missals. Others said rosaries or offered devotional prayers. The priest read the epistle and gospel in Latin as he faced the altar. While the laity's participation was minimal, throughout the ceremony I never doubted that the Chinese people were at prayer all around me.

Recently, while crossing the north quad in early September sunlight, I saw a Zhengde t-shirt dart in front of me headed for the Huddle. It must have been ten years old! It was a hand-me-down, treasured for whatever reason—possibly the winning score in large numbers on the front, or the image of Lou Holtz on the back. Seeing the t-shirt again reminded me that I had one, too, in my bottom drawer in Farley. I resurrected it, amazed at how good it still looked. They were good shirts with a fine printing job in nine colors and produced by a local man who was able to buy a whole new press as a result of the national sale.

I turned the shirt from front to back and back to front as though I had never set eyes on it, while my thoughts went rushing back to China. I couldn't resist. I pulled the shirt over my head, hoping against hope that Zhengde was holding his head high as best he could, making his daily way in his wheelchair—a young man with a message for all the physically handicapped in China.

TEN

Father Ted

Fr. Ted Hesburgh, president of Notre Dame throughout my rector years, had his own history with Farley Hall, having moved into the rector's quarters in the late 1940s when the plaster was still wet. So coming to Farley on a Sunday night in the fall of 1973 put him in a pretty familiar space as he prepared to celebrate the Eucharist with some of the first women to grace the north quad.

Walking once again into Farley's rector's room, he quickly spotted the large wooden desk, declaring it military surplus. "We probably paid a dollar for that, Jean." He found the government label still readable, hidden on the side of a top drawer, as he continued to comment on how heavily Notre Dame came to depend on army surplus materials following World War II days. He also spotted a small inconspicuous end table, "Oh, I used that all the time."

He admitted that he still feels a tinge of pain whenever he enters Farley, remembering how he suffered decades ago when he fell on the newly waxed corridor floor and broke some ribs. "We had no carpeting in those days," he explained, "and the hallways were filled with personal lockers lined up next to doorways of individual rooms." Fr. Ted recalled having 340 students in postwar Farley compared to the 250 present occupants. "They were hanging from the rafters—all freshmen." He quickly pointed out his agreement to do away with all-freshman halls in the late 1960s. "Imagine all that homesickness under one roof. It was terrible," he exclaimed.

Light switches on the south wall also grabbed his attention. He reminisced about each of them, relics in their own right, still in working condition. Fr. Ted used one switch "years ago for lights-out purposes." Each evening he was able to cut the power in every room at a designated hour, after which he settled down and wrote a theology book. The other switch activated what was then known as the class bell, manually operated before and after each class period, reminding residents to get to class on time. I was told to use it as the fire alarm signal. However, as I explained to Fr. Ted, I discovered during our first fire drill that half of the alarms, placed behind screens high on corridor walls, had been cleverly adjusted. The arm of the unit was bent back so far that it never reached the bell attachment. While sleep went undisturbed for many students in days gone by, we had some unbending to do in the name of fire safety.

After the celebration of the Eucharist, Fr. Ted found some literature still in the sacristy cupboard from his days as chaplain to World War II veterans and their wives and children who lived in Vetville behind Farley. He stood amazed, remembering Farley's chapel as the vets' "parish church," where he baptized a long line of babies and regularly gathered young families around the altar.

Stepping back into the present moment, Fr. Ted asked for time to finish praying his breviary in the rector's room before joining the Farley women for refreshments in the basement lounge. Walking into a sea of feminine faces, he found himself mixing with the daughters of fathers he had known and taught. Cameras flashed as the first generation of undergraduate women asked, "What was Farley like when you were my dad's president?" Word was out that one coed had providentially landed in her father's room.

In later visits to Farley, especially during the annual January celebration of Pop Farley Week, Fr. Ted joined the residents, sketching a bit of a biography as well as cherished local stories about Fr. John Francis Farley, CSC, the hall's namesake. Fr. Ted added to an oral history passed on by eyewitnesses such as Fr. Charlie Sheedy, CSC, who had also been a rector of Farley Hall and the dean of the College of Arts and Letters; Edward "Moose" Krause, former director of Athletics; and Prof. Paul Fenlon, former teacher and resident of Sorin Hall for more than sixty years. All of these people had seen Pop Farley in action as their rector.

During Fr. Ted's winter visits to Farley, the women were attracted to a series of patches sewn on the front panels of his red down jacket. These patches represented some of his major travels that never ceased to be conversation pieces. While he liked to tell Antarctica tales, I often put in a request for his account of his SR-71 flight. The thought of traveling at supersonic speed (Mach 3.35, which translates into 2,193 miles an hour) at an altitude of some eighty thousand feet in a pitch-black atmosphere, and breaking a world record in the process, never failed to grab imaginations, including mine. I would always find myself saying under my breath, "This man is a daredevil!" In time I began to realize it was this kind of energy that went into the shaping of Notre Dame.

Fr. Ted was invited to Farley Hall in January 2000 to celebrate an evening Eucharist, not only because it was Sunday, but also to celebrate Pop Farley Week for the twenty-fifth time. Amazingly, Fr. Ted led the first such celebration in 1976. This time he mingled submarine tales with his Pop Farley repertoire.

He had just returned from spending a week in a nuclear submarine that traveled from California to Hawaii. The trip was a gift from the U.S. Navy. Fr. Ted and his brother, Jim, who had been a naval officer, climbed aboard as the only guests with a crew of 120 men navigating the sub in the ocean depths. Elated at the thought that he had been able to celebrate Mass at such depths, he was also captivated by the character and manner of navy men chosen to serve on a submarine where everyone lived, worked, relaxed, and ate in such close quarters—and then slept in snug sleeping quarters three layers deep. Fr. Ted came away from the experience full of respect and admiration for the men. "And what a feeling it was when we surfaced in Hawaii, and opened the hatch—I saw the blue sky and took a deep breath of earth's air." He stays a daring man at the age of eighty-three.

Fr. Ted was always a study for me as I watched him walk across the stage in Washington Hall each fall to deliver his address to the faculty. I attended my first Fr. Ted address in October 1973 as a rector and adjunct instructor in theology. Seated in the eighth row, I quickly realized there wasn't a single woman seated in front of me. There had to be some behind me, but I never had the courage to count. We were so few, but we did multiply.

I learned a lot about the university from Fr. Ted's overviews and updates in the early 1970s. He dipped back into Notre Dame's history, explaining where it had come from and its destination in terms of faculty growth. He laid out new domestic and international academic programs; addressed sensitive student, faculty, and staff issues that needed attention; assessed new building projects on the drawing board; indicated speakers and visitors expected to visit campus; and reviewed travel highlights and personalities he met along the way.

One such address has lingered a long time with me. Fr. Ted spoke about the many universities in Europe that date back to the Middle Ages, when they were known as outstanding Catholic institutions of learning. Over time, he explained, they grew financially insecure and finally lost their Catholic identity as they became state-supported schools, although various ones retained at least a school of theology. This kind of historic background gave him good standing and gave me a long memory about why he committed himself so strongly to the task of making Notre Dame financially sound. He never wanted the same tale told of the University of Notre Dame in the United States. He started down that financially sound path and never turned back.

Fr. Ted, fresh from the airport, stepped out of a car one day in front of the Administration Building. I happened to pass by and greeted him. He quickly asked me what the date was. I could tell he had a lot on his mind as he realized out loud that he had crossed the international date line, lost track of time, forgot the calendar day, and lamented a missed appointment. His arrival home to Notre Dame from elsewhere around the world made me more aware than ever of a familiar student chant:

> Ted the Head,
> Is never home in the Dome.
> Probably on his way to Rome.

Or the joke often told:

> What's the difference between God and Father Ted?
> God is everywhere.
> Father Ted is everywhere but Notre Dame.

Fr. David Tyson, CSC, who traveled with Fr. Ted on various occasions as his administrative assistant, confirmed the local color that surrounded the president's travels. On one flight across the country, Fr. Ted lost a gold inlay, which fell to the airplane floor. Fr. Dave got out of his seat and stooped to search, attracting the flight attendant who joined him. After the inlay was recovered, Fr. Ted dipped the filling in his drink and replaced it, adding that he really needed it for the rest of the trip. Shortly after the commotion in the aisle, the captain of the plane appeared at his side introducing himself as a 1958 Notre Dame graduate and classmate of Fr. Don McNeill, CSC. "I heard you were on board, Fr. Hesburgh, and had to come and say hello."

I met Fr. Ted one afternoon when he had just returned from Washington, D.C. This time his mind turned immediately to campus issues. He was forever expressing a keen interest in how women were adjusting to Notre Dame, especially in those earliest years of coeducation. Abruptly he became more personal with me, and thoughtfully asked about my well-being and about my Franciscan community. In particular he wanted to know how often I was able to be with my Franciscan sisters. "I would feel terrible if your ministry here would ever endanger your relationship with your community in Joliet, Jean." He was as happy as I was to hear that two more Joliet Franciscans had recently been hired as Notre Dame rectors for the following years. The topic changed and lightened quickly, "Jean, I never realized before that you have two different-colored eyes," at which point I tried to explain that one had a large freckle in it.

Fr. Ted was hardly a micromanager, but he had ways of seeing and knowing what was going on around him. I was duly impressed when I heard him say that if there's serious trouble with the athletic department, blame the president; he's ultimately responsible. Fr. Ted believed strongly that collegiate athletic programs were not separate entities on a university campus. He had his own unique way of dealing with team scores that reflected losses. After a major football defeat I was within earshot when an *Observer* reporter asked him how he deals with such a spectacle. He replied simply, "Sometimes it can be good to lose. It purifies the whole system."

There were always some fun encounters with Fr. Ted. Around 11:00 one night, I met him at the back door of the Administration

Building. He was going in to start his midnight correspondence. I was on my way out after a long committee meeting about a five-year evaluation of coeducation at ND. As he bade me goodnight, he pulled a six-inch piece of white string out of his suit coat pocket with a bit of surprise at finding it there. He lightheartedly asked me to guess what it was. Without thinking I retorted, "A piece of a basketball net?" It was! He was flabbergasted that I knew what it was and so was I. He asked me how I knew. I had no clue, except I said, "whatever was in your head, just flew into mine." I hadn't been to any recent games. "For guessing correctly," he said, "I'm going to give you half." Notre Dame had beaten the University of San Francisco in a historic upset and Fr. Ted got a "piece" of the victory. He searched for his penknife but came up with a cigarette lighter. He burned the string into almost equal pieces. While I could never prove to anyone that my souvenir was anything more than a snippet of butcher's string with a scorched edge, I know I have a piece of the spoils. Better yet, I know who did the burning and kept the other half.

I stay fascinated with the phenomenon of Junior Parents Week (JPW), which Fr. Ted blessed in its infancy the first year of his presidency in 1952. From the start, he put the holiday into the hands of students. They chose February as the best month and the Morris Inn as the best place for the event. February was not chosen for weather patterns that range from a touch of spring to a full-blown blizzard, but because there were fewer activities on campus during that time of year. For many reasons, JPW was destined for success.

Fr. Ted knew that juniors were ready to host their parents. Having been a rector himself, he realized a weekend visit in February would allow parents to experience the campus in the midst of an academic semester—no moving in or out. They could spend a good piece of time sharing the campus with a daughter or son, going to a class, and meeting professors. There were roommates and friends for parents to meet, and a host of activities to share. Parents and their children could talk and listen, dine and dance, and pray together in ways they never had before.

JPW sells itself. It has been known to beckon parents to campus from across the country and around the world, year after year. When

Michael Ford of Palos Park, Illinois, heard the news that his second child was admitted to Notre Dame, one of the first things he exclaimed to his wife Trudy was "And we get to go to Notre Dame for another Junior Parents Weekend!"

Fr. Ted welcomed junior parents for thirty-five years, watching the crowds outgrow the Morris Inn, the North Dining Room, and Stepan Center, finally moving into the spacious Joyce Center for many of the events, including the Eucharistic celebration and a dinner served at more that four hundred circular banquet tables. Even the hockey rink gets covered over. It is the biggest dinner of the academic year—and one of Fr. Ted's most cherished legacies.

Before I left for China to visit former student Zhengde Wang, Fr. Ted told me not to hesitate to go to church in Tianjin, a city of seven million citizens. And so I did as he said.

After Sunday morning Mass in a Chinese church building that looked so much like the Basilica of the Sacred Heart, I stepped outdoors into a warm June sunlight, squinting in the midst of a crowd of worshipers. Feeling very secure within this humanity, I became lost in a sea of unfamiliar Chinese words and sounds as I waited for Zhengde's brother to pick me up. Suddenly, an older gentleman presented himself to me. He bowed and I bowed a bit. Looking me straight in the eye, he said distinctly and slowly, "U.S.A." He was right; that's exactly how I felt in this overwhelming crowd of Chinese worshipers. I was "the U.S.A. in person." I confirmed my citizenship with a smile. He very deliberately stood still and kept me in his gaze. I felt a bit uneasy. Then I smiled one more time and said, "No Chinese." And he returned with, "No English." A rather significant impasse; I figured the encounter was over. But it wasn't. He stepped forward and stunned me with another word, which in an instant set up parameters for friendship, "Hesburgh." A bit astonished, I repeated it twice adding the word *Father* to the third pronouncement. He kept nodding his head in agreement.

But then we felt helpless again, unable to go another phrase until, out of the church crowd, a young woman appeared with a child in her arms. She greeted this man warmly with a short exchange of words. Turning toward me she explained that she knew some English and perhaps could help with our language deadlock. Her kindness and skill let us easily slip into each other's lives. I quickly learned with overwhelming amazement that I had just met Ren Wan Cai, who had just finished reading Fr. Ted Hesburgh's autobiography, *God, Country, Notre Dame,* in a Chinese translation.

Still more astonishing was Ren Wan Cai's personal story. Our interpreter informed me that Ren and her father studied together in the seminary for twelve years. They were preparing for their ordination when the Chinese government collapsed and the Communist party came to power. All ties with the Vatican were severed and their ordination was forbidden. With this disclosure, Ren bowed his head. I asked for a blessing. He shyly refused but finally agreed to give me his address so that I might pass it on to Fr. Hesburgh.

When I returned to campus and met with Fr. Ted for a China debriefing, I learned that Archbishop Jin of Shanghai had made arrangements with Fr. Ted for a Chinese translation of his autobiography. One of those twenty thousand copies had landed in Ren's hands. Some days later Fr. Ted wrote to Ren expressing his surprise and delight that we had met and that Ren had read his book. Fr. Ted also added a poignant postscript, "I know of tragedy in your life but I also know you are still a priest at heart."

During my debriefing visit with Fr. Ted, he shared a story from one of his trips to mainland China before the country "opened up" under Deng Xiaoping's leadership. He was traveling with government officials and interpreters. One of the tours took them into a church building, which at the time was not allowed to be open for worship. Fr. Ted noticed a man sitting quietly by himself in the back of the church. He walked toward him, aware that he might be a priest but wondering how to communicate with him without getting him into trouble. Fr. Ted decided to speak in Latin, knowing that if the man were a priest, he would answer. While government personnel were in a bit of a quandary as to what was taking place, the two priests slipped easily into a Latin conversation. Fr. Ted explained that he felt frustrated—there wasn't much he could do for this fellow priest who had admitted that he wasn't sure if he was still a priest in light of all that had happened in the Chinese Church. Fr. Ted went on to offer him the sacrament of reconciliation, which the Chinese priest accepted immediately. For some brief moments, at least, the Latin in their lives brought them together as priests in prayer.

Fr. Ted had his own inimitable ways of stepping up to a challenge. When asked by student government officials Duane Lawrence and Bruce Lohman to address a group of student leaders in the fall of 1985, Fr. Ted offered them his "Ten Commandments for Student Leaders" with wit and wisdom and a Mosaic touch, "composed at two o'clock in the morning"—

1. Look upon all of it as a learning experience.
2. Mistakes are inevitable. You have to learn to live with them and so do I.
3. Don't get caught up with global issues, such as remaking the whole University and outgunning the Trustees. Politics is the art of the possible, so pick out some realistic goals and really go for them.
4. Try to strike up a friendship with the administration. They aren't really bad guys and you might have something to learn from them. Also, they are not automatic adversaries. Believe it or not, they like you and want to be helpful as you mature into real leaders.
5. The common good is terribly important. It means the common good for students, faculty, and for the whole University community. You are part of it, so work for it.
6. Be honest, especially with yourselves. Integrity is probably the best quality of a leader.
7. Be open-minded. No other attitude makes learning possible. As Winston Churchill said, "All complicated questions have simple answers. However, they are all wrong."
8. Be fair even with grown-ups. Fairness will win them more than anything else.
9. Don't be cynical. A cynic accomplishes nothing. All of us have to be shocked by the injustices we face in life. Cynicism will never conquer them and attain justice.
10. This will probably sound silly, but my bottom line is laughter and love. It is important to be able to laugh at ourselves, which means not to take ourselves too seriously, whether we are President or freshman. Somehow laughter gets us through the most

> difficult of situations, but love is important, too, because in a very real sense, we can't work together unless we respect and love each other, young and old.

From the moment of their first unveiling, these two-o'clock-in-the-morning commandments were destined to hold legacy status, having appeared since then in *The Source*, the student leader handbook, and requested by other schools in the country.

The day John Glenn orbited the globe in his seventy-seventh year, by mere coincidence I found myself finishing lunch in Corby Hall when Fr. Ted joined me as he began his. I had been thinking of him that morning as I listened to Walter Cronkite offer color commentary on Glenn's flight, knowing how much Fr. Ted wanted to ride the shuttle and celebrate Mass in space. It wasn't hard to tell him how I wished he could have been the one. His words came quickly, "I do too, Jean." Apparently the moratorium on space travel, following the shuttle accident in January 1986, lasted too long and "I got too old too fast and missed my chance." He explained that he was ready at sixty-two when he passed NASA's physical and psychological astronaut tests. He mentioned that there were two people in line before him marked for space travel, Walter Cronkite and James Michener. "I was the youngest, but still, too many birthdays passed me by."

On various occasions I have thought of Fr. Ted as a daredevil after hearing some of his exploits on land, sea, and in the air. I must admit that the thought crossed my mind in a very winsome fashion the day I went to the university beauty salon for a haircut, only to hear that Fr. Ted had just been there, fresh from a trip from Israel. It was new territory for him. He couldn't find his regular barber, Frank, in the men's barbershop nearby, and he was desperate for a haircut. So Debbie Annis, the hairstylist, took care of him. At the end of the cut, she asked, as she always does, if he would like to have his hair blow-dried. He hesitated a moment, saying he had never had that experience before, but "I guess I could try that"—and he did.

Fr. Ted moved with ease and appreciation among the few hundred women who came to campus during the spring of 1998 to celebrate their arrival twenty-five years earlier. They were a special attraction back then and always will be, as the first undergraduate women admitted to Notre Dame.

Fr. Ted was recognized and honored, formally and informally, throughout the weekend for playing such a major role in admitting undergraduate women. As one alum put it, "Without him, our Notre Dame degrees would simply be a figment of our imaginations." He joined in many of the major anniversary celebrations, including the placement of a large, engraved stone (which he blessed) near the foot of the grotto's altar that declares a major change in the course of Notre Dame's history:

In thanksgiving to the Blessed Virgin Mary
1972
We are and will forever be grateful
daughters of Notre Dame du Lac

While the spirit of the group was infectious across campus throughout the weekend, it reached a peak during an evening banquet in the South Dining Hall. Gathered around tables from all parts of the country and the world, these feminine celebrants caught up on twenty-five years of living, with great doses of Notre Dame memories added for good measure. Cochairs of the event, Jamee DeCio and Mary Ann Grabavoy gave official welcomes. The Honorable Ann Williams was the dinner speaker. Special guest speakers were President Edward "Monk" Malloy, CSC, and President Emeritus Theodore M. Hesburgh, CSC. Many of their words focused on the significance and accomplishments of these women who stepped into the history of Our Lady's University. A number of the women had followed their grandfathers, fathers, uncles, cousins, and brothers to campus. Some women were "double-Domers," having earned both their undergraduate degrees and graduate or law degrees from Notre Dame. It was an evening filled with gratitude and good cheer, dotted with the phrase "Thanks to Father Ted."

As the dinner came to an end and each woman came forward to accept a certificate indicating "First Notre Dame Woman" status from Fr. Malloy, president, Fr. Hesburgh stood nearby adding his greetings and receiving warm gestures of appreciation. It was a study in reciprocity, an exchange of gratitude and affection. Fr. Hesburgh was grateful for each one of the women, and they were appreciative of him and his eighty years of life and dedication—and his decision to make Notre Dame coed.

A final spontaneous story brought the historic ceremonies to a close as Fr. Ted took the microphone, commenting that "being here with all of you this evening makes me think of my novitiate days." I sat straight up in my chair wondering where he was taking us this late in the evening. But we all went with him as he told us about his novice master who often gave talks on the three vows of poverty, celibacy, and obedience. After the novice master's talk on celibacy, Fr. Ted explained to the group that he raised his hand to ask a question: "What about kissing women?" Having just witnessed a great show of affection, the crowd in front of him offered a ripple of laughter. It seemed to take him a bit by surprise since his story wasn't finished. He continued, indicating that his novice master was a fine man, "a wise man, who stopped and thought for some moments before answering me." We felt the pause in the room. "Finally," Fr. Ted went on, "the novice master explained that kissing women was all right as long as you were kissing all of them." With that, the room exploded with laughter as Fr. Ted tried to add his last phrase: "I guess I'm still kissing all of them." He received a standing ovation.

Speaking of women in Fr. Ted's life, I have often heard him refer to Mary, the Mother of Jesus, in very familiar terms, especially after watching the university come through a difficult and stressful time. He would easily pay her tribute publicly, explaining to his listeners that "the Lady on the Dome takes good care of us!"

A sad piece of news landed right in the midst of the Baccalaureate Mass petitions on May 19, 2001: We were asked to pray for Monsignor John Egan who had died earlier that day. A slight gasp was heard in the crowd of twelve thousand who had come from across the country and beyond for graduation. Many knew his name and work; others knew him personally, such as Msgr. George Higgins, who was among the guests scheduled to receive the Laetare Medal the next day during graduation ceremonies. The medal honored him for all of his accomplishments in the area of social-justice work—so like the work to which Jack was dedicated. They were good friends.

Jack had been ill, but those who knew of his illness never wanted to face his death notice. We wanted him around forever to prick our consciences and to carry on with his good works. He lived in the cardinal's residence in Chicago after he left Notre Dame, and so it was fitting that he was laid in state in Holy Name Cathedral.

I knew this had to be a hard loss for Fr. Ted since he had invited Jack Egan to come and spend a sabbatical year at ND while he was having lingering difficulties with Cardinal Cody during the 1960s. Jack took Fr. Ted up on his offer, little suspecting that he would serve the Church at large from Notre Dame from 1970 to 1983, assisting Fr. Ted at times until the day Cardinal Bernadin invited Jack "home" to Chicago.

A few days after Jack's death, a procession of Notre Dame folks drove to the city to pay their respects. Michael Garvey and I arrived for the wake and prayer service the night before the funeral. On our arrival, we met Fr. Ted in front of the church, emerging from his car driven by Marty Ogren. We entered the cathedral and approached the middle aisle, taking turns to sign the memorial book. Fr. Ted leaned over and thoughtfully said, "Jack was like a brother to me." He walked ahead of us into the midst of friends and admirers who recognized him, then straight to the right side of the casket. Fr. Ted stood alone, looked long and hard, then he placed his hand on Jack's shoulder. As he turned away, he was met by members of Jack's family and his secretary, Peggy Roach.

Michael and I lost any sense of where Fr. Ted was in the crowd until Marty Ogren found us with the message that Fr. Ted wanted us to join him and Marty for dinner before the evening service. Outside the cathedral, Fr. Ted instructed Marty to find a good restaurant where we might tell Jack Egan stories and dine in his name. Marty led us to the neighborhood place where Jack often ate his way through his own stories.

Everyone had Jack Egan stories. One of the best focused on his insistence on having a collection taken up at his funeral Mass for his most recent social-justice cause, with specific instructions that the collection should begin with the clergy at the altar. Rumors spread that a Jack Egan story could surface in his own hand. Apparently, Jack wrote a letter expressing his beliefs on why the Church should ordain women priests.

Fr. Ted stayed the night in the cathedral rectory so he could attend

Jack's funeral Mass the next morning. Before the day was out, he flew to Land O'Lakes to fish and celebrate his birthday. It was an annual excursion. When I asked him the date of his birthday, he quickly offered May 25, then thoughtfully explained that Jack Kennedy and he were born a few days apart. But that was only the beginning of what was on his mind. He looked me straight in the eyes and said, "I just can't imagine Jack Kennedy being eighty-four years old—and looking like me."

ELEVEN

Forever Our Alums

"Those are Annie's eyes," I murmured to myself as I shoved my coffee cup to the right and set the *Chicago Tribune,* dated December 11, 1999, on the table for an early-morning read in the Huddle. Her eyes stared up at me from just above the half-fold mark of page one. When I opened the paper full length, her face was three columns wide and four inches deep, crowned by a headline that was all Annie: "True to Herself."

I sat back with a heavy sigh filled with awe. U.S. District Judge Ann Claire Williams, my first assistant rector in Farley, was approved by the U.S. Senate to serve as a judge on the Seventh U.S. Circuit Court of Appeals. My coffee waited until I read my way through more than fifty inches of print and photo.

Ann and I met in late August 1973, the first year Farley opened its doors as a women's residence. I was assigned as rector; she, as a second-year law student, was to be my assistant. We were to take the helm of a once male bastion and create a new community of young women scholars. Since there was next to no time for long introductions, we put our heads together immediately, trained a new staff of resident assistants, and prepared for 130 freshmen who arrived on our doorstep only hours after we did. They were followed by another hundred residents a few days later, mostly sophomores and some upperclassmen, including transfer students from St. Mary's College.

A few weeks later, Ann and I sat outside on a Farley bench one hot September night to review hall business. In the midst of our business, we wandered rather graciously into conversation about each other. It seemed the perfect moment to tell her my concerns about working with "a wonderful gung ho black woman," as someone had described her, who got on so well with faculty and fellow students. She eyed me closely as I strung my words together: "I must confess that I kept wondering if I had prejudices that would suddenly surface and cause difficulties between us." To my delight, she instantly took hold of the conversation: "Well, you should have seen me when I heard that I was going to be working with some nun!" Our laughter that moment spearheaded us into more than twenty-five years of friendship.

As I finished reading the *Tribune* article about Ann, I settled with pride and affection into the fact that I now live in her former quarters in Farley Hall, while Ann now lives near my roots in Chicago (not far from the University of Chicago) with her husband, David Stewart, son, Jonathan, and daughter, Claire.

It was a great day in the new millennium, January 21, 2000, when we were all reunited at Ann's inauguration, celebrated in the world of judges. A contingent from Notre Dame led by President Rev. Edward Malloy, CSC, along with family and friends and political leaders, gathered in a large courtroom in the Dirksen Building in downtown Chicago. I caught up with Ann's parents, Dorothy and Joshua, in Ann's judicial chambers, although I had first met them in Farley Hall. It was in Farley that I learned that both of them had gone to historically black colleges but were unable to find jobs after graduation because of racism in their hometown of Detroit. It was many years before they were offered teaching positions. Although Ann's dad was trained in psychology, he drove a bus for twenty years, while her mom worked for ten years in a home for delinquent children.

Watching Ann accept her judicial responsibilities reminded me that there was no end to the gifts and talents in the women I came to know at Notre Dame. My first hall staff reflected such bounty: Patricia Brines became a physician; Ann Therese Darin Palmer, an attorney; Deborah Romann Fischer, a linguist; Holly Zadoretsky, a biologist; and Marianne O'Connor Price, a metallurgical engineer, named the first Notre Dame woman valedictorian. Ann's judgeship also reminds me of five other Farley residents who served on the bench, including Kathleen

Kearney ('80), who became a circuit judge in Broward County, where Florida's governor, Jeb Bush, discovered her courtroom work on children and families and appointed her to his cabinet as secretary of the Department of Children and Families in January 1999.

Upon completing her ND law degree, Kathleen became a public prosecutor, much to the dismay of her father who thought she should go into corporate law and gain more financial security, especially in light of her educational loans. There was strong disagreement between them at that time, so much so that he couldn't bring himself to come to her law school graduation. The day after the ceremonies, when it was time for fond farewells after seven years in South Bend at St. Mary's College, I drove her to the airport, aware of some of her anxieties. As we hurried to the boarding area, we discovered we were standing in line right behind our president, Fr. Ted Hesburgh, on his way to deliver a university commencement address elsewhere. Naturally, we quickly fell into conversation with him. In his inimitable way, he found out the essentials of Katie's story and assured her not to worry, "Your dad will come around," which he did. In the meantime, Fr. Ted congratulated her and declared his delight at being the one to take her father's place for the moment and escort her into the next phase of her life as they boarded the plane together.

Other Farley judges serving across the country include Tracy Kee ('78) of Dallas, now in her second term as a district court judge, which in the Texas system is the highest-level trial judgeship. Mary Kay Rochford ('76 and '79) occupies the bench as associate judge of the Circuit Court of Cook County. Ellen Dauber ('82) serves as the circuit court associate judge in Belleville, Illinois. New Mexico claims Martha Vazquez ('75 and '79) as a U.S. district court judge.

A few more judges might be waiting in the wings, especially when I think of all the budding attorneys that walked the halls of Farley. Meg Hackett ('79) and her triple-Domer sister, Patricia ('81, '83, and '91), initially followed in the legal footsteps of their mother who served as a Michigan judge. Some Farley attorneys stand tall professionally in firms with their fathers, including Colleen McCarthy ('77) and Greta Roemer Lewis ('86). Many combined their law careers with marriage and family responsibilities, as Sheila Shunick Burton ('84) has, sending annual Christmas photos to prove it.

Leslie Griffin ('78) first earned her Ph.D. in ethics from Yale and later a J.D. from Stanford, which brought her first to ND's theology department for some years, then to the University of Santa Clara as a law professor, and most recently to the University of Houston as an ethics professor.

In addition to law degrees and specialties, Farley women with M.D.'s specialize in all sorts of practices: anesthesiology, nephrology, ophthalmologist pediatrics, neurology, endocrinology, plastic surgery, internal medicine, emergency medicine, otolaryngology, family medicine, dermatology, obstetrics, and gynecology! On a bet one evening, I counted twenty-five women who lived in Farley during the first ten years of coeducation who grew up to become doctors. Coletta Miller, our first hall president, from Pocatello, Idaho, seemed to set a trend, becoming an oral and maxillofacial surgeon.

While these women took their doctor daydreams seriously as Domers, they also managed to make good friends, play basketball, dance hard, fall in love, bake cookies, phone home, do laundry, gossip, make an urban plunge, go to the movies, eat in the north dining room, run the lakes, and sleep a bit. As we went our daily ways from one season to the next, I just never thought of them as the future doctors of America—and all the time, they were.

A ten-year Farley roster of M.D.'s would probably begin with Patricia Cahill Brines ('74), an ob/gyn specialist, and end with Susan Trompeteer ('83), who practices internal medicine. Central to the lineup would be Liz Berry Kavis ('79), whose special interests were pediatrics and neurology. Liz remains notorious among her peers as the only undergrad to score perfect sevens in two semesters' worth of quizzes in the chemistry classes of the legendary Prof. Emil T. Hofman.

Farley women have also chosen a variety of other professions to which they brought unique talents. Laura Nymberg Ulrich ('77) traveled the world as a geophysicist for Enron Oil and Gas International. Running into Laura and her husband Mark ('75), who were on campus during reunion days, was one big surprise. The other was discovering that she searches out the best spots in some thirty countries around the world for the placement of oil rigs, each with a twenty million dollar price tag. I couldn't resist reminding her that I knew her as a freshman who ran a birthday cake service out of Farley.

I stopped in my tracks early one morning when I heard the name Nancy Cox on a National Public Radio newscast. I had an immediate recall of a lovely blond Farleyite, who, as an overall-wearing undergraduate, drove back and forth to her southern Illinois home in her baby blue pickup truck. One of her claims to Farley fame (which I did not know at the time!) was that she drove a truckload of Domers to the 1977 Cotton Bowl in Dallas, Texas, where Farley Hall President Tracy Kee reigned as the Notre Dame Cotton Bowl princess. As the NPR announcer added more biographical information, I realized he was talking about the southern Illinois "hick" (as she often called herself) whom I knew.

Nancy Cox Epstein, an associate professor of human genetics at the University of Chicago, was making headlines in the year 2000 for the part she played in discovering a type II diabetes gene. As a member of a team of three, it fell to Nancy, as a statistical geneticist, to make her way through the entire human genome map. She discovered various sites along the way that were associated with diabetes, then finally pinpointed the diabetes gene now referred to as the Calpain-10 gene. Up until then, no one analyzing a complex disease through genetic mapping had been able to discover the specific gene carrying a specific disease.

As Nancy explained, "We knew the proximate location of where the gene was that increases the risk of type II diabetes. But then we had to sift through huge amounts of data. To use a comparison, it was as though we gradually went from looking at the whole world, to finding Indiana in the United States, then locating the Notre Dame campus, arriving at Farley Hall, and opening the door to room 307." Further, she explained that it was up to her to carry the computational responsibilities of this gene identification project. "I worked in a 'dry lab,' so to speak, with pencil, paper, and computers. Since it was possible to do some work at home on computers, my young daughters, Bonnie and Carrie, were able to watch over my shoulder and have fun helping with graphs."

Nancy, who arrived at the University of Chicago in 1987 after earning her Ph.D. in human genetics at Yale University, claims that there is still so much she doesn't understand. "But it's exciting to see this discovery happen," she explains, with scientific exhilaration, "because the same kind of paradigms that were developed for this project will be used to identify genes for other disorders, like asthma."

While Barbara Frey ('78) enjoyed a special history with women's basketball at Notre Dame before varsity days, it was her close association with Notre Dame's Center for Social Concerns that pointed her professionally toward the issue of human rights. Having been one of the student founders of the Urban Plunge program, she made a few plunges herself. She went on to complete a summer service project in Oakland, California, where she trained to become a community organizer.

After graduation, she was selected to be one of the five original Holy Cross Associates. This was a group organized by the Congregation of Holy Cross priests to attract lay volunteers among university graduates to serve the Church by assisting Holy Cross priests in their ministries. Barbara was assigned to work in Portland, Oregon, as a community organizer in areas of poverty and housing, all of which helped to spearhead her into the study of law at the University of Wisconsin, where she more closely examined the ways law and policy can effect social change.

Following a six-month affiliation with the Congregation of Holy Cross in Chile, where she observed human rights issues and learned Spanish, Barbara accepted the position of executive director of Minnesota Advocates for Human Rights, with headquarters in Minneapolis. During her tenure, this enterprise grew from a small volunteer group to one of the largest U.S.-based international human rights organizations, with more than twelve hundred members and fifteen active programs. In the course of such expansion, Barbara has become a leading expert on international human rights law and policy, traveling to various places around the world to investigate human rights violations.

Some twenty years after her first urban plunge, Barbara remains close to Notre Dame and her mentor Fr. Don McNeill, CSC, serving as chair of the board of directors for the Center for Social Concerns. She has recently accepted a newly created position as director of the Program on Human Rights in the College of Liberal Arts at the University of Minnesota. Wife and mother of three, Barbara is an adjunct professor at the University of Minnesota in both the Law School and the Institute for Global Studies.

For years I watched Notre Dame men return to campus with all that it takes professionally and personally to pass the university on to another generation by serving in administrative positions. One day, I became aware that Notre Dame women had begun to do the same.

Alisa Hardiman Fisher ('77 and '79) serves as the associate director of Admissions. Angie Rick Chamblee ('73) is associate dean of the First Year of Studies; while Ann Stockman Firth ('81), who also earned an ND law degree in 1984, was the first director of Residence Life and now serves as special assistant to the vice president for Student Affairs.

On her return to Notre Dame, Katie Walsh Anthony ('85 and '96) was appointed director of Audit and Advisory Services. As the millennium approached, she became the director for Y2K Compliance, better known as the "Y2K czarina." Katie now serves as director for M.B.A. Alumni Relations. Missy Conboy ('82) earned her J.D. at the University of Kansas and returned to Notre Dame where she serves as the associate director of the Athletic Department.

Ann Rathburn Lacopo ('87) is the first woman to be appointed as a director in the Development Office where she oversees the university's relations with foundations. After graduation, Frances Shavers ('90) worked in the Alumni Office as an assistant director of Alumni Clubs. She went on to serve as the coordinator of the Life Skills Program for the Athletic Department before leaving Notre Dame to pursue Ph.D. studies at Harvard University.

Chandra Johnson ('96) returned to undergraduate work after being employed for some years on the West Coast. She now acts as an assistant to the university president and as assistant director in charge of special activities in Campus Ministry.

Finally, three alumnae returned to Notre Dame to minister in residence halls. Kate Sullivan Barrett ('85 and '90) was the first female alum to serve as a rector, assigned to Lewis Hall. During and after leaving that position, she was also a member of the Campus Ministry staff. Cathie Lohmuller Cicchiello ('86 and '91, with an M.A. in theology from Creighton) arrived back on the campus scene when Pangborn became a women's residence hall, where she served four years before returning to hospital administration. Heather Rakoczy ('93) with her master of divinity from Vanderbilt, is presently a rector, assigned to Pangborn Hall.

Farley women stayed in touch in many surprising ways. There were wedding invitations and Farley brides walking down the aisle of Sacred Heart Church or into the Log Chapel. Christie Herlihy Starr ('77) holds the distinction of spending the night before her summer wedding in my rector's room while I was away from campus. "I lit your prayer candle and spent a wonderful kind of retreat evening before the big day." Actually, I saw this wedding day coming for a long time. I remember hearing the first "signs" of it on the fourth floor in the T-wing corridor one wintry evening when a snowball hit Christie's window. I gasped. It was a high throw. Someone nonchalantly mused, "Oh, that's just Bill Starr, the baseball player, looking for Christie." As planned, I arrived back on campus just in time to see Christie and her bridesmaids cross the north quad in brilliant sunlight to meet the baseball groom and his team of groomsmen.

There were always love stories in the air and anniversaries to mark them. In South Bend's bagel shop, Studebagels, one Sunday morning after Mass, Chrissie ('79) and Roger Klauer ('75) reminded me that they were close to celebrating twenty-one years of marriage. Our eyes grew wide at the double-decade count, which led Roger to recall his former visit to my Farley rector room on a Friday night before a football game. He made the trip from the Mayo Brothers' clinic in Rochester, Minnesota, where he was serving as an intern, and where he became convinced that it was the time, and Notre Dame was the place, to ask Chrissie Romano to marry him. Standing tall in my Farley doorway, he asked to use my place "to freshen up a bit." Later, he showed me the engagement ring that he wanted to give to her at the grotto. Fidgeting a bit, he explained how he must first find the father of the bride-to-be, a former Dillon Hall man, Mr. Buddy Romano ('50), who was in town for a football game with his wife Florence, "to ask for their daughter's hand."

We remembered it all in living color. But in this Studebagel setting, Roger suddenly put a question to me: "By the way, did you ever wonder why I chose to come to your room? I knew many other people on campus where I could have gone." I had to confess that it had never crossed my mind, but apparently, he had given a lot of thought to his approach to campus that night. "I didn't want to go to anyone who would start philosophizing to me and pose all kinds of questions and put obstacles in the way of what I wanted to do. I was ready to act on my convictions. They were deep, and it was so clear to me what I should do. I thought you would understand." All this was spoken with morning coffee, and three of five Klauer children listening to us sort out history.

As we all parted and I drove back to campus, I went back twenty-one years one more time. Roger was right, to a point. I had known and understood their love for each other, and I was happy for them then. But I wondered for some moments about what those obstacles were that someone might have put in front of him some twenty years ago. Regardless, as I drove down Ivy Road, there was a thrill of grace in me as I thought of how their lives have grown so full of meaning and how their love has deepened.

The e-mail era naturally brought many former students much closer. Carol Latronica ('77) often sent me "new mail," so present to my senses with a trail of memories.

> I'm in my office thinking fondly of ND and all the wonderful times there. I'm sorting out thirteen years of student affairs files and you entered my mind. So, I surfed the net and found you on the Student Affairs page! As you can tell, I am still in the student affairs field and love my work. It's definitely a vocation for me. I have maintained the contact with students and my work with Newman Center and the local churches. There are not too many dull moments—that's for sure. I think about the Easter liturgy celebrations at ND and remember what an impact that had on me. Just wanted to drop you a short note—I will try to write sometime and fill you in on the past 23 years!

Marian Sullivan sent an e-mail invitation that possessed all the elements of a Gospel parable held together by her life:

> Sister Jean,
>
> I hope you might remember me. I was one of your Farley girls way back in 1973–77. We have seen each other twice since I gradua-

ted (the only two times that I have been back on campus). Anyway, my husband, Joe, and I are blessed with three beautiful adopted children, who will be baptized in the Log Chapel on campus on July 11th. I was hoping that maybe you would be able to join us for that special ceremony. If, by any chance you will be around that day, and not too busy, the baptism is at 1:00 pm. Only our little family and my long time friend Dr. Chuck Kulpa, will be present. It would be special to have you there, and I know you would love these kids.

Fondly,
Marian Toth Sullivan ('77)

After catching up with Marian and Joe in the Log Chapel before the baptismal ceremonies, I learned that the children were siblings, the oldest ready to turn eleven. Marian and Joe had met them in an orphanage in Latvia, and on a second visit there, had created a family of five on the spot and brought them "home" to America in 1998. On this summer day two of Marian's former ND professors of biology were present with special roles to play in their lives. Prof. Charles Kulpa became godfather for David, Lydia, and Billie, while Father Jim McGrath, CSC, officiated at the baptismal ceremonies.

On a much more personal and difficult note, Mary Palladino ('74) e-mailed me to tell me that she would be on campus during the last weekend of the semester to spend time with her daughter, Sue, who lived in Howard Hall. Mary wondered if we might get together. However, in the process of sending one e-mail message, Mary included another:

The countdown has begun! Some forty-eight hours until the moving truck arrives. This has been a difficult time. There was a wonderful article in ND Magazine this fall, written by a female professor who was widowed at a young age, too. It hit so close to home. I felt like I could have written the article myself. Right now this house is in such a state of upheaval that I think I will be relieved to get out of here. Actually Bob only got to live here for three years. For me, I saw the kids grow up here and learn to drive and go on to college. So, it is part of my life that is ending. I am turning melancholy as I sit here. I should be packing boxes! I am looking forward to next weekend! I will be ready for a little "vacation." I arrive late Friday morning, so I will try to find you.

Love,
Mary

Male friends of Farley women also sent surprise e-mail letters, like Mark Bruggeman, whose message carried details long forgotten:

Sr. Jean,

This year marks 20 years since I graduated with a B.Arch., and I'm now reading my alumni magazine cover to cover. You were referenced in the most recent issue, and it brought back some memories for me.

I was graduating at mid-year, and somehow we met for the first time. Whether it was through one of the Farley residents or other circumstances, I don't recall. I do recall that you recognized at that time (much more than I) the significance of an ND graduation and the personal magnitude of the moment. We struck up a conversation and even a brief friendship, shared dinner, and you even ushered me through a chance encounter and an informal ceremony where I met Fr. Ted briefly, in the University Club. All in all, I remember the circumstances as providing a truly meaningful commencement to my years at Notre Dame.

At face value, it doesn't sound like much of a memory. It's a small thing, really. But at this stage, I'm finding myself being drawn more and more to the ideals of my education, and in large part basing it on the little memories which surface from the great underlying truths of ND. We're raising three girls now, all proud sweaty occupants of Alumni Family Hall these past few summers, and "family values" has taken on meaning separate from a political slogan. At the same time, as we squirrel away the 401k for the projected tuition, I'm hoping we can instill the same values I learned all those years ago on campus from the people who make the place what it is.

Thanks for the memories.
Mark Bruggeman ('78)

Once I had an overwhelming dream that one hundred thousand ND alums were only a phone call away. I woke up realizing that it was true!

Tony Grasso ('75) was a member of the population who called now and then just to "catch up on life." When he phoned one Saturday afternoon, his voice had a definite significant edge, "Jean, do you realize that we've known each other for over twenty years?" It was so easy to answer, "Yes, Tony, and as some students would say, it's been a ton of grace all the way."

Tony's Notre Dame days stay ever fresh in my mind. He had been an award-winning weightlifter who looked to Terry Lally, CSC, as a mentor for many reasons, including the fact that Fr. Terry was capable of bench-pressing three hundred pounds. While Tony claimed me as his theology teacher, I felt a special trust when he asked me to sew his ND insignia on his weightlifting suit when he qualified for a special match. The suit was made of a stretchy material, spandex, which rolled into the size of a softball. I had to stretch the suit across my knees in order to sew on the ND emblem. For a fleeting moment, I felt like Betsy Ross with a needle in hand and stars and stripes in my lap. Those tricky stitches, and the time spent discussing the strengths and weaknesses of Tony's theology papers, proved to be the basic ingredients for a lasting friendship.

Tony transferred to Notre Dame after two years of engineering at Indiana University. He was never sorry for the move, but he always felt like he was "catching up" with himself. In fact, he found it hard to graduate from Notre Dame. He felt "undone," so "unfinished," as he put it, with his undergraduate work. But his academic record indicated otherwise. Ready or not, he was a graduate with a major in engineering. As the years went by, Tony often wondered if he ever deserved a Notre Dame degree. I could hear the doubt in his voice during some of his phone calls, but he always came round with refreshing philosophical and theological holds on life. He never gave up hope. As a resident of Texas, he became quite fluent in Spanish and went on to marry Ana Maria from Mexico. Together they raised three daughters through some challenging times. Somehow there were always blessed breakthroughs.

This Saturday afternoon was another breakthrough moment. Tony called to tell me that he was sitting in their family room with two boxes filled with his Notre Dame "stuff." His wife had just discovered the boxes that very day as they prepared for a garage sale. "I can't believe what I have in my hands: papers I wrote for Prof. Joe Evans and for you. They were right on the top of the pile. I had to call. I'm sitting here realizing that things really have started to fall into place in my life." His voice was strong. "I've lived long enough; I took on the challenges. I'm ready—I am a Notre Dame graduate." He had never heard himself say it like that. For years he had been afraid to let people know he was an ND graduate, fearing he could never live up to what they would expect of him. He finally took on a truer identity as I clutched the telephone, hundreds of miles away, honored to be a witness.

"Have to go, Jean. Ana can't figure out what's keeping me!" What kept him was the insight of a lifetime that grabbed him right in the middle of a garage sale. I knew he meant his final words, "We'll keep in touch," which we do, with special focus on his daughters, Anna ('02), a budding architect, and Stefanie and Michelle, students at St. Mary's College and Holy Cross College respectively, across the road.

Some phone-calling alums have colorful grotto requests. Capt. Alan Perry ('86) who was commissioned into the U.S. Army at graduation during the same hour that he was inducted into Phi Beta Kappa, went off to administer a military hospital in Vincenza, Italy, during the Gulf War. While traveling in Italy, he called one day from St. Peter's Square in the Vatican asking if I would light a candle for him and a special intention at the grotto. I reminded him that he was at St. Peter's, a shrine unto itself, with lots of candles. But he insisted that nothing could take the place of a candle with his prayer at Notre Dame's grotto.

After leaving the army, Alan went on to earn his Ph.D. in Italian studies at the University of Wisconsin, and he recently accepted a tenure-track position at Gettysburg College. At Gettysburg he still makes candle requests for special intention, the latest being that he might develop into a strong teacher and a really fine professor, "like those I had at Notre Dame, Fr. Jim Burtchaell, CSC in theology, and Prof. Robert Kirby in history. They continue to inspire me to be the best."

My sense is that many students on campus have "grotto request" stories to tell. John Burchett ('84), of Zahm Hall, told me of a midnight call he received from an alumnus who explained that he had lived in John's room many years before. The gentleman remembered the telephone number and called to see if the present student occupant would "please go down to the grotto and light a candle" for his very good friend who was a dying Notre Dame alum.

Alumni, of course, come in all ages with strong ND attachments and unique needs. Bill, an octogenarian alum in my summer Elderhostel class, took me into his confidence one afternoon before class, explaining that he had just come from Cedar Grove Cemetery where he had backed his car into a headstone and picked up a sizable dent. He was so frustrated with not being able to fully complete his cemetery mission. Once out of his car, he had searched but couldn't find the grave of his good friend Prof. Frank O'Malley. "I knew he was buried in the vicinity, but I just couldn't find him," he lamented. "So I called out, 'I know you're there somewhere, Frank. I'm in town and stopped by to say hello again.' That visit counts, doesn't it?" he queried. As he took my hand, I assured him that it did—and the dent gave it double affirmation.

At the end of one of the Elderhostel classes, I was escorted back to Farley Hall by another ND graduate of forty years. Along the way, he confessed that he had had some hard times at ND as a student and had stayed away all this time. "Why did I ever do that to myself? Look at this place. It could have been a mainstay in my life." There was only one thing left to say, and we almost said it together, "Begin now."

Some alums who live on the edge of campus, a stone's throw from Farley's neighborhood, have become family and feed my soul and body. Steve Moriarty ('69), a professional specialist at the Snite Museum, and his wife, Kathleen, a secondary teacher in South Bend, along with Michael Garvey ('74), assistant director of Public Relations at Notre Dame, and his wife, Margaret, who heads Protective Services in the South Bend area, have kept me close to my Franciscan moorings. They allowed me to help them in whatever limited way I could with their work for Cambodian and Vietnam refugees, and those needing the hospitality of the Catholic Worker House on Notre Dame Avenue. I learned so much about Jean Vanier and the L'Arche community, and I stayed close to Margaret's work with Protective Services, which is designed to help those mentally and physically unable to care for themselves.

There were evenings when we discussed the life and influence of Dorothy Day and Archbishop Romero and the plight of the people of El Salvador. We traded books and had some of the best conversations of our lives late into the night about crucial topics that were disturbing us deeply or filling us with life. We prayed together on many special days when Fr. Jim Burtchaell would celebrate baptisms, First Communions, wedding anniversaries, or the memory of departed loved ones. I gathered often at their tables for birthdays and graduation celebrations for Michael, Joseph, and Monica Garvey, and with the Moriarty children, Elizabeth ('00), Sarah, and Daniel, my godson. To be invited to their tables was to stay open to an endless surprise of guests. It might be Peter Steinfels of the *New York Times* or Trappist monks from New Melleray or Georgette and Hanna Eid, former residents of Palestine who opened our worlds to the plight of their people. Monsignor Jack Egan was a cherished friend and mentor in their midst. Steve and Kathy met years before as young volunteers in his west-side Chicago Presentation parish during serious racial tensions, and they remained close friends with Jack and his secretary, Peggy Roach. Their hospitality was contagious and their homes were always opened to university, staff, faculty, and Holy Cross priest friends, along with young people the same ages as their children.

These days, short notes on Christmas cards from Farley alums are beginning to multiply, announcing that they will be bringing their freshmen offspring to campus "next fall." Double-Domer parents Kathleen Buckley Murren ('76) and husband Phil ('76), as well as Sue Grace Murphy ('78) and husband Don ('78), have sons in the class of 2004. This forward movement in time has encouraged some Farley women to look back and remember—and pass it on.

Donna Crowley Campbell ('76), one of the first women presidents of Farley Hall, offers an early perspective:

> We thought we were such pioneers in 1973 when women came to the North Quad. The male students didn't quite know how to handle women in the dining hall and walking "their" quad. . . . But we learned to co-exist harmoniously, enough even to play touch football on the quad with Joe Montana—a fact that causes my children still to shake their heads in disbelief! . . .

I fondly recall the evening Masses celebrated in Farley Chapel. It was a powerful source of refuge and solace after a day of classes, studying and otherwise hectic pace. To be able to experience the real presence of God in our midst through the Eucharist was something very special—we were a community within a larger community. My twin Denise ('76) and brother Dennis ('78) celebrated our parents' 25th wedding anniversary, their love for each other and love for Notre Dame in Farley's chapel. . . . When my Dad (a ND grad) died suddenly, we had a stole made in his memory for the Farley chapel, with the design from his memorial prayer card. Fr. Griffin blessed it at Mass. . . . Whenever it was used, I felt my Father's life was being memorialized with us and his beloved Notre Dame.

I realize that the friendships I made at Notre Dame were extremely important then, and continue to be now. . . . My sister Denise and I and five of our friends met our husbands at Notre Dame; . . . it's our good fortune to be able to share so much of the Notre Dame experience in these relationships.

There are so many memories . . . I wish I had kept a journal—my scrapbook helps. . . . With age, one realizes how precious our time on earth is! May we all glorify God through Notre Dame our Mother!

From Phyllis Provost McNeil ('77 and '83), law graduate and former resident assistant:

My goodness, a quarter of a century! And to think I was there at the beginning with you, Sister Jean. . . . We inaugurated Farley as a hall for women. It was a terrific time for me. . . .

Since the 1997 Directory was published, I have had another baby—Duncan Andrew Provost McNeil who has joined his brother Douglas. Such a different life style now!

After 22 plus years in the work force (US Navy–CIA–Harvard–Presidential Commission–and back to Harvard), I am now reduced to cleaning bottles and changing diapers at 44 years of age. There is something definitely skewed with this picture. But on most days I am having a ball. I am curious, but unable to predict, what the next bend in the road holds for me. My first son, Douglas, will begin kindergarten this year, while most of my classmates have their offspring entering college! Scott, my husband, puts it this way: "Douglas, the five-year-old, kept us young. Duncan, the 13-month-old, is killing us!"

How well I remember

—being captain for the Farley intrahall softball team, the precursor to the women's varsity team that won the championship three out of four years; the hall basketball team that won every year and was also the precursor to the women's varsity basketball team.

—Becky Banasiak climbing into the firehose cabinet and shutting the door just to prove she could fit.

—screams of agony wafting across the Quad at midnight or the Thursday before Emil Hoffman's Friday morning Chemistry quiz.

—Fr. Griff and his dog Darby O'Gill.

—Fr. Ted the Head, as we irreverently called Fr. Hesburgh, but we think he actually liked the moniker!

—touring the campus at night and pointing out the "jump Mary Jesus" statue and "the wizard" church tower.

—swinging from the wooden swings still hanging from the rafters of the old Field House at 2 a.m.

—praying at the grotto . . . walking around the lakes for quiet time.

—sledding down the steps of the Administration Building on cafeteria trays during one of many snow storms.

—cherishing the camaraderie and sense of belonging that I always felt from being a part of Farley Hall.

From Tracy Kee ('78), former president of Farley Hall:

My favorite memory of Notre Dame are the friends that I made and the enduring quality of those friendships.

I vividly remember walking into that one room triple, wondering how on earth we would fit three women and all of our stuff in that room. Kathleen Kelly arrived shortly thereafter and was upset that she ended up with a roommate from Texas. She wanted to broaden her horizons. . . . Marge Meagher, our other roommate, arrived and announced "I hate blue" at the sight of the carpet we laid. . . .

Marge, Kathleen and I became close friends with Nancy Cox, Keelin Garvey, Molly McGuire and Vicki Lopez. Throughout my four years in Farley, I stayed with those roommates, in various combinations depending on the luck of the draw. . . .

We spent four years getting to know one another, our families, our fears, our loves, our hopes and our dreams. We spent a lot of time talking about the guys—the freshman dog book was searched for the good-looking ones. . . . I flushed terribly whenever one guy was around and Marge and Kathleen teased me unmercifully. We visited the guys in pairs or threes when one of us wanted to try to get to know someone better. We helped each other when a heart was broken by some cad. . . .

We argued politics and debated the hot topics of the day. Occasionally we even helped each other in our studies. We planned parties, discussed upcoming Farley formals. We started the spoof-filled debutante ball. We organized intramural teams and did pretty well. We made great Halloween costumes. We played our music loud and danced. We shared each other's clothes.

I'm glad that the dorms at Notre Dame were not coed and I liked the fact that parietals kept the men out of the dorms late at night. That gave us freedom to be ourselves without worrying about the guys all of the time (which is a huge preoccupation for women in college anyway!). I think it helped us to become closer friends. . . .

We have continued to be there for each other through weddings, births, funerals and other momentous events in our lives. If not in person, we keep in touch by phone, by mail, and now by e-mail. We stay together at ND reunions—those dorm rooms seemed even smaller than I remembered—and had a blast. We celebrated our 40th birthdays during a weekend in New York. . . .

Notre Dame's spiritual side and the intimacy of Mass in the dorms is something that has not been surpassed by any of my experiences as a Catholic in a parish. I loved Mass with Father Griff and was delighted to read that the men at Stanford Hall have decided to call themselves "Griffins" in his honor.

At the end of her reflections, Tracy reminded me of a note I sent to her after I heard of her parents' tragic deaths as the result of an automobile accident while they were driving home from the Dallas airport. It touched the heart of Notre Dame rectoring:

Thank you for the note about my parents. They always felt that I was in good hands when they left me in your care.

Love,
Tracy

Some weeks before the new millennium, former resident assistant Dr. Mary Ellen Burchett Fausone ('79), of ob/gyn fame, who has delivered hundreds of babies and has had a few of her own, reflected back on ND, ironically scribbling her thoughts on paper marked "Patient's Progress Notes" from Northwestern Memorial Hospital (in Chicago) as she awaited the outcome of a surgery:

> For many years after college, Notre Dame was not much in my thoughts. I was busy—physically and otherwise. I spent most of my 20's in medical school, tackling a very demanding residency with a new husband in my life as well.
>
> A year or two after starting private practice, my twins arrived, and so began my career as a mother. Now the twins are nine, and in these last few years, Notre Dame has begun to re-emerge in my consciousness.
>
> Three years ago I moved to Wilmette, Illinois, where I found myself living a mile away and in the same parish as Maria Choca. Our friendship, which had suffered the effect of time and busy schedules, blossomed again. She continues to be one of the most amazing people I met at Notre Dame. She is totally unassuming, friendly, open, refreshingly common sensical and funny, all in spite of her many tragedies since Notre Dame—losing a mother suddenly to Legionnaires disease, a father to lung cancer, an infant son who died in her arms, and a brother slowly succumbing to AIDS. How does one person not only survive all this, but continue to love, give, raise a family, and never ask anyone for sympathy. She has and will continue to be an incredible source of inspiration to me. (Of which, I am sure, she is totally oblivious.)
>
> That same year, I got together with many of my old Farley friends at Carol Lally Shield's home in Philadelphia. Our husbands tolerated us, our kids played together. (It was summer and my kids still talk about the "slug race" conducted with slugs the kids collected from the yard.) And again Notre Dame reigned. . . .
>
> Last year I took my 8-year-old son to his first Notre Dame game. We parked in the usual back lots, then cut across to Moreau Seminary and walked around the lake. It was early and we were alone on the path and all was quiet. "Mom, this is so beautiful!" he kept saying. We eventually turned and made our way up to the old bookstore. In two minutes we went from perfect solitude to being one of hun-

dreds—the quad crowded with the band, jugglers, hawkers, barbecuers and fans. He looked at me in amazement. I don't think one can quite appreciate the magical quality of an ND football Saturday until you've seen it through the eyes of an eight year old.

So, after so many years, Notre Dame is part of my life again and there are memories that stand out—

. . . the Lally Literary Festival, held in the community bathroom. We had such culturally enriching topics as simultaneous readings and guest appearances each year including David Huffman, of football fame. How wonderful to do something so totally loony! Carol Lally helped make my Notre Dame/Farley experience unique. Who else had a roommate who could dream up such a Festival, then go on to become a world class eye surgeon?

Farley Football—I have no idea if intramural girls flag football still exists, but in '76 we went at it with a vengeance. Flags were thrown and tempers flared, since like all good Domers, we took the game seriously. We obviously needed an outlet and this provided us one. Makes me so happy there are women's sports at Notre Dame.

I remember as a freshman, being accosted by those strangely dressed alumni. More than once I heard, "Enjoy these years, they are the best years of your life!" I was always troubled by those words. If the best years of my life are already here, then what was I suppose to do for the next 40 years! Was it all downhill? Anyway, I didn't necessarily think being 18 was the greatest. I didn't have an inkling who I was or what I wanted to do. I wasn't even sure who my friends were.

Looking back I realize that my new appreciation for Notre Dame isn't because I had such a great time there, although there were great times. I think I am more comfortable with Notre Dame because I am becoming (finally) a bit of the person that Notre Dame always encouraged me to be, but at the time seemed so hopelessly out of reach.

I am sitting in a hospital room, waiting for my mother to come out of surgery, the surgery that will hopefully cure her breast cancer. My siblings are all in their respective cities awaiting phone calls from me. I think this is when we finally think we are grown—when we take charge of and take care of our parents. Maybe I am learning the lessons of life that will allow me to be a mentor, at least in some way, to young women—the way you, Joe Evans, my biostats professor, K.B. Buckley, my first R.A., and Jean Gorman, my assistant rector, were for me.

The combination of your letter and my Mom's diagnosis opened up in me a need for reflection—and this letter is a start. Thank you for listening. You are in my prayers as I hope I am in yours.

Love,
Mary Ellen

TWELVE

Football Weekend Fringes

True, Notre Dame alumni carry football tickets in their pockets and cheer their "Irish" down to the last seconds through rain, sleet, snow, and blistering hot sunny days. They make it quite clear that they want the next national championship. It's all a given. But for ND alums there's always so much more to returning to campus as they take long walks, long looks, and simply sigh, "Ah, it's good to be back here again."

It's not too hard to get inside their words. On any game day, alumni are notorious for spinning tales of what life held for them between seventeen and twenty-two years of age, remembering mysterious and sometimes bewildering moments of growth and change. Many can give dates, hours, and colorful details about when and where they were most challenged and stretched in every direction of the heart and mind.

They made close friends, fell in love, and talked about everything under the sun into the night and early mornings. They made mistakes, hurt others, got hurt, and felt pain at all levels. They studied hard, and some would say they played harder than they studied. They got mono and toothaches, sprained arms and ankles and necks. Some broke bones or became deathly ill. They read and wrote and read some more. They worked math problems into the night and in their sleep. They dialogued and argued and got angry with professors and mentors and adults who confronted them and cared about them. They walked the lakes "to get their brains together," to slow down, to focus, to watch the sunset. They questioned God in ways they never had before. They ranted and raved. And they reached down deep to pray. At one moment in time, Notre Dame was all theirs, in their faces, in their hands, and under their feet.

No wonder a memory gets tagged so much on a game day. You catch comments in crowds, at hot dog stands, down at the grotto, or waiting for the band concert to begin on the steps of the Main Building. "This place is full of my life. I meet myself back here in ways I never think of myself in any other place. It makes me reflect on what I've done with my life," one man declared. A younger alum commented to his friend, "Strange, but I never come to a game without filling up with gratitude for this place and for everyone who had anything to do with my landing here." My nephew, Michael Ford ('89), arduously shared with me one day five years after graduation, "I'm just now beginning to realize what happened to me here."

Many have admitted that in coming back to campus, they don't "just remember," they actually get "renewed." Rich memories get richer. It's endowment of another kind as young men and women invest their four years, then watch the place become theirs, to learn from and care about for the rest of their lives.

Before and after each game, there's a bit of drama at every turn as family and friends search for each other or come face-to-face by sheer coincidence. Some shout their surprise and walk into bear hugs. Others stand absolutely stunned in the presence of a long lost-friend they haven't seen in years. Words finally come. Affection hangs heavy in the autumn air.

Since personal relationships are at the heart of most Domers' ND experience, reunions of every kind swirl around football games within a hundred-mile radius, involving former roommates, rectors, classes, professors, ND regional clubs, athletic teams, Holy Cross Associates, ACE Volunteers, international study groups, glee club, band, and a host of ND families from across the United States and often beyond.

Football Saturdays were a perfect setting for the Abowd family. Laden with favorite Lebanese food, the late Richard Abowd ('49), a former design engineer with Ford Motor Company, and his wife, Sara, drove down religiously from their home in Dearborn, Michigan, for twenty-one years. During that time, nine of their children attended Notre Dame, some becoming double-Domers: John ('73), Anthony ('74 and '75), James ('75), Rosemary ('81), Michelle ('82), Stephen

('84), Gregory ('86), Peter ('88), and Paula ('90 and '91). Three other children, David, Elizabeth, and Marypat, were also accepted at Notre Dame, but found it best to attend college closer to home in light of an economic crunch that accompanied the oil embargo years. All scholars, nine of the twelve Abowd children were valedictorians of their high-school graduating classes.

For the Abowds, football Saturdays were a grand occasion for reuniting "before the older children left home," and then "after almost everyone did leave home." With a mother's touch and thoughtfulness, Sara would call ahead to Farley, reserve the kitchen, and arrive in time with her husband, Dick, to spread a Lebanese feast. During the feast, everyone caught up with each other's lives, having traveled back from graduate schools and career positions across the country. By the time Paula, "the baby," graduated in 1990, a bevy of spouses joined in the football rendezvous, while a third generation ran among them, singing the Fight Song forward and backward.

Many other families with three and four generations of built-in fans targeted football weekends for family "huddles," including the Hugh ('39) and Jane Garvey family from Springfield, Illinois; the James ('43) and Margaret McCaffertys from Cincinnati, Ohio; the Tony ('47) and Jeanne Earleys from Long Island, New York; the Buddy ('50) and Florence Romanos from Chicago; the Bob ('51) and Mary Clemencys from Milwaukee, Wisconsin; the Jerry ('51) and Joyce Hanks from Moline, Illinois; and the Ray ('65) and Milann Siegfrieds from Tulsa, Oklahoma. All of these families touched my life and the lives of those in Farley and many other resident halls.

Actually, one sees, hears, and feels football Saturdays long before a fan is sighted. Scribbled signs emerge with a familiar theme—"Needed 2 GA [general admission] tickets." Evening lights burn bright on fields where the team and band practice hard to make it all happen. Homemade banners declaring team support are hung from student windows. Guests begin to dot the scenery lugging bags full of bookstore booty. Parents slip onto campus, saunter the pathways, snack in the Huddle, and relax on outdoor benches as they watch the student body come and go to class. Grills, barrels, tables, and wooden sawhorses are dropped off at strategic locations, and student chefs will turn it all into concession stands and feed the game-day multitudes hot dogs, hamburgers, and brats.

The pace increases. A Friday night rally begins in the Joyce Center, starring eleven thousand fans who huddle around a determined football team and coaching staff, led on by a marching band with a fight song that almost plays itself in the presence of Irish fans. "They hear it before they hear it," someone once quipped. It lingers in bones and bloodlines from game to game, in and out of seasons. One football weekend I watched a child, who could hardly reach the keyboard on a baby grand piano in the new bookstore, bring shoppers to a veritable standstill as she played the fight song with one strong, stubby finger.

During his younger years, my godson Daniel Moriarty and I made it our business to show up at a Friday night rally each season. Crowd control manager Jim Murphy, who insisted on calling Daniel "Spike" and me the "legendary sin fighter," always found us good seats. One rally night, unbeknownst to us at first, he sat us next to Heisman Trophy winner Johnny Lujack, who graciously greeted us, and upon request, lifted eight-year-old Daniel onto a chair so they could pose for a photo that will probably last a Moriarty lifetime. Daniel usually stayed the night, rose early on game day, and waited at my Farley window for the sight of the first football player to finish breakfast next door in the north dining hall. He would make a beeline with pen and the latest *Sports Illustrated* for as many autographs as possible. As he got older, he became more selective, looking for his favorite players.

Fans who want a whole day's worth of a football Saturday arrive on campus in the early hours, walking from far-flung parking lots. Not only do they get the first cups of coffee in the Huddle, but they also enjoy the band's wake-up version of the Notre Dame Victory March as it crosses campus, heading for a final practice session in open fields, while eighty thousand people speed to campus by wheels or wings, sure of a seat.

Although I've walked through thick local color on campus football weekends, I suspect I know it all more intimately by way of my Farley Hall room where I've lived these past twenty-seven years. With perfect sun exposure for people and plants, it offers a sweeping view of the north quad. For much of the year, I have a clear view of Mary, as she stands in sight on the Dome with her left shoulder toward Farley. My south windows fill up with Breen-Phillips Hall and a collection of bikes between us that sometimes speaks to me of China, but always reminds me of campus expansion.

On game days, voices of early-morning fans outside my window lead me into consciousness, while blaring strains of "Hike Notre Dame" and the alma mater, played over window loudspeakers, mix with the Prayers of Lauds. Real drama sets in with coffee and toast as amplifiers fill the north quad with historic recordings of announcers giving breathtaking plays—quarterback runs, long kicks, great passes—that led to national championships or went down in history as incredible gridiron moments against such teams as Michigan, Miami, and USC (the University of Southern California). From my windows in Farley, I often watch fans stop in their tracks on the sidewalk to listen with a cocked ear to the all-time favorite Knute Rockne and his locker-room pep talk.

I'm further steeped into the mood of football by listening to Bob Lux, host of WSBT's live radio show on game mornings, broadcast from the Ramada Inn, and more recently from the Varsity Club, where former Heisman Trophy winners, all-Americans, quarterbacks, linemen, kickers, coaches, administrators, band members, cheerleaders, or captains of the Irish Guard will step out of the crowd, take the mike, and tell a tale that takes listening audiences back to football lore of the 1920s, 1930s, 1940s, and 1950s. Certain voices became familiar: Paul Castner, Fr. Ned Joyce, Moose Krause, Fr. Jim Riehle, Coach George Kelly, Ziggy Czarobski, Leon Hart, Johnny Lujack, Ara Parseghian, and Chuck Lennon. Now and then the reigning Leprechaun took the microphone.

While football Saturdays bring the ND family together, they also entice my own family to campus. My mother delighted us often with the fact that she and my dad had seen the Irish play in Chicago's Soldier Field in front of one hundred thousand fans or more in the late 1920s. In 1989, at eighty-one, she attended her last ND home game in her raccoon coat and hat seated in row fifty-two across from the student section. We shared a well-worn ND stadium blanket, which I had received for serving on an historical committee that evaluated the first five years of coeducation at ND. The Irish trounced USC, and the student body stormed the field, as did Brian, my twelve-year-old nephew, who returned with a handful of field sod as a souvenir. It was a cold day in

November that required portable stadium lighting for the crowd of fans that lingered long and listened to every note as the band played on.

My nieces and nephews rolled through season after season of fall leaves right outside my Farley windows on game days. Once I discovered my nieces "playing Mass" in the chapel with "wacky wafers" for Hosts. They grew up learning the campus, capable of giving tours. With their parents, Ray and Ethel Lenz, Jack and Pat Lenz, and Mike and Trudy Ford, they saw their share of Friday night pep rallies, crushed in crowds in Stepan Center, on basketball courts behind the Flanner and Grace Halls, and finally in the Joyce Center. Young and old ate their share of meals in the Morris Inn, at the University Club, and in the Pay Caf, where they learned the stories of the grand murals on surrounding walls, including the fact that our uncle Harry Wilke supervised the construction of the tallest smokestack connected with the power plant. They fed generations of ducks and carp in campus lakes. And at the grotto, they lit a myriad of candles where they knelt to pray, while the children in all of us delighted in relighting the candles that campus breezes puffed out.

On game days they arrived in a flurry of excitement, heaping my bed with hats, coats, stadium blankets, seat pads, rain gear, and all it took to make the day go well. They often honored me by wearing one of the Notre Dame sweatshirts and caps I had given for birthdays. On their arrival, there was fresh coffee and rolls for some, while others were ready for our buffet lunch on my handy ironing board, somewhat disguised under a long tablecloth—a Farley version of a tailgater.

In the midst of such dining, there were always former Farleyites moving in and out of the scenery. Sometimes whole families filled the doorway. Former hall president Michelle Kelly ('80), her husband Andy Herring ('80), and their four children arrived decked out in ND wash-and-wear. They posed for pictures on the edge of Farley flowers very near the first-floor window where Andy used to reach high to scratch Michelle's screen when they were seniors. As Michelle's rector, I remember waking up one morning wondering if I had just dreamt it, or whether they really did elope in the night. It was only a dream.

In addition there were always visits from relatives and friends from the south side of Chicago, and annual visits from members of my Franciscan community who cheered the Irish. For many years running I welcomed a college classmate from Columbus, Ohio, Dee Allen, and her husband, Bill, parents of four Domers: Susan ('77), Diane ('80), Maureen ('83), and Christopher ('88), each of whom received a prestigious Joyce Scholarship.

To complete this mixture of game-day humanity, there were always former Farley men who would ask to walk the hallways to show their wives, children, and grandchildren "my room." However, during my first year, Farley men arrived in shock to learn that the hall had become a women's residence. Some became suspicious as soon as they encountered the scent of perfume as they entered the building, "Oh, no, they took Farley." One Saturday I walked from my bedroom into the main room of my living quarters only to find a group of men drinking and eating hot dogs. They were a bit astonished at my sudden appearance, wondering what I was doing there. They thought the room was a lounge in their old dorm and had no idea women were on the scene. Their upset somewhat subsided when we realized that we were all from the same parish on the south side of Chicago.

As campus quads fill with fans, as well as with the aroma of barbecued hamburgers and hot dogs, the wide-open spaces fill with children playing football or frisbee. Some tots run in circles, shouting at the top of their lungs, while others run as fast as they can away from parents. On nice days many alums and visitors wander about without ever seeing the inside of the stadium. They take long walks with their children on their shoulders or in strollers, stopping in the Huddle or the Pay Caf to catch the score. Some speak of the campus as a grand state park that happens to have a stadium on the fringe.

The sporting events are hardly the only things that take place on campus during a game day. A weekend *Program of Events* guides fans to the right time and place for a glee club concert, a drama production, a Folk Choir program, or possibly an Emil T. Hofman Lecture, inaugurated nine years ago in honor of a cherished teacher of chemistry who was once informed by the university registrar that he had taught thirty-two thousand Domers over the years.

As guest of honor, Emil attends these early game-day lectures that are always delivered by someone he taught who became a physician. William Bell, M.D. ('57), a researcher and professor of medicine at the

Johns Hopkins School of Medicine, one of the world's leading hematologists, was the first speaker in 1993. William C. Hurd, M.D. ('69), world-traveled ophthalmologist, delivered the millennium lecture, "A Bird's Eye View of Ophthalmology: From Memphis to Madagascar."

The 1995 Nobel Prize winner Eric Wieschaus, Ph.D. ('69), Squibb Professor of Molecular Biology at Princeton University, attracted unique attention when he lectured before a football game in September 1996. As usual, Emil duly congratulated him but went on to remind Eric that he hadn't earned As in Emil's chemistry classes. At that point, the legendary chemistry professor rose to the occasion, confessing that in the face of a Nobel Prize, he was moved to do something he rarely did. He changed Eric's chemistry grades from Bs to As! Proof of the proceeding appeared in a document that Emil obtained from the university registrar, which in turn he officially presented to Eric with congratulatory trimmings. Some months later, Notre Dame's Nobel Prize winner told Emil that he kept the registrar's document on display in his Princeton University office, using it to explain to his students what it took to get an A in chemistry at the University of Notre Dame.

While many of his former students track Emil down on football Saturdays, some find him in other, faraway places. Recently, when his back needed the attention of the Mayo Clinic in Rochester, Minnesota, a group of doctors held a special reception for him. They were all his former chemistry students.

However, on a game day, an "Emil audience" is quickly swept into a south quad crowd, moving in amoeba fashion toward the front steps of the Main Building, ready to see and hear the marching band in mini-concert. All of this gradually leads hundreds of fans to arrange themselves along a "God quad" path to wait for the shrill of a whistle that sets the oldest university band in the country into marching cadence. A chorus of trumpets, trombones, baritones, tubas, clarinets, saxophones, piccolos, flutes, drums, cymbals, bells, and glockenspiels are led by cheerleaders and a company of Irish Guards, including its first woman member, Molly Kinder ('01), who will strut and stride in colorful uniform with serious intent, clearing the way as the band strikes up the "Notre Dame Victory March" to lead fans to "the house that Rockne built."

Even inside the stadium there's more taking place than a football game as four generations of fans sit in tight formation on wooden benches steeped in strong tradition, passing on a passion for the place. Fans pay tribute to America and hoist her flag on high with patriotic songs. Sometimes very special guests like former President Gerald Ford, carry the American flag to the northeast corner of the stadium for such ceremonies. The Goodyear blimp, filled with technological innards that send campus images across the world, swims through the heavens like a gigantic whale in a deep sea. One day the blimp treated me to one of the most insightful optical illusions of my life. In the middle of a game, a gorgeous monarch butterfly, full of color and the miracle of life, flew very near me and momentarily filled my view, eclipsing the high-flying blimp. It took my breath away and left me with the lingering thought that God's creations forever upstage anything we dare to manufacture.

Children are always making stadium debuts. I listened to a former Dillonite direct his seven-year-old son to watch the student section do the "William Tell Overture" routine. He reminded him of the photo back home in their family room which commemorates the Irish win thirty-one to twenty-four, during the "game of the century" between #1 Florida State, and #2 Notre Dame. He carefully showed the lad how to move his arms in the same direction, over his head, and out in front of his chest, in sync with the crowd. I could tell this was the beginning of a long relationship that involved much more than the gridiron scene. As the little fellow got into the act, he too had a hint of the bigger picture: "Dad, we gotta win today. It's my first game here."

A grandfather standing behind me impressed me as he tried to stay calm and reasonable when his granddaughter asked him about why the TV official kept holding up the game when he appeared on the field. In a hot dog line, at halftime, I overheard an alum trying to explain to his daughter why the seniors were throwing marshmallows at each other. I came close to asking him if he was a psychologist.

In the midst of an exciting play during one game day, an eight-year-old sitting next to me forgot he hardly knew me. He grabbed my arm when the reality of the moment became filled with much more than a football game, "I'm at Notre Dame! My dad told me on the way coming here that it's my school now!"

While the student body can be full of fun and energy in the stadium, standing as they do throughout the entire game and wearing the same colored t-shirts, they often find unique ways to make their more serious thoughts known. During a November 1997 game, all of the students removed their shoes during the singing of the national anthem to express their concerns over the United States' use of land mines. They also sent a petition with hundreds of signatures to President Clinton urging him to sign the land mine treaty.

Now and then, right in the middle of a game, I catch myself seriously wondering about stories that I've heard regarding people whose ashes are buried in the stadium, one in particular on the fifty-yard line. I suspect there's a bit of truth to this myth. More than once I've been told that individuals have requested such arrangements for loved ones who spent some of the happiest hours of their lives in the stadium. I have no confirmation of any such requests being granted, but I have been told that "only God knows how many fans are buried in the stadium."

Halftime events have always held a variety of surprises. Notre Dame's first astronaut, U.S. Navy Capt. James Wetherbee ('74), stepped to midfield in 1990, during halftime of the Notre Dame–Air Force game, to receive the Corby Award from the Alumni Association for exemplary service in the nation's armed forces. To everyone's amazement, he had just served as pilot on his first spaceflight, during which he carried Notre Dame's prestigious Laetare Medal received in 1925 by pioneer aerospace researcher Dr. Albert Zahm. Dr. Zahm was a professor of mathematics at Notre Dame a century ago, involved with extensive study related to methods of launching airplanes, eleven of which led to the first air flight sponsored by the U.S. government. Sitting in the stands that October halftime, and celebrating Notre Dame's first man in space, I had faint recollections of Jim Wetherbee running into Farley Hall as a carefree senior to see his sister Jule ('76), who had followed him to Notre Dame. She was among the very first undergraduate women to earn a Notre Dame degree, which sent her on her way to becoming a cardiologist—as well as the Domer sister to a Domer astronaut.

Since his halftime appearance more than a decade ago, Notre Dame's veteran astronaut, Capt. Wetherbee, has made history as mission commander for four additional shuttle flights into space: one on *Columbia* (1992), one on *Atlantis* (1997), and two on *Discovery* (1995 and 2001). He also served as commander of a 2002 space flight. Our NASA astronaut has established an ND tradition in outer space these years, taking with him some significant Notre Dame mementos on each flight, only to return them to campus as historic keepsakes.

In the fall of 1992, some of the final scenes for the *Rudy* movie, which has become one of the top-ten sports movies, were filmed during halftime. Fans watched Notre Dame play Boston College that day for the first half of a regular game. Players then headed for the tunnel and their locker rooms, only to be replaced by "movie star" teams who ran through the tunnel in the opposite direction and onto the field with actor Sean Astin depicting Rudy Ruettiger ('76). The 1975 movie teams of Notre Dame and Georgia Tech filled the field in vintage uniforms as fifty-seven thousand fans served as extras and cheered on the actor playing Rudy. Rudy Ruettiger played for twenty-seven seconds in the last home game of his senior year, fulfilling one of the dreams of his life—all of which was poignant enough to be made into a movie. Cameras rolled under the direction of David Anspaugh and screenwriter Angelo Pizzo as they produced what some have declared a TriStar classic with fairy-tale or parable trimmings.

Halftime shows held surprises often associated with the opponent of the day. When the Naval Academy came to town during the 1995 season, Notre Dame alumni officials took advantage of the moment and presented their Corby Award to Vice Admiral Kent J. Carroll ('46) for his distinguished service throughout his long naval career. It was an eye-catching scene to see five other admirals flank their comrade on the field for the occasion—all commissioned from Notre Dame.

Every three years or so there's a halftime drama that's hardly a surprise, yet it delivers a powerful surge of emotion into eighty thousand fans who see it coming. Some one thousand Domers, all past or present ND band members, stretch across the field, playing everyone's favorites one more time: "Stars and Stripes Forever," "Notre Dame Our Mother," and the forever engaging cadence of the "Notre Dame Victory March." Former drum majors and members of the Irish Guard join the lineup as the band struts itself into breathlessness. Word has it that a few alums in the ranks have been expectant moms.

The Four Horsemen, Jim Crowley, Elmer Layden, Don Miller, and Harry Stuhldreher became the focus of a special seventy-fifth anniversary celebration during the 1999 football season. Members of their families were contacted by the athletic department and were hosted at a reception in the press box and given tickets for the game. At halftime, over two hundred members covering four generations of the Four Horsemen's families stood tall on the field, paying tribute to the ND legends that stay fresh in their genealogies.

During a halftime show in the 2000 football season, special attention was given to Ken Dye, the director of the Notre Dame Band. A composer in his own right, he produced all of the band music for the Parade of Athletes, which took place at the opening ceremonies of the 1998 Olympics in Nagano, Japan. The program included forty-two musical pieces, one for each country that had thirty or more athletes competing. The total length of the composition for the Parade of Athletes was ninety minutes, a musical feat in itself.

Halftime also gives fans a chance to catch up with fast food, as well as with family and friends spread around the stadium. It always gave me the perfect opportunity to seek out Ernie Stark when he came to town from Glen Ellyn, Illinois. Ernie sat in one of the wheelchair sections added at the time of stadium expansion. His confinement to his wheelchair, due to multiple sclerosis, never prevented him from becoming a certified Irish fan during his younger brother Joe's four years at Notre Dame, nor did it deter him from bundling up in layers of clothes against the wind and rain to cheer with parents and friends.

Ernie stayed on one weekend to watch his brother Joe play as a member of Knott Hall's 1999 championship interhall team. As was the custom, this final game was played in the stadium for a much smaller crowd. ESPN was on hand to document the traditions of this annual game, capturing all the miniversions of a ND band, cheerleaders, and coaching staff. As we all rushed onto the field at the end of the game to celebrate Knott Hall's victory, the ESPN camera focused on Ernie who was in the midst of us all—the quintessential loyal fan.

A new tradition slipped into place with the opening of the expanded stadium. Every former football player is now invited to help form a tunnel for the football team as it takes to the field for its first game of the season. Also, the Monogram Club focuses on the last home game by inviting all returning monogrammed athletes of all sports to sit as a group on the field in their blue letter jackets.

At game's end—after team members hold their golden helmets on high in front of their student body, after the Irish Guards do their last jig step (i.e., if we win), after the singing of the alma mater, after the band plays one last march of the day through the campus and heads back to band quarters—many fans move in traditional directions to such familiar places as Sacred Heart Basilica or residence hall chapels in Alumni, Dillon, Sorin, Farley, or Keenan-Stanford for a celebration of Mass. Of late, hundreds more fans crowd into Stepan Center. There are untold numbers for whom the celebration of Eucharist stays at the heart of the university.

Later, celebrations carry on in family restaurants around South Bend, such as Rocco's at the edge of campus where Julia and Rocco have fed generations of Domers since 1951. Their restaurant is like an extension of home for many Notre Dame faculty, staff, and off-campus students, along with Parisi's, Francesco's, Sunny Italy—all of which boast strong family ties to the ND community.

Sunday mornings dawn with very little sound. ROTC folks rise early and help maintenance crews clear all signs of debris that lie in the wake of eighty thousand fans. Students slip into a heavy study day, which closes in late evening in residence halls with the celebration of the Eucharist.

I very rarely missed home games. They had their own way of unknotting my emotions after challenging days in Farley Hall and later in the Office of Student Affairs. An exhilarating force cleared my head and heart while standing in that stadium in any kind of weather—sunny autumn days or raw cold ones, complete with blinding snow now and then. Sometimes rain fell hard in rivulets down my poncho and off the tip of my nose. But among stadium friends, Henry ('56) and Linda Dixon of Dixon, Illinois, to my right, and Dr. Robert Devetski of South Bend and his family, to my left, I cheered the team on, shouting at times at the top of my lungs and soaking up the tenseness of cliff-hanger endings, such as the one starring Harry Oliver ('83). Harry shocked himself when he kicked his longest field goal—fifty-one yards against Michigan in 1980, with no time left on the clock—against a wind that lost its gusto for the moment. Fans had slipped into an eerie silence as Harry stepped up to the task, only to erupt into a ground-swelling uproar that took them, and everyone else in the world listening or watching, into the land of euphoria as the football slipped over the edge of the uprights. Along the way I learned how to lose, but oh, those wins stayed around forever.

I came to know players like Alan Pickett, Steve Orsini, and Dave Huffman, who had friends in Farley while I was rector. And I crossed paths with coaches along the way. Although Ara Parseghian was getting ready to leave coaching when I arrived on campus, I met him through his son Michael ('77) who met Cindy Buescher ('77) of Farley Hall as a freshman; they became good friends, fell in love, and married. Little did I realize how much of an inspiration they would become through the years as they raised their four children, Ara, Michael, Marcia, and Christa, three of whom were diagnosed with a terminal illness, Nieman-Pick disease. Nor did I realize that while I had admired Ara so greatly as a coach, I would come to admire him even more as he and his wife, Katie, along with their friend Arthur Decio, president of Skyline Corporation, became a major force in the formation of a research foundation called the Ara Parseghian Medical Research Foundation. The foundation was established to find a cure for Cindy and Michael's children's rare disease. Ara senior serves as chairman; Cindy, president; and Michael is secretary. Ara's past players and friends across the country continue to offer support, including ice-skating stars and other celebrities who sponsor benefit shows for the cause.

I spent an evening in the Parseghian home one football season when Michael and Cindy traveled in for a home game from Tucson, Arizona, where Michael practices as an orthopedic surgeon. The Parseghian family gathered for a grand family dinner. I watched Michael and Cindy's small children, Michael Jr., Christa, and Marcia, who were beginning to show signs of their illness, move among those who loved them dearly. Dinner conversation filled with family stories that at one point came to focus on Ara, who reminisced about some of his navy days and his coaching years at Northwestern University. He led us all to the moment that he drove down Notre Dame Avenue, between the maples, to become head coach at Notre Dame, distinctly remembering "how his spine tingled" at the sight of the Golden Dome.

I had little contact with Dan Devine, although I was introduced to him and his wife and children seated at a round table in the Morris Inn just after they had arrived in South Bend. While our paths crossed again when he came to Farley to forecast one of his most successful seasons, it was his late-night return to campus (with that victorious team that beat Alabama seven to zero during a regular season game in November 1980) that gave me Devine memories forever. Domer residents ran shouting and screaming from their residence halls at the end of that Alabama game. Long-distance phone lines overloaded. Students danced on cafeteria tables during the supper hour as toilet paper got wound round bushes and trees. As evening wore on, students were told "to get to the circle" to meet the team. Band members began leaving residence halls, bundled to their ears and swinging their instruments. I arrived at the circle entrance about 10:30 P.M., engulfed in circus atmosphere and stadium energy.

The Morris Inn was aglow. People hung from windows and perched on the canopy, with a perfect view of TV Channel 16 van parked right in front of the Mary statue on the circle drive. Bright lights glared down Notre Dame Avenue as rolls of toilet paper unfurled high in the night sky. The area was filled with fans waiting for team buses to come out of the dark. A cabdriver tried to deliver a passenger but gave up, stopping his cab in the curve of the road. The passenger paid his fare and, with his driver, got lost in the fun and frolic of it all.

Suddenly in the distance, headlights turned onto Notre Dame Avenue, triggering loud cheers from the crowd. Students began to run into the street as team buses rolled toward them. A feeling of embrace filled the air. Buses were forced to stop near the University Club. Players in ten-gallon hats peered out of windows, some full of wonder at the surge of humanity. One by one players emerged, a few a bit bashful. Some crawled jubilantly onto the roof of the bus, while others were swarmed by fans as they headed for the circle. Television cameramen were eager to capture players in the flush of fresh victory, while band members huddled in absolute disarray, playing their hearts out. The "Notre Dame Victory March" declared the truth of the moment, over and over and over again.

Suddenly Coach Dan Devine appeared on the shoulders of players as they carried him to the top of the television van where he waved both arms, then offered the crowds the "#1" gesture. When the band struck up the Irish jig, Devine put his feet to music, presenting his creative rendition against a brightly lit Golden Dome. Students cheered themselves into an uproar, and with extra exuberance and pride sang the fight song one more time. Recognizing a most unique moment, one student, wearing a bright red jacket, jumped behind the life-sized statue of Mary, depicted with hands folded in prayer. In the shadows of that cold November night, he stood behind her pretending his waving arms were hers and conducting the crowds in their song.

I first met Lou Holtz when he came to the Office of Student Affairs early in his Notre Dame career to meet with John Goldrick, then associate vice president for Residence Life. As it turned out, John was not available due to a scheduling mix-up. Since it was April 1, the coach's humor went right to work declaring the mix-up an April Fools' Day joke and was about to leave most graciously. As John took time to explain his dilemma, he proceeded to bring Coach Holtz to my office on a moment's notice. John explained that he was sure I had some business to discuss with him.

I had just returned from Easter weekend in Chicago where a very respected high-school teacher had tapped me on the shoulder as I knelt in the wake of high-spirited alleluias following the Easter Vigil. He wanted to warn me about a few high-school football stars, apparently being recruited by Notre Dame, who had very questionable personal reputations. "Be careful!" I was told. On Easter afternoon my sister, under the instruction of all her neighbors, quietly cornered me in the family pantry to deliver the same message. I never thought I would pass such news to Notre Dame's head coach in person, assuring him it was not an April Fools' prank. Time proved the Easter messages were on the mark and they did receive serious attention.

I was delighted to be mistaken for him on one wintry day. Conning tower personnel at Palwaukee Airport near Chicago took for granted that Bill Corbett ('52), one of Notre Dame's pilots, was flying Coach Holtz into the Chicago area in the university plane, probably on a recruiting mission. In the course of landing, I received greetings fit for a winning coach before the truth of my identity surfaced and laughter made way for our landing.

I had heard so many good things about Coach Holtz' wife, Beth, and was delighted to finally meet her, in Cedar Grove Cemetery at the end of Moose Krause's burial service. Beth stood near a crowd of historic football heroes and coaches who circled Moose's grave to the final note of the "Notre Dame Victory March." The sight of that coaches' lineup made me realize how much I had watched each of them accept the pressures of their work, the disappointment of their losses, and the thrill of the win.

It's impossible to be at Notre Dame for any length of time without running into Knute Rockne legends, which have an intriguing way of winding themselves into endless lives. The lore caught me by surprise in the person of Paul Castner ('22), one of Rockne's legendary players who possessed fascinating Franciscan connections. During June 1979 reunion days, Paul Castner approached me in front of Sacred Heart Church as I, with a few of my Franciscan sisters, was wheeling Sister Gerarda Jonik ('34) through campus on a minitour as part of her return to campus after years away. As a graduate student, Sister Gerarda had worked closely with Dr. J. Arthur Reyniers at the outset of his biological research which led to the discovery of how to raise germfree animals, all of which developed into LOBUND (Laboratories of Bacteriology at the University of Notre Dame).

Paul greeted us and, in the process of introductions, realized, to his great surprise, that we were "his" Franciscans. He had all the facts at his octogenarian fingertips. His grandfather, Dominic Moes, and the foundress of our congregation, Mary Catherine Moes, were Luxembourg cousins. He knew of her Joliet Franciscan foundation but had never met any of the sisters. So, from that day forward, Paul Castner never came to campus without getting in touch. On one of his visits he met and prayed Vespers with four of "his" Franciscans who were rectors of residence halls: Sisters Verene, Kathleen, Annette, and myself.

In time I discovered that Paul had maintained a close relationship with Knute Rockne until his fatal plane accident. While a student, Paul was one of Rockne's outstanding players, known for his running and kicking records, some of which still stand. He played on the field with George Gipp and the Four Horsemen, starring on teams in 1920, 1921, and 1922 until he shattered his hip. Paul was named an all-American fullback in 1922. He also had strong interest and talent in hockey and was pivotal in establishing a hockey program at Notre Dame. In addition, he played baseball on campus and later pitched for the Chicago White Sox, where, as a rookie, he faced Ty Cobb in a memorable game. It has been said by some that Paul was probably one of the best all-around athletes in Notre Dame's history.

On many of his visits back to campus, Paul drove a large recreational vehicle that served as a home-on-wheels during his travels across the country from his Minnesota home, especially as he visited and interviewed former "Rockne men" for the book he wrote in 1975 with John D. McCullum, *We Remember Rockne*. He felt right at home driving the RV through campus to the dismay of many ND security officers, often parking it in the Morris Inn lot. During one such visit, he presented me with a copy of his Rockne book. However, it was the inscription he added to a flyleaf that forever put intriguing pieces together in his own hand:

> To Sister Jean Lenz
>
> Sister, I am pleased to share these wonderful memories of Rockne with you.
>
> The book is a portrait of a beautiful man who was a great spiritual leader—I loved him like a father.
>
> Yours in Christ,
> Paul Castner
>
> P.S. How fortunate our pleasant meeting before Sacred Heart Church at Notre Dame where we learned that my grandpa Dominic Moes, and Mother Alfred, (Mary Catherine Moes) your foundress, were cousins. PC

It seems that such words granted Joliet Franciscans an eternal Knute Rockne connection.

THIRTEEN

Burying Griff

"Griff died."

For days I heard the message coming. Holy Cross priest Father Bob Griffin, former rector, university chaplain, and minister to multitudes for thirty-three years on and off Notre Dame's campus, had been suffering physically and mentally for three months due to serious complications from diabetes. The last week of his life was agony.

I helped him hold and eat a small seventy-fourth birthday cake two weeks earlier on the feast of Our Lady of the Rosary, October 7, 1999. In the course of a short visit, he passed me a copy of Henry Nouwen's biography by M. Ford, which might have been the last of many books Griff finished reading: "Let me know what you think about this." At his request, we blessed each other. As I reached the doorway, ready to leave, he called after me, "Jean, if anyone wants to know how I am, tell them I'm just fine."

But he wasn't fine. One foot was almost completely wasted away, and the other was discolored. Doctors had warned him over and over again what the prognosis was, but Griff would not relinquish even a toe, which was the first surgical plan. Yet he looked me straight in the eye one day and said, "Jean, I think I'm being fitted for a harp."

Griff vehemently protested any surgery that involved amputation. He could not see fit to mutilate his body. "First the toe, then the leg, Jean." He pensively listed classical literary figures who were one-legged men, dwelling on the character of Ahab who moved through one of his favorite tales, *Moby Dick*. He did not want to be added to that list.

And so he suffered, vacillating between acceptance and denial of his condition. Eastern Province seminarian. Vinnie Cappola and others, who tended him daily, caught direct questions and poignant comments: "Am I dying?"; "Will I die?"; "I'm afraid"; and "I know what I've chosen and I must see it through to the end." In the midst of it all, he would kiss a hand and give a blessing to dear friends. Sometimes he would ask a blessing. How carefully he would say, "I love you."

Months then weeks before he died, medical authorities regularly updated him on the progress of his physical deterioration and his need for surgery. "I hear what they say, and then I have such terrible demons through the night," he admitted. I could hardly stand the thought of Griffin, filled with pain and poison, taking on demons in dark hours. I became feisty as I tried to convince him that he had wonderful memories he could call upon to fill his mind and heart in the middle of the night. So, I made him an offer, "Griff, let's talk about some of those memories right now so they'll be fresh and you can latch on to them quickly." We called some up, one by one. A few had Farley trimmings and others were filled with London lore. He chose classic moments. At the outset of our next visit, he recounted some of his midnight meanderings that put the demons totally out of commission. "I thought about Henry Nouwen and our prayer group a good long time last night." While I wouldn't vouch for his Nouwen notions, I knew that he could have immersed himself quite easily in refreshing laughter and tears that got loose in our prayer group of earlier years. That group included Dean of Students Jim Roemer and his wife, Mary Ann, who worked with Student Volunteer Services; Father Don McNeill, CSC, director of Student Volunteer Services; and Sister Vivian Whitehead, OSF, rector of Breen-Phillips Hall.

While he slept fitfully in his final days, moaning, talking, and sometimes having nightmares, he died very peacefully in the brightness of a noonday with his Holy Cross brothers and close friends praying at his side. Griff went home to God before the rest of us, and we were left with the adventure of trying to bury him.

Over the years he told a multitude that he wanted to be buried at Notre Dame. Members of that multitude began calling campus when they heard that Griff's wake and funeral were already posted at Stonehill College in North Easton, Massachusetts, while plans would be made for a Memorial Mass to be celebrated at Notre Dame at a later date. An eruption of calls to the Eastern Province requested Griff's burial at Notre Dame.

But Griff was a member of the Eastern Province of Holy Cross. It was a long-standing community practice for Holy Cross members to be buried in their provincial cemeteries. Griff had lived and ministered at Notre Dame for a grand total of thirty-three years, but he didn't share his burial plan with any of his provincials. There was nothing in writing. In the midst of all those years, he never requested a transfer from the Eastern to the Indiana Province, which gave all the arrangements a curious touch. And so the plan stood, Griff would be buried in the East.

One early suggestion was to have his body cremated so his ashes might be split, with some buried in each place. I had serious doubts about that. Griff was adamant about not giving up his toe. As it turned out, we learned he did not want to be cremated, so splitting his ashes never became an issue. There was some fanciful talk among alumni members about stealing his body from the local undertaker's and sending an empty casket to Stonehill. But that was very short-lived. The compromise was a Notre Dame wake service and memorial Mass of thanksgiving for the life and gifts of Robert Francis Griffin, CSC, before his funeral and burial in the East.

On a gorgeous October Sunday afternoon, Griff was laid in state in the middle aisle of Sacred Heart Basilica. The late afternoon sun turned stained-glass windows into color drama as folks from all walks of life paid tribute to a man who had touched their lives through the celebration of sacraments, over the radio with his *Children's Hour* program, by way of his books, and through columns written in the *Observer*, *Notre Dame Magazine*, and *Our Sunday Visitor*. Some in attendance were friends whom Griff met along the way with Darby, his ever faithful, taffy-colored cocker spaniel.

Sitting on the edge of the middle aisle, it was hard to realize that Griff was in the coffin. I was imagining the Urchins' Masses, during which Griff invited children's participation, and the baptisms and weddings he celebrated in this holy space. The stories of some of them crowded my brain. He once told me that he would never begin a wedding ceremony without first seeing the whites of the eyes of both bride and groom, since he had the unhappy experience of watching one bride walk down the aisle only to discover the groom's absence. On another day he picked up the hand microphone instead of the aspergial, dipped it into holy water, and began to bless the wedding rings, all of which sent a noise through the church that sounded like a natural catastrophe. The memory settled me down into smiles mixed with tears and a great sense of thanksgiving for Bob Griffin's life.

Pews filled with people who came to celebrate Griff's life. Some sixty members of the Holy Cross community emerged from the sacristy singing with full voice. Fr. Don McNeill served as main celebrant, while Fr. Ted Hesburgh delivered the homily. Some of Griff's fellow priests had hardly set down their traveling bags from fall break. Fr. Patrick Gaffney was fresh from the Congo as he read the death notice on the Corby Hall bulletin board and headed for the ceremony. He slipped into a pew too late to take part in the formal procession.

In his homily, Fr. Ted masterfully captured Griff's character and ministry, stating "every campus needs a Griffin." He called attention to the many students Griff served over the years, the amount of writing he did, the radio shows he hosted, and the hours he gave to those in need, including his special summer ministry among the street people in Greenwich Village. Looking out over a church filled with Griff's friends and admirers, Fr. Ted thoughtfully remarked, "people came to talk to Griff hoping that perhaps they would learn to talk with God."

If anyone was missed at this special Mass, it was the Notre Dame Glee Club for which Griff served as chaplain and traveled thousands of miles over some twenty-five years. They were on their way home from their fall tour but could not make it back in time. Instead, they dedicated their fall concert to him on their return and sang his favorite songs.

Before the end of Mass, Luis Gamez ('79), professor of English at Western Michigan University and former student musician for Griff's Urchins' Mass, let Fr. Griff "speak" in his own words when he read the following passages:

> I don't dislike kids. I bear no grudges against frisbees; but kids throwing them make me restless. The very sight of them causes absurd images to spring up in my mind. I think to myself: I wish I were a frisbee thrown by the hand of Christ. I wish God would send

me skimming high over the earth into the path of the sun, spiraling me in an arc so graceful that observers might almost think that I had wings. It is silly for a man to wish he were a frisbee, but I don't think it is silly for a man to wish that God would do graceful things with that man's life.[1]

It was past midnight, and the young man had been sitting on my couch for a long time. Finally, as he was leaving, he said: "It may seem strange to ask this, after the time you have given me, but do you really care?" . . . I am not young enough to remember if caring has a birthday. I'm not old enough to know if caring will ever die. Faith teaches that there is an eternal heartbeat in me that belongs to God; it keeps me from getting weary when I am needed to care. Yet even for the professional Christian, caring can get dull, like any other duty. Sometimes the best I can do is give a professional attention, wanting to care deeply, yet knowing that in all my attention, there is nothing really personal. Eventually, with God's help, I touch the place where the nerve ends quiver; I find the spot where the pain shows through. Then my experience is like that of St. Thomas, when he put his finger into the side of Christ; a personal bond is established because I know how someone has suffered. Sometimes it's not the hurt that people show us that induces our tears. Sometimes it's the hidden wounds—the wounds that a man hides even from himself—that convert us to caring. . . .

I've never found a person whom I needed to love whom I couldn't love, if I am patient enough.[2]

"I would like to be immortal," says Woody Allen, "by living forever." Forever would be nice. But as long as priests are ordained, I will be part of the forever of Holy Cross. If Notre Dame survives for 1,000 years, the neat crosses in the cemetery will identify the holy dead. The living members continue to give their service to the campus, trusting in the continuing love affair that binds Holy Cross in a covenant of affection to Notre Dame.[3]

In the midst of such words it became clearer than ever that as much as Griff wanted to be buried here, and as much as we wanted him buried here, he was Holy Cross at heart, and would rest in peace in either cemetery. So he lies in a lovely cemetery on the campus of Stonehill

College in North Easton, Massachusetts. But I must admit that at the hour of his burial out East, I walked to the community cemetery on the edge of Notre Dame's campus and stood at the spot where he might have been laid to rest: "We really tried, Griff."

Robert Griffin was an easterner with deep roots in Maine. As a young man he converted to Catholicism, which seemed to come at a great price for his Methodist family. He once told me that he thought his conversion had a lot to do with his father's untimely death. "There are times I think I killed him, doing what I did." On the other hand, Griff's mother outlived her husband by many years and she also converted to Catholicism before she died, unbeknownst to her priest-son. The first Mass Griff celebrated for his mother was the Mass of the Resurrection.

I came to know Griff when he was the well-established rector of Keenan, although his path to such a post had unique twists and turns. He actually came to campus some years before, on a temporary basis, from the Eastern Province to recuperate from a serious illness in Holy Cross House, a medical facility for the community on St. Joseph's Lake. He ended up walking across campus and staying for the rest of his life.

He wrote his way into many lives through his campus and national columns—and he found out more about his own along the way. On Saturday mornings he hosted *The Children's Hour*, a radio show that highlighted storytelling and offered classic children's literature. He celebrated a Sunday liturgy referred to as the Urchins' Mass, arranged for children. He often visited Morningside, a low-income housing facility where he visited the residents and celebrated the Eucharist. Griff found ways to reach all age groups, on campus, in South Bend, and on the streets of New York in the summertime.

For years he weighed 350 pounds or more, a burden that he carried in distinct pear-shaped fashion. Many a Halloween eve he threatened to go trick-or-treating, dressed as the Golden Dome. But the day came, to many people's astonishment, when he made it his business to shed some weight, hoping for the day when he could buy regular-sized clothes from a regular rack, especially a Notre Dame blazer complete with the university emblem.

Since Griff celebrated a late-evening Eucharist in Farley's chapel four years running, residents stayed close to his weight-loss victories. Everyone could see that he was shedding pounds gradually and starting to look lost in his oversized clothing. His pants grew more than baggy and his belt actually grew a foot too long for his waistline. One wintry evening an observant coed offered encouraging words with a back-handed challenge: "Fr. Griff, I bet two people could fit into your over-coat these days." Standing nearby, I was invited to test the truth of the matter as he backed me into his grand old overcoat and easily buttoned it up, giving everyone reason for a great round of applause and volley of laughter.

Griff would leave Farley after the 11:00 P.M. Mass and walk with his dog, Darby O'Gill, in tow, to the basement lounge of LaFortune on the coldest, wettest, windiest, loveliest nights of the year, to stay until dawn "in a clean and well lighted place," as Hemingway put it. He would spend these hours with students destined to pull all-nighters, but, more importantly, he was there to lend his good ear, fine mind, and big heart to those needing someone to talk with for one of a hundred reasons.

His daytime ministries included celebrating a noontime Lenten Mass in LaFortune Center that attracted off-campus students, some faculty, and staff. Many slipped into the alcove off the first-floor lounge to pray with him. He knew many simple Christian hymns, including "Jesus Loves Me," "Were You There When They Crucified the Lord," and a Quaker favorite, "Lord of the Dance," and he easily led a group in reflective singing before, during, and after a Lenten Eucharist. Now and then, following the last blessing and the beginning of "Lord of the Dance," he would invite students to take a partner. Once I was his, totally amazed at how light on his feet he was in view of his bulk at that time in his life.

Following one memorable Ash Wednesday liturgy in LaFortune, Griff joined the traditional lunch line in the Huddle, picking up food along the way for himself and for Darby, whereupon he reached the beloved, middle-aged, vivacious cashier, Vi, known and loved by hundreds of Domers. As he paid his bill, she wondered out loud if he happened to have any leftover ashes with him, since she was going to be unable to get to church that day. Her word was his command; he dug into his coat jacket for his plastic bag of blessed ashes, into which he dipped his finger and crossed her forehead with full formality and the blessing, "Thou art dust and unto dust thou shall return." She blessed herself carefully as the entire line of hungry Domers came to a Lenten standstill in the face of the age-old holy ceremony.

Griff was hardly ever seen without his dogs, Darby O'Gill I, II, or III, who appeared in consecutive years at his side, often leashed but sometimes free "to run and make love to the squirrels." Many campus onlookers never quite realized when his pet replacements occurred, since the taffy-colored cocker spaniels were all namesakes and look-a-likes.

Griff always claimed that his dogs contributed significantly to his ministry. He told intriguing tales about individuals who first met and talked to Darby, only to turn a corner and walk into Griff "waiting for his mutt." These scenes offered Griff untold opportunities to meet students or street people in New York, some eager and others a bit hesitant to talk about their lives, to express gratitude, to share serious regrets, to talk about God, or to ask a blessing. The Darbys of his life led Griff down some colorful, grace-filled paths of people that led to Gospel territory and came to life in his homilies.

When Darby II reached the end of his days, the vet cremated him. He called Griff, knowing how much the dog meant to him, and directed him to send a container for Darby's remains, if he so desired. Mulling over the matter, Griff called me about the vet's request. "I'm wondering what he has in mind—maybe he just needs a large envelope!" Then he went on to explain that he was sitting there looking at a Christmas canister that I had filled with mints hoping they might help him quit smoking. He wondered if I would mind if he used the canister for Darby's ashes. I felt curiously honored.

As it turned out, all the ashes fit in the canister. At 3:00 A.M. one morning, with the aid of a broken golf club, Griff and two alum accomplices, Rick LaSalvia ('75 and '79) and John Sweeney ('80 and '84), proceeded to a spot near the grotto where they dug a hole and buried the canister, a significant final resting place for a good dog. However, as time went on, Griff began to question what he'd done, worrying that some day a major renovation of the Grotto area would take place and there would be great consternation over whose ashes were in the Christmas canister. So, in the wee hours of another long night, Darby's ashes were exhumed with the help of another friendly accomplice, emptied from the canister, and placed in good clean earth, covered over with one of Griff's personal handkerchiefs marked with his first initial, an embroidered *R*.

Griff's third taffy-colored cocker spaniel outlived him and found a home with Jean Benedett ('79), her husband, Nick Matich ('81 and '82), and their two children in Alexandria, Virginia, both of whom assisted Griff with the Urchins' Mass when they were undergrads. They took Darby into their home when Griff became too ill to care for him. Not too long before Griff died, he finally and quite officially declared Jean and Nick Darby's new owners.

Some folks found Griff a rather shy man, which he was. But his layers of shyness seemed to dissipate as he settled into writing. He often dug deep inside of himself, sharing intimate thoughts that sometimes made headlines, as well as offering heartrending insights into some of his family difficulties, reaching back into personal history and personal struggles. He let the whole world in on the deep lessons he learned as he revealed what hurt him deeply and what filled him with genuine joy. And Griff shared it all with a great array of images that continually tumbled out of him. I once started to collect his columns with the intent of doing an article on "Griff the Image Maker."

His shyness also seemed to vanish in the face of delicate questions and topics that he often tossed out for discussion because of his interest, care, and concern, or a refreshing, gnawing curiosity. One day Fr. Don McNeill and I invited ourselves to have lunch with Griff when he was living in Corby Hall. He hadn't been feeling well, but he seemed up for a visit. As we settled in at a table he remarked that we both looked good, and then, without wincing, he glanced at me pleasantly across the table and asked, "Jean, did you get a face-lift?" Don gasped, "Oh, no! Griff!" The question dramatically redirected our conversation from his health, but only long enough to allow me to catch my breath, say no with a lilt of laughter, and explain that I had slept well the night before—and besides, it was a good hair day.

No matter where Griff and his curiosity moved on campus, his room always had a whale motif, reflecting his Maine roots and one of his favorite pieces of literature, Melville's *Moby Dick*. He taught that classic at Stonehill College, where it seemed to get into his bones before he came to Notre Dame. Most whale gifts that he received over the years, made of whatever substance—metal, wood, glass, cloth, ceramic, plaster, paint, or paper—seemed to make a hit with him. While some kidded him about his whale collection, they understood it belonged to the great mix of this Maine man, born and bred close to the sea. Sometimes Griff gave whales away. While attending to daily mail, I use his gift of a wide-eyed, open-mouthed, steel whale, shaped into a handy letter opener!

Griff was probably the best-read person I knew on campus, harboring broad interests in literature, theology, philosophy, and history. It was not unusual to see him sitting in the midst of a few piles of books in his room, which was crammed with bookcases holding favorite volumes and old resources, including a collection of Shakespeare's plays—mine. He borrowed it once, and years later finally announced that he thought he had earned it for keeps. I surrendered. Eventually he traded it for a Chesterton collection, a biography of Gerard Manley Hopkins, Fr. Jim Burtchaell's *From Synagogue to Church*, and Fr. Charlie Sheedy's favorite book, *God's Fool*, the life of Francis of Assisi by Julien Green.

Following Griff's rector years in Keenan Hall, he stayed on as a chaplain, first in Keenan Hall, then in the newly constructed Pasquerilla Hall, and finally in Stanford Hall. He was actively involved in a myriad of ministries during these years with students, alumni, and friends who forever scouted out his whereabouts. It was Griff's move to Stanford Hall that marked the beginning of his major decline in health. He suffered congestive heart failure, and, in time, developed diabetes, all of which slowed him down dramatically and limited his writing. After some recuperative months in Holy Cross House, he requested to move back on campus and live with the Corby community as long as possible, which he did.

Over the years, Griff, who was "on loan" from the Eastern Province to the Indiana Province for thirty-three years, took on a more and more Midwestern Holy Cross identity and grew close to members around him in his own inimitable way. As always, while he may have shied away from direct words to his Corby confreres, he often found ways to describe such poignant relationships, for example in a column, for all the world to see: "One day, when you are praying or eating or hearing a conversation, love overtakes you by surprise as the honest mood of your soul. You think of the people you live and work with and it is as though God were singing a song inside of you."

However, in the end, Griff lost all vestiges of a double-province identity. He was simply steeped in Holy Cross brotherhood, which stood at the heart of not one, but two Eucharistic celebrations, filled with dramatic traces of the East and West pieces of his life. And Darby O'Gill II stayed buried at the grotto.

NOTES

1. Robert Griffin, "Letters to a Lonely God," *Observer*. March 26, 1976.
2. Robert Griffin, "Letters to a Lonely God," *Observer*. September 14, 1979.
3. Robert Griffin, "In the Shadow of the Dome," in *Reflections in the Dome*. ed. James O'Rourke (Notre Dame, Ind.: Juniper Press, 1985), p. 200.

FOURTEEN

A Band of Men

In the spring of the new millennium, I did something I've never done before. I took a slow walk through the rows of gray crosses in the Holy Cross Priests' Cemetery on St. Mary's Road, where I counted 165 graves of those who have died since I came to Notre Dame in 1973.

The first time I walked this sacred ground, I went searching for a single grave marked "John Francis Farley, CSC," which I discovered near the large crucifix at the head of all the graves. I read his tombstone so carefully that day: "Born Feb. 15, 1876, Died Jan. 15, 1939." It stood lined up with so many others that belonged to complete strangers. Nonetheless, they were the communion of saints, and I prayed hard that Father Farley and all these men of God buried there might bless each one of us so newly moved into Farley Hall.

However, on this new millennium cemetery tour, I was hardly in the midst of strangers. I walked among graves of Holy Cross colleagues and friends whom I had come to know, admire, and cherish over three decades. I knew many of their tombstones by heart and could go directly to the spot where they were buried. We had walked the same halls, taught the same students, served on the same committees, attended the same meetings, and prayed the same prayers. Having watched many of them in their various ministries, I knew a myriad of stories that they had added to the local color of the twentieth-century communion of saints.

These men were laid to rest in every kind of weather following a sudden death, like that of John Van Wolvlear, while playing tennis; a lingering illness, like Michael McCafferty, after suffering through a bone-marrow transplant; or after long life, like Jerry Wilson, who went home to visit family at Christmastime and died in their midst. They were accompanied to their resting places in solemn procession by their brothers in Holy Cross, family members, friends, and colleagues. The majority went on foot from Sacred Heart Church following the Mass of the Resurrection, walking past the grotto, skirting St. Mary's Lake, and traveling through the woods on St. Mary's Road.

Those processions invariably reminded me of the deaths of my Franciscan sisters buried a hundred miles away. The ceremony would push me to think about the similar realities found at the heart of both women's and men's religious communities: the reality of vocation, the vowed life, the daily dynamics of community, the multitude of ministries, chapter meetings, elections, and international missionary endeavors. Looking back, I realize more clearly that as a Franciscan woman, I really never felt outside religious community life during my years at Notre Dame. I was surrounded daily, supported, accepted, and included in fitting manner by many Holy Cross members who believed in so many of the same things I did. We were living out similar commitments. They can never fully know what an inspiration so many of them have been for me. I have wept at times thinking of their influence.

Of all things, there was something I did intensely miss at times—the daily Franciscan liturgical calendar. A Franciscan household fills up with a great array of Franciscan feast days that focus on men and women with every degree of grace and goodness stretching from the Middle Ages—especially the great Feasts of Francis and Clare, which took on special meaning, prayers, and trimmings within Franciscan circles. These were the days when it seemed best to make such longing a simple practice of poverty.

It's hard to imagine that I knew nothing about the congregation of Holy Cross and its relationship to the University of Notre Dame during my adolescence on the south side of Chicago. I suspect if anyone tested me along the way, I might have guessed Notre Dame was run by the Jesuits, a belief which fits into that somewhat legendary story about how the Jesuits took a poll to find out—among other things—which of their universities was considered the most well-known, only to discover that Notre Dame had landed the top spot. But Holy Cross was in my life long before I knew it.

When I first came to campus as a graduate student, I met a college hero, Father Louis Putz. I simply knew him by name and reputation, which did not include his Holy Cross identity. He was a significant figure in my life all through college as the authority on YCS (the Young Christian Student movement), which he brought from France where he had been mentored by Abbé Lebreton and Abbé Cardijn. I had read and reread his series of pamphlets on the lay apostolate which dealt with the importance of Christian leadership in the world and the place and value of the inquiry method based on three strategic steps: observe, judge, and act. During weekly college YCS meetings, I also learned about his influence in establishing CFM (the Catholic Family Movement) and Fides Press at Notre Dame.

Another legendary figure who traced Holy Cross history and traditions for me in my student and earliest rector days was Fr. Henry Glueckert, a retired professor of Latin and Greek who took some meals in the Pay Caf and collected leftover bread from the dining hall for the ducks. Some called him Father Duck. When he came to realize how new I was to campus, he made it his business to give me "history lessons" that often lasted past dessert. He wasn't too clear on more recent developments, but he knew the past like the back of his hand. I became intrigued with the French history of Holy Cross priests as I first heard of Basil Moreau and the young missionary Edward Sorin.

It was always moving to hear of the simple, colorful, and sometimes dramatic beginnings of Notre Dame, for example, the bartering for education—chickens for arithmetic and spelling classes—brick making, cholera cases, devastating fires, weekly baths, "minims," candlelight, public outhouses, farmland, and barns and livery stables. Father Henry, who lived most of his hundred years at Notre Dame, constantly set movie plots in my path, making it clear to me that a host of unsung Holy Cross heroes put their lives on the line for this place known as du Lac.

And so it was that Fr. Louis Putz and Fr. Henry Glueckert set me on my way into the world of "the CSCs." During my graduate studies in the late 1960s, I became acquainted with a generation of Holy Cross men back on campus as faculty and staff with fresh Ph.D.'s and other graduate degrees, including Jim Burtchaell, John Dunne, Gene Gorski, and Don McNeill, who were members of the theology department;

David Burrell of the philosophy department; John Gerber from English; and Ernie Bartell of economics. All of the men lived in residence halls, some as rectors and others as assistant rectors. They all wore the traditional Holy Cross cassock and cape.

I first came to know many of them as celebrants of the Eucharist in residence halls. During the regular academic year, a group of graduate students gathered daily in Morrissey Hall where David Burrell was rector. While the first female professors at Notre Dame, Suzanne Kelly in philosophy and Josephine Ford in theology, and graduate lay students Margie Geib and Dave Zangrelli were often in attendance, most of us were religious women in full habit, showing only slight signs of modification: shorter skirts and veils and a few wisps of hair. The major impact of Vatican II on the Church at large, and religious life in particular, was just beginning to show.

In the spring of my graduate year, I ventured out at 11:00 P.M. for the first late-night liturgy of my life, celebrated by Jim Burtchaell in Dillon Hall's chapel, which was packed with students. I sat in the shadows of the chapel dressed in full Franciscan habit along with my religious confrere Sister Miriam Hudak, who was working toward a master's degree in French. I was pinned with a green shamrock to mark St. Patrick's Day, praying with young people so enthusiastically engaged in good liturgy. I listened to my first dialogue homily, filled with Vietnam War overtones.

Six years later when I returned as rector of Farley, I stepped into another world of CSCs who were colleagues through the Office of Student Affairs: Richard Conyers, Carl Ebey, Jim Flanigan, Greg Green, Robert Griffin, Gene Gorski, Tom McNally, Don McNeill, John Mulcahy, Matt Miceli, Claude Pomerleau, Tom Tallarida, Bill Toohey, and David Schlaver. Many ministered in twenty male residence halls and campus ministries. Entrenched as I was in CSC territory, I began to receive mail with *CSC* after my name. Now and then I received French correspondence addressed to Rev. Jean Lenz, CSC. There was always a slight struggle to hang onto my identity.

In the mid 1970s, another generation of Holy Cross priests came into my life, quite fresh from ordination, with all their wit and wisdom and strong ministries. Among them were Daniel Jenky, Bob Krieg, Edward "Monk" Malloy, Tom McDermott, Tom O'Hara, Peter Rocca,

David Tyson, and Michael McCafferty. Three of these men would become university or college presidents: Malloy at the University of Notre Dame; Tyson at the University of Portland in Oregon; and O'Hara at King's College in Wilkes-Barre, Pennsylvania. After serving as rector of Dillon Hall and rector of Sacred Heart Basilica, Daniel Jenky took his place in our midst first as Bishop of South Bend–Fort Wayne, Indiana, then Bishop of Peoria. Peter Rocca resigned from the Office of Student Affairs to succeed Bishop Jenky as Basilica rector. I watched Tom McDermott leave campus ministry work at Notre Dame and turn to missionary work in Africa, where he served as pastor of Holy Cross parish in Jinja, Uganda, and directed the minor seminary. Michael McCafferty became professor and assistant dean at the Notre Dame Law School before he passed away at the age of forty-one.

I gained another Holy Cross perspective by watching ND graduates at close range. With multiple career potential, they made major vocation decisions that brought them to Moreau Seminary to carry on the congregation's traditional ministries in the Church. Near the turn of the millennium, former Student Body President Tom Doyle was ordained and celebrated his first Mass in Sacred Heart Basilica, where the loudest and most colorful fuss was made by the undergraduate men of Keough Hall (where Tom served as rector).

And the stretch of manly dedication goes on. As I serve as a member of the Moreau Seminary formation team these days, assisting with the precarious and holy task of preparing young men for priesthood at a time when priesthood is under scrutiny and pastoral needs keep mounting, I stay aware of the impact that Vatican II has had on the Church at large, on priesthood, and on religious life. Watching drastic changes take place, and seeing glaring signs of more change to come, I feel challenged to consider what it means to rethink, refound, and look ahead to what religious life might look like in the future, and how priesthood might be "reconfigured." Who should be called forth for ordination as we move into the third millennium? It is a question that never goes away.

These days, whenever I walk through the Holy Cross Community Cemetery, I purposely, with sweeping glances, try to take in all the crosses and all the lives, reminding myself of how much I have leaned on Holy Cross inheritance these past three decades. While I have, at various times, been aware of some of the personal, communal, and institutional missteps and burdens these men of God have carried, I am always utterly amazed at all the goodness that has come to life and flourished because of them. In curious ways, they have made me very conscious of the actual force of their goodness. In fact, I can hardly say the word *goodness* by itself anymore without adding the word *force* to its meaning. I want to make it a phrase—the force of goodness. Symbols of such force keep catching my eye, such as the flower that gets through rock formation or asphalt. I even sat up straight and moved to the edge of my chair when I heard the phrase at the end of a late-night movie. It was *The Razor's Edge*, based on W. Somerset Maugham's classic novel. Actor Herbert Marshall posed as Maugham in the film, reminding Gene Tierney in a closing scene that she must never forget that the greatest force in this world is the force of goodness.

More to the point, Edward Sorin, CSC, bestowed a genuine sense of the force of goodness in a letter he sent to the Very Rev. Basil Moreau, founder of the Congregation of Holy Cross. I caught the words on the cover of the memorial Mass booklet for the Memorial Mass of Archbishop Emeritus Mark McGrath, CSC ('45), of Panama City, Panama, celebrated in Sacred Heart Basilica at the opening of the academic year 2000–2001:

> Will you permit me, dear Father, to share with you a preoccupation which gives me no rest? Briefly, it is this: Notre Dame du Lac was given to us by the bishop only on condition that we establish here a college at the earliest opportunity. As there is no other school within more than a hundred miles, this college cannot fail to succeed. Before long it will be one of the most powerful means for good in this country. Finally, dear Father, you cannot help see that this new branch of your family is destined to grow under the protection of Our Lady of the Lake and of Saint Joseph. At least, this is my deep conviction. Time will tell if I am wrong.

Time does tell. More than a century of dates pressed into cemetery crosses prove Sorin right in many ways, in many lives, and in the force of goodness that has emerged, one Holy Cross generation after the other.

We ask how we might follow, and we found many footprints on the road. A great band of men had passed this way, men who had made and lived by their vows, men who had walked side by side in their following of the Lord. They beckoned us to fall in step with them. We wanted to be part of the family they formed in order to share in their life and work.

—Constitutions and Statutes of the Congregation of Holy Cross, #1

Epilogue

I thought that I was the only one in Farley Hall on one of the hottest June nights in South Bend history. Near midnight there was a knock at my door by a young scholar, Amalia Meier, who was a bit overwhelmed with organic chemistry and the heat. "Would you run through the sprinklers with me? I heard them swish on outside, but I don't want to go alone." For a moment I stood still with a stare and an open mouth. Then I simply closed the door behind me and we left the building laughing.

There was a great full moon in a hazy southeastern sky that night. I felt a touch of mysticism in the air. We ran south, taking the long way around the Peace Memorial through great sprays of water that arched every which way over the sidewalks, into our faces, and over our bodies. Then we ran north along Cavanaugh and Zahm halls, catching a glimpse of the Dome drenched in midnight lights. In all, we "did" the north quad as we say, finally arriving back at Farley's south entrance—drenched, laughing, out of breath, a bit exhausted, and so refreshed.

Curiously, that precious midnight moment has settled in me more and more as a fitting image of my years of ministry at Notre Dame. Having lived almost thirty years in Farley Hall, there are quiet moments late at night in all kinds of weather when I feel drenched in laughter or sorrow, out of breath, a bit exhausted, or so refreshed. Names and faces come out of nowhere. My thoughts latch on to memories at the blink of an eye. Phone calls from alumni make past events seem like they happened yesterday. At times I think of the students I have taught or come to know or of all the women who have lived in Farley, and I pray for them and others like them, not able to see their faces all at once or to say all of their names. There are moments when I recall with much affection the ten Franciscan Sisters from my Joliet community who also joined me in rector ranks over the years. I clearly remember so many deeply cherished Holy Cross colleagues. I think of my friends often, my best friends and my dear family. At times I muse about all of the conversations that have swirled around the walls of my Farley room and my office in Student Affairs over the years—a grand chorus of grace-filled stories hidden in plaster forever.

In the midst of some late-night musings, especially when the heat hangs heavy, I think that I've heard a knock at the door. I seem so ready for another run through the sprinklers, in midnight moonlight, with hopes of catching a glimpse of the Dome over my left shoulder. But down deep I know so well that it only happens once in a lifetime.